Employing Nietzsche's Sociological Imagination

How to Understand Totalitarian Democracy

Jack Fong

LEXINGTON BOOKS

Lanham • Boulder • New York • London

Published by Lexington Books
An imprint of The Rowman & Littlefield Publishing Group, Inc.
4501 Forbes Boulevard, Suite 200, Lanham, Maryland 20706
www.rowman.com

6 Tinworth Street, London SE11 5AL, United Kingdom

British Library Cataloguing in Publication Information Available

Library of Congress Cataloging-in-Publication Data
Names: Fong, Jack, 1970- author.
Title: Employing Nietzsche's sociological imagination : how to understand totalitarian democracy / Jack Fong.
Description: Lanham : Lexington Books, [2020] | Includes bibliographical references and index. | Summary: "Harnessing the empowering ideas of Friedrich Nietzsche to read the human condition of modern existence through a sociological lens, this book confronts the realities of how modern social structures, ideologies, and utopianisms affect one's ability to purpose existence with self-authored meaning"— Provided by publisher.
Identifiers: LCCN 2020007660 (print) | LCCN 2020007661 (ebook) | ISBN 9781793620422 (cloth ; alk. paper) | ISBN 9781793620446 (pbk. ; alk. paper) | ISBN 9781793620439 (epub)
Subjects: LCSH: Nietzsche, Friedrich Wilhelm, 1844-1900—Political and social views. | Sociology—Philosophy. | Political science—Philosophy.
Classification: LCC HM479.N54 .F66 2020 (print) | LCC HM479.N54 (ebook) | DDC 301.01—dc23
LC record available at https://lccn.loc.gov/2020007660
LC ebook record available at https://lccn.loc.gov/2020007661

Contents

Preface

Many thinkers have claimed and credited German philosopher Friedrich Nietzsche (1844–1900) for inspiring new trajectories for their discipline. His ideas on empowerment are, if I may, simply too empowering to be contained within the provincialism of one discipline. As a member of the sociology discipline and after much immersion in his works, my view is that sociologists are justified in framing Nietzsche as an adept and prescient sociological thinker. Nietzsche's ideas do have many profound sociological themes in spite of his discontents toward the discipline and its relationship to modern society and modernity overall. My polemical work thus attempts to present Nietzsche as an informed observer of society, in the process crediting him for making visible the architecture of existential sociology, a sociology that considers possibilities for a new self vis-à-vis social systems experiencing crises and decline.

At a time when the leaders of the "free" world can run systems in an authoritarian manner, replete with their jingoisms and subtexts of internal colonialism, it is rather urgent that we demystify democratism, one that in its current iteration in the United States has enabled the emergence of what can be seen as a totalitarian democracy; additionally, where informal cultural forces coexist by punishing one another through, say, the panopticons of identity politics, we can also argue that this is a form of totalitarian democracy. The tragic irony of modernity is how it has become bloated in its systemic, panoptic, and cultural enforcement of democratism, creating a variety of contradictory pieties and tensions within society. This theme will again be visited toward the conclusion of my work, one that requires an elaboration of Nietzsche's sociological insights before we give his views a *crescendo*: by considering how modern social systems of all manifestations, including democratism, can be overcome by the self contesting their dysfunctional states as they exert control through the promises of their utopianisms. Nietzsche remains one of the few who predicted the consequences of being duped by such modernist utopianisms and dared to offer some radically new considerations about self and social change. In this regard, he remains a very dangerous philosopher—and if my attempts at rendering Nietzsche's sociological imagination are successful—a very dangerous critical sociologist from *beyond* ideologies. Here, I share Karzai's sentiments about Nietzsche's legacy, namely that "sociology can no longer turn its back on Nietzsche's critical social thought. . . . Without Nietzsche questioning the entire Western canon there would be no critical theory in the social sciences in the form that it presently exists" (2019, xv).

An exegesis of all of Nietzsche's writings, along with his unpublished notes, is beyond the scope of this work, however. That said, excellent scholarly works and biographies already exist to further enrich understanding of Nietzsche; one cannot fail to find a suitable piece that highlights his deepest foci in well-translated volumes. Instead, I hope to make operative his most sociological insights through his major published materials so that we can dive into their rightful sociological contexts with little haste. Honoring Nietzsche's tendency to explicitly state the particular type of readers he prefers, I should note that my work is composed for those who acknowledge, if only intuitively, that many ideological, cultural, and institutional components of industrializing modernity exist to our detriment, uncritically reified as atavistic expressions of impossible utopias. Drawing from Nietzsche's major publications, my work illuminates the contours of modern systemic decay and how this enfeebles the collective and the self, steering members toward adopting meaningless and repetitive institutional scripts for security. No longer allowed to author or purpose one's own existence, I argue that in such a context Nietzsche's "overcomer" becomes *the* praxian agent able to engage with social change: by injecting self-authoring and emancipation life projects directed toward securing meaning in a nihilistic existence. My work thus discusses processes of social and institutional decay, those ensuring their degeneration by promoting conformity to convention, and how the overcoming self as ideal type and variable can prevail in spite of such social deficits. By making visible that Nietzsche had all along predicted the glaring contradictions of modernity's *isms* (democratism, socialism, capitalism, atheism, Darwinism, and feminism, to name but a few) and its negative effects upon lived outcomes, my work argues that we need to urgently demystify democracy in order to redeem it. Such an undertaking requires us to harness the sociological imaginations of Nietzsche's complex existential philosophy to "read" social problems of our modernity, a modernity replete with institutionalized yet dysfunctional panopticons that continue to impose their ideological and cultural demands upon the population. Suffice to say for now, since his birth in Röcken in 1844 in what was then the Kingdom of Prussia, until his mental collapse in 1889 in Turin, Italy, and death eleven years later in Germany in 1900, Nietzsche did attempt to demystify and desacralize the accumulated reifications and teleologies we internalize from the outputs of our social systems, reifications that for our philosopher emanate from religious as well as other major social systems of modernity.

Nietzsche sharpened his ideas and profundities as a young professor and a former medical orderly in the brutal Franco-Prussian War where he witnessed vulgarized deaths from warfare. His ideas were also nourished when Nietzsche's wanderlust saw him as sojourner of Europe open to romance yet seeking transcendence, in the process vehemently rejecting the nascent German nationalism and nation-state construction of his day. He composed music, wrote poetry, and admired composer Richard Wagner and was brotherly to his younger sister, Elisabeth Förster-Nietzsche, both of whom he would later experience a falling-out with due to their subscription to German nationalism. Nietzsche had also fallen for Russian psychoanalyst Lou Andreas-Salomé while confronting the emotional and nihilistic dangers in his search for truth, a process that haunted him during his solitary periods in later life, one that was further exacerbated by his chronic physical ailments. He never healed from witnessing during his childhood his father, Karl Ludwig—a well-loved Lutheran pastor—die of brain degeneration, and a younger brother, Ludwig Joseph, who died not long after at the age of two. Yet Nietzsche climbed mountains, took long hikes, and found his solitude and need for life affirmation transformative. He confronted himself and taught us that knowing the self in a conformist society is a fearsome process, one that nonetheless creates the conditions for purposing one's own emancipation and existence.

Nietzsche never ran from his pain and suffering. Instead he dove into them, embracing them as catalysts for renewal and rebirth. Nietzsche, in spite of his prescriptions for great overcomers, was very human, but an exceptional one. Exhibiting a brilliant intellect shaped by the tempestuousness of life struggle, sociologist Anas Karzai notes that Nietzsche is unequivocally a "philosopher of life, of the present and future, of love and joyfulness, and of laughter and affirmation" (2019, xxvi). Philosopher Jan Sokol echoes similar sentiments, poignantly describing of Nietzsche: "Behind all his tough and vicious words—he himself was a shy, warm-hearted and quiet person, who was called the 'hermit' by his neighbors in Sils Maria—[yet] you can find him being horrified to see the abyss to where civilized humanity was heading" (Bergmann et al. 2007, 17).

The suffering and tragedy that befell, and perhaps haunted Nietzsche when he was most taken by personal matters, transformed him into a warrior for a war he saw on the horizon, one that few could envision, let alone fight. Alone in confronting his animus, a nihilism stemming from a godless universe, and almost able to overcome it through his active embrace of its teachable dimensions, Nietzsche maintained his campaigns against religiosity, nationalist Germany, the herdish side of modern cultures, and the dysfunctions of the Western tradition in ways that empower actors to face the failed utopianisms of their modernities. Nietzsche simply desired that we learn the art of maximizing our freedoms by authoring our sovereignty and by purposing our existence as the integrity of systems degenerate around the self. Nietzsche most certainly philosophizes like a hammer, one he employs to systematically destroy the false façades of modernity's pieties.

A Nietzschean existential sociology, then, continues to presciently make visible the contradictions and vulgarizations that exist in many nuances of the social experience. Existential sociology, heavily informed by a Nietzsche lens, is thus more than a sociology of self and society. Instead it is about a self with agency to still prevail and overcome in spite of the pathos of social dysfunctions and decay that pull other actors down with them. For one of the earliest proponents of existential sociology Edward Tiryakian, existential sociology is thus "vitally concerned" with humanity "in the totality of his situation" (1962, 6). Nietzsche, then, taught us about how utopian onslaughts upon the actor can function as catalysts that set into motion the making of a new free-spirted overcomer, one empowered and optimized to continue being *and* becoming in an age that sociologist Jürgen Habermas (1986) describes as exhausted by utopian energies.

— Jack Fong

Acknowledgments

When one decides to write a book about the ideas of a brilliant yet subversive thinker a network of supporters greatly enhances the undertaking. In this regard, I am eternally grateful for the wonderful insights offered by Dr. Kevin McCaffrey with whom I communicated frequently a variety of Nietzschean themes. I also express my gratitude to sociologists Drs. John Moss, Anjana Narayan, Steve Nava, Piyasuda Pangsapa, Christine Payne, Michael Roberts, and Anthony Villareal. All of you have heard about the content of this monograph in more ways than one and I am grateful. My gratitude also extends to Dr. Gabriele Plickert who has been instrumental in ensuring that I accurately convey the semantics of different German expressions. Dr. John Brown Childs, a deep soul and a great friend, is also much deserving of my gratefulness. His notion of a shared humanity through the ideas of transcommunality underpin the important ethos that members of society should always engage in creating new communities of dignity and respect.

I am also grateful to Drs. Maudemarie Clark and Julian Young for being wonderful sources of inspiration. Drs. Patrik Aspers and Anas Karzai have also been supportive of this effort and are wholeheartedly deserving of my gratitude. All of your analyses and accounts of Nietzsche have been influential in generating a variety of cues about how to approach his philosophy as a sociologist. I also express much appreciation and gratitude to Lexington Books' excellent editors Courtney Morales and Shelby Russell for ensuring a smooth publishing process. This work is also inspired by former friends, colleagues, mentors, and wonderful people who have now left us: my father Leo S. W. Fong, Drs. Dilip Basu, Ben Crow, Fouad Kalouche, and Wally Goldfrank. I express my heartfelt thanks to all of you.

A warm thank you must also be directed to John Ambrose, MD—an admirer of Nietzsche—for granting me the rights to use his 2017 oil painting of our philosopher for the cover. The abyss our philosopher stares into is hauntingly captured in an evocative and uncluttered scene, perhaps not unlike the solitary evenings in Sils Maria when Nietzsche engaged with his existence, our existence—humanity's existence. Finally, I thank my spouse Thasanee and my son Pattarakorn: without the patience and support from both of you, this work would not have materialized.

Introduction

Many readers and thinkers who encounter the philosophy of Friedrich Nietzsche (1844–1900) have come away with, perhaps, an alternative rendering of one's emancipation, or some sort of reworking of its definition of self in ways that strengthen corporeal and emotional constitution toward life and struggle. That scholars and writers have often referred to Nietzsche as a "prophet" of modernity speaks volumes about his prescience in envisioning what it means to exist with self-mastery in an era of hyper-clutter, polarized ideologies, and constraining cultural scripts. For Nietzsche, self-mastery in such an existence requires the self to author one's own values and morality, especially in a human condition framed by nihilism, a scenario that reflects how "advanced" societies of modernity, its technocracy, robotic efficiency, and emphasis on reason and rationality, have indifferently robbed from actors meaning and awareness of the human condition. Even though such a nihilistic society is seen as having no inherent meaning or purpose, Nietzsche argues that members of the community unwittingly reproduce this nihilism through their own conformity, sycophancy, and deference to social systems that, in turn, author superficial meanings about existence for them. Yet, lamented Nietzsche, many do not even realize this aspect of the human condition and, instead, actively enable their own vulgarizations of what it means to exist in society, further reinforced by social systems that require them to remain members of a captive audience for life. Such a problematic defined Nietzsche's search for answers, an undertaking that has resulted in works that even for today's readers offer a "rare and intoxicating experience" into the mind of a philosopher whom many feel an "immediate, intimate contact with," according to philosophers Robert Solomon and Kathleen Higgins (1988, 4).

   Nihilism is seen in this work to be alive and well in the twenty-first century. Of concern, however, is that some actors overlook the catalysts generating a nihilism tied to what Zygmunt Bauman (2000) describes as a "liquid modernity," one distinctly different from the "heavy" modernity ushered in by industrialization and early capitalism at the end of nineteenth-century Europe, yet one that continues to develop a modernity through globalized economies of mindless consumption and revanchist geopolitics. Such hyper-living forces upon the actor shifting lifestyles, a process that for many will be littered with stressors and emptied of depth and meaning. Like the heavy modernity that ushered in what Nietzsche believed was the death of god, conceptualizing a liquid modernity—a modernity of hyper-stimuli with new and quickly shifting power centers beyond the state—allows us to see how Nietzsche's philosophy offers up new considerations for the self in society, a self that currently chafes under the constraints of politicized cultural scripts and corporatocratic regulations. It is here that Nietzsche's ideas can still have much utility in reminding readers about how one can still self-author meaning with aplomb, self-mastery, and self-overcoming. Thus, the boundary of a heavy and liquid modernity will be blurred in this work, yet nonetheless chronologically sequenced, to reveal the power of Nietzsche's philosophy as it forges from old to new horizons in conceptualizing how the self exists in modernizing societies under duress.

   But why is meaning so important for the human being? Such a query has befuddled great minds of previous epochs regardless of whether it stems from prophets, philosophers, poets, artists, or visionaries. The question of meaning continues to astound and confound the individual thinker as the daily grind of an arithmetic and quantifiable life shaped by finances, profit, income, stock dividends, and materialism can no longer satiate a hunger for a purpose and a calling, nor provide a cushion for that person who falls into the abyss of personal trials and tribulations, some to never again emerge. Yet some thematic cues do cohere into a center of gravity that informs the function of meaning. For Nietzsche, life experiences—especially hardships—provide for the individual access to self-mastery and overcoming in ways that are further enriched by a courageous handling of suffering. The profound discontents in life experiences are what creates, if one is made mindful, life-affirming meaning and purpose for existing—but only upon overcoming the precarious corporeality of existence, even if they usher in the most painful energies and sentiments. In an opinion piece in *Physicsworld.com*, philosopher Robert P. Crease notes how Nietzsche's philosophy is based on reminding readers that "if you simply banter about abstractions without connecting them to the life source from which they arose, you can say anything you damn well please, because you have lost track of life itself" (2018).

The importance of introducing new cues for navigating one's journey through life is significant not least because reason and rationality, expected of how institutions of modernity should be administered, have reached their limits in illuminating depth and content for the self. Nietzsche felt these concerns viscerally and envisioned an exemplary human being that, according to Richard Schacht of *Human, All Too Human*, would still be able to exhibit the acumen and tenacity to forge ahead with purpose and meaning even though the pathos of modernity—an impoverishment of both aforementioned states of being—characterize the void of nihilism (cited in Nietzsche 1996, ix). For Nietzsche, such an elevated human being could thus stare into the valley of nihilism and awake from what has been a deep slumber, one instilled and reinforced by modernity's clutter of cultural scripts and other forms of ideological domination. Failing to usher in such a great being traps us in a decadence that nourishes nihilism. Yet how Nietzsche sloganeered the importance of overcoming nihilism is inimitable, and his books "are highly idiosyncratic, born of questioning in the face of pain and death, a kind of crystallized spray from massive brain waves" (Middleton 2007, xi).

For some scholars, nihilism contains objective historical content. Donald A. Crosby, for example, observes that nihilism can be seen as trends in the thought of our times. Even though the roots of nihilism lie "in the beginning of the modern era," its salience "in the last one hundred years and particularly in the period since World War I" is most pronounced in cultural expression (Crosby 1988, 5). As content informing a means of conceptualizing the world, Crosby describes existential nihilism as a view that "judges human existence to be pointless and absurd" (1988, 30), a view that sees life as leading to nowhere and amounting to irrelevance, to nothing. For Crosby, "it is entirely gratuitous, in the sense that there is no justification for life" (1988, 30). With such a view:

> The only feasible goal for anyone who understands the human condition is the abandonment of all goals and the cultivation of a spirit of detached resignation while awaiting life's last and greatest absurdity, an annihilating death that wipes us so cleanly from the slate of existence as to make it appear that we had never lived. (Crosby 1988, 30–31)

Some of Nietzsche's contemporaries, like Leo Tolstoy, added to this dismal state a dose of cynicism:

> I could give no reasonable meaning to any single action or to my whole life. . . . Today or tomorrow sickness and death will come . . . to those I love or to me; nothing will remain but stench and worms. Sooner or later my affairs, whatever they may be, will be forgotten, and I shall not exist. . . . One can only live while one is

intoxicated with life; as soon as one is sober it is impossible not to see that it is all a mere fraud and a stupid fraud. (cited in Crosby 1988, 31)

Succumbing to any attribute of such nihilistic states of being, where vital energy for life and living is sapped, is what greatly concerned Nietzsche. A key consequence of nihilism to Nietzsche in *On the Genealogy of Morality* is that humanity has retreated into predictability and complacency. Challenging the self as a project for life and living is abandoned for creature comforts as modern humanity descends into exhaustion and hollow apathy, where the sight of fellow human beings now "makes us tired," according to Nietzsche, and as such we no longer love and respect humanity, prompting him to remark that "what is nihilism today if it not that?" (I, SEC. 12 / 2006a, 25).

Political scientist Bruce Detwiler credits Nietzsche for recognizing that "an unswerving adherence to tradition turns easily into a stultifying conventionalism repressive of life," and that "the greatest benefactors of mankind have often been the destroyers of tradition" who, by "toppling old boundary markers," create "new standards of values" for vanquishing nihilism (1990, 7). Rolf-Peter Horstmann of *Beyond Good and Evil* offers a view of a Nietzsche terrain that is a "chaotic dynamic process without any stability or direction," a context the sovereign being will need to overcome in the process of remaking the self in society (cited in Nietzsche 2002, xvi–xvii). The free spirit tasked with navigating this terrain, according to Nietzsche, is therefore someone who can teach us the art of enduring life through self-authored empowerment, freed from decaying social systems that amplify nihilism. The process forwarded by Nietzsche advocates a will to power to construct new values and purpose in a nihilistic universe, for as Crosby argues, in a nihilistic age where there is "no prior plan, purpose, or meaning to life," we are also "released from all barriers of inhibitions to freedom" and "no scale of value constrains us" (1988, 34). Such a process can be made to vanquish the dysfunctions outputted by society, and in ways that allow the sovereign actor to be made operative and optimized in different modernities. Such a sovereign overcoming actor, for Nietzsche in *On the Genealogy of Morality*, is fully aware of their power and freedom, one who has a conscience *and* consciousness informed by that "rare freedom" radiating from "power over himself and his destiny," a power that has "penetrated him to his lowest depths" to become "an instinct, his dominant instinct" (II, SEC. 2 / 2006a, 37).

The notion of how the flow of modernity exacerbates the aforementioned dilemmas has rarely been addressed through an amalgamation of existential philosophy and sociology. Thus, my work attempts to address the self engaged in the process of empowerment by establishing meaning of existence beyond the dictates and influences of impaired or failing social systems. It is a work, however, that behooves us to harness the ideas of arguably the most dangerous thinker of existence that is Friedrich Nietzsche, even though existential thought has inspired a rich panoply of thinkers to comment on the nature of existence in ways that spanned the end of nineteenth-century and early twentieth-century Europe.

Alternative conceptualizations in existential thought can be seen, for example, in Arthur Schopenhauer's variant of existentialism which was pessimistic, Søren Kierkegaard famously argued that subjectivity is *the* truth, authors such as Albert Camus, Franz Kafka, Fyodor Dostoyevsky, and Leo Tolstoy conveyed their views on how existence can be absurd, while Jean Paul Sartre coined the term "existentialism" in the twentieth century as he offered his own notions of oppression and freedom. Yet it would be Nietzsche, in my view, that was most courageous, daring, and incisive in illuminating the "insides" of societies as they fail the self, a decadent society in Nietzsche-speak. Because systemic breakdown and social discontents against such outcomes are indicative of the human condition of modernity, it is not surprising, then, that many thinkers such as Hannah Arendt and Simone de Beauvoir applied Nietzsche's view to attend to unresolved issues of society related to politics and gender, respectively, while sociology's classical greats such as Max Weber and Georg Simmel relied on Nietzsche's existential observations to "read" the angst of our social world. Detwiler adds that "in the field of social and political thought alone, we can detect Nietzsche's presences in the writings of thinkers as diverse as . . . Sigmund Freud, Carl Jung, Georges Sorel, Karl Mannheim, Ortega y Gasset, Ruth Benedict, Albert Camus, Michel Foucault, Jacques Derrida, Jürgen Habermas, and most of those associated with the Frankfurt School" (1990, 6). Theodor Adorno, an important member of the Frankfurt School, had remarked that "of all the so-called great philosophers I owe him [Nietzsche] by far the greatest debt—more even than to Hegel"; Michel Foucault shares similar sentiments, noting in 1998 that "no doubt . . . my archeology owes more to Nietzschean genealogy than to structuralism properly so called" (cited in Karzai 2019, xxiii–xxiv). For Karzai, Nietzsche is categorically a consummate "critic of culture . . . of civilization and politics, a poet, a historian of ideas, and a sociological thinker in his own right" (2019, xiii), one of the "most free-spirited thinkers with a clean conscience that ever existed or ever lived" (2019, xxvi).

Although the aforementioned list of Nietzsche admirers is not exhaustive, what merits consideration is that since the Industrial Revolution a variety of thinkers have sought to illuminate contours of meaning in a world where technocratic efficiency, financial calculability, and the embeddedness of Ferdinand Tönnies's notion of a self-serving *gesellschaft* have become the framework of our lives, creating a variety of discontents in the self as it negotiates with a bureaucratic society further hollowed out by rampant consumerism. Although nineteenth-century romanticists may have set this critique into motion, it would be Nietzsche's ideas that are most praxian for understanding the agency of individuals as they journey through different iterations of a decaying modernity.[1] Indeed, in Kotarba and Johnson's sanguine assessment, a key distinguishing feature of existential sociology is how it "gives us a romantic way to appreciate life" (2002, vii). In this regard, few other thinkers were more incisive in adamantly rejecting the institutional demands and scripts of the modern world, along with its rampant nationalisms and *faux* cultures, all in hopes of assembling the self-determining sovereign human being who can overcome all travails with utmost passion and fortitude. In this regard, Nietzsche is a bona fide sociological thinker. That he dared argue how one's will to power fuels an actor's agency toward society in ways that contest *dis*empowering systemic dysfunctions along consumerist, cultural, and political dimensions pulls our philosopher into the sociological cannon. Detwiler holds such a view, arguing that "there is something problematic about propounding Nietzschean ideas without exploring their ostensible political dimension" (1990, 5):

> We can say of Nietzsche's politics here that in every case he assesses the political sphere from a theoretical framework that adjudges the issue of cultural vitality and decline to be paramount. In every case he favors the kind of politics he associates with cultural vitality and the enhancement of man. For Nietzsche the problem of the Western world is ultimately a problem of decadence, and this is reflected in the political sphere. (1990, 8)

Nietzsche's ideas were unscrupulously appropriated by his sister, Elisabeth Förster-Nietzsche, a German nationalist and later, Nazi sympathizer, to promote values palpable to the nascent German nationalism of her day. Yet Nietzsche should by no means be associated with the political right. He was an ardent anti-nationalist at a time when nation-states were being imagined and constructed. In fact, as notes Bernard Williams of *The Gay Science*, many modern groups and their ideologies, from socialism to feminism—the latter two also drawing the ire of Nietzsche as we shall see in subsequent chapters— have found much support and inspiration in the philosopher's writings (cited in Nietzsche 2001, xi). Across his major works such as *Untimely Meditations* (1997b), *Human, All Too Human* (1996), *The Gay Science*[2] (2001), and *Ecce Homo* (2005, 2007b), Nietzsche makes emphatically clear the decay of culture, community, and individual freedom can be seen in the social dynamics fostered by nationalism. In *The Gay Science*, Nietzsche warns of the dangers of nationalism because it enabled if not advocated racism, a "scabies of the heart," a form of "blood poisoning" that European nations deploy to "delimit and barricade against each other as if with quarantines" (V, SEC. 377 / 2001,

242). Historian Peter Bergmann is correct to note that Nietzsche's urgent concerns about nationalism are derived from how the philosopher viewed it as a "new secular religion" (Bergmann et al. 2007, 29). For philosopher Frantisek Novosád, a sacralized nationalism is no better than Christianity, which Nietzsche saw as a "religion of resentment [*ressentiment*]" (Bergmann et al. 2007, 11). Nietzsche was a pan-European who believed that an amalgamation of all ethnic, racial, and sacral identities would favor the attainment of culture "both in nations and in individuals," according to Nietzsche scholar Walter Kaufmann (1950, 288).

Nietzsche's sense of urgency about overcoming the dysfunctions of modernity are thus his redeeming qualities as a thinker, one that can, as will be posited in this work, generate alternative considerations for constructing a self in the midst of social decay even as society imposes its worldviews and scripts on uncritical adherents. By embedding Nietzsche into sociology, efforts by sociologists to begin new conversations about actors who find agency in the midst of what Nietzsche perceived to be the essence of modernity, social decay, can be realized. Although the conventional practice by sociology is to highlight group dynamics that promote social change through systemic resistances or contestations, the view forwarded at the outset of this work establishes that a new type of human being is required for praxis, especially when social systems experience what sociologist Jürgen Habermas (1975) terms as legitimation crisis, a situation where public confidence declines in regard to how it views a society managed by its political, economic, and legal spheres. To what extent nihilism results from such decay and systemic dysfunction is one focus of my work. In such malfunctioning contexts, a new type of human being will need to be actively engaged in the process of overcoming with one's will to power, two key attributes that underpin Nietzsche's conceptualization of the superb human being with agency to vanquish life struggles.

My work thus employs Nietzsche's existential ideas in ways that presume most readers are thematically aware of his philosophy and existentialism in general. Juxtaposing Nietzsche alongside other influential existential thinkers for comparative purposes (for example, Jean Paul Sartre, Simone de Beauvoir, Arthur Schopenhauer, Albert Camus, to name but a few) would be beyond the scope of this work. Instead, I hope to discuss what Robert Antonio (1995) describes as Nietzsche's "antisociology" in ways that contribute important insights toward critical sociology itself. Within this context I harness Nietzsche to make sense of how the self relates to defective social systems. Thus, the elaboration of existentialism in this work will be amalgamated with what I highlight as Nietzsche's sociological ideas. Such an amalgamation is intended to set into motion a Nietzschean critical analyses of contemporary society's institutions and systems and how the self withstands their paroxysms. My orientation should be seen as significant if only because it makes visible how social systems in decline exhibit numerous contradictions. Yet, "repairing" such a society with another script, another formula—as in a revolutionary overthrow of capitalist society for the sake of establishing communism—is deemed unacceptable by Nietzsche.

Nietzsche's elaboration about the death of God, death of Christianity, the inefficacy of political ideologies to offer true emancipation, and the dangers of automaton-generating features of modernist culture, can be seen to offer an existential sociology for the actor who desires to still exist and prevail against a society experiencing decline. As it stands in sociology, social systems are assumed a priori to have staying power in ways that do not require maintenance or repair. We theorize on social systems by assuming they will frequently be available for scrutiny. Yet societies are fragile and vulnerable, and very mortal. Nietzsche saw this with scathing clarity. Thus, the variant of existential sociology informed by a Nietzsche lens is not only about existing beyond modernity, but is also postpositivist and postfunctionalist (Kotarba and Fontana 1984). In this regard, Nietzsche's existential sociology can be made to portray human beings "confronting life in its situatedness and staggering complexity" (Kotarba and Fontana 1984, 11).

The core orientation of my work attempts to make visible Nietzsche's sociological imagination, one that derives from the progenitor of the concept C. Wright Mills in his eponymous work (1959), yet employed to view the self experiencing systemic crisis, to be understood as when social systems exhibit acute contradictions that disrupt their ability to legitimate social ideals. The process will be challenging because one must carefully interpret Nietzsche's scathing excavation of the human *being* and *becoming* in hopes of locating that sovereign individual in a universe without gods. It will also be challenging because sociology orients its gaze toward group dynamics operating inside social systems. How then, can sociology insert the self beyond the collective for sociological analyses? I am of the view that we can employ Nietzsche sociologically by situating the self within a society experiencing some form of social degradation. And thus, lies one of the goals of this work: to employ sociological concepts to make visible the contours of systemic crisis-ridden modernities through Nietzsche's philosophy, one that warns of the consequences of nihilism when modernity's most promising utopianisms are exhibiting dysfunctions. By confronting this problematic, my work considers social obstacles that overcoming types will need to contest if they desire to retain the sovereignty of a free individual.

Because Nietzsche saw modernity and its manufacturing of consent through the state as problematic in more ways than one, he had no qualms attacking convention, conformity, and sycophancy since these state-generated forces are seen to annihilate the individual. In Nietzsche's time, Germany was experiencing such dynamics through industrialization and the power plays of Prussia's Otto Von Bismarck, creating a heavy modernity derived from science, steam, steel, bureaucracy, and nationalism, all of which required mass participation, while in the background the old European order of Napoleon Bonaparte would come to an end after the Franco-Prussian War, a "modern" and brutal war that saw Nietzsche's participation. The discontents of capitalism were also emerging: Nietzsche lived in a time where *gesellschaft* dynamics shredded *gmeinschaft* sensibilities, where the working classes in many parts of Europe were agitating for revolution. At the age of 26, Nietzsche was aware of the Communards and their fate in the traumatic Paris Commune of 1871, an uprising launched in the immediate social discontents of the Franco-Prussian War. In the rear Christianity desperately tried to stay relevant yet continued its ignoble decline by enabling the continuation of life negation, as Nietzsche's views will reveal.

Exposed to such epic events, events that birthed nation-states but reduced the individual to automaton status, Nietzsche saw how the modernity of his time harnessed the mass populace to usher out the old order, transforming Europe quickly and violently through culture, residual religiosity, and politics. Nietzsche's philosophy had something sociologically vital to say about society in such contexts. We can offer some important Nietzsche propositions about self and society to set the tone for further discussions to take place in subsequent chapters: a) all social systems, be it the state or its outputs of culture, religion, and politics, are mortal, and b) the self must author its own philosophy of power to overcome social systems experiencing their mortality. However, Franz Solms-Laubach argues in *Nietzsche and Early German and Austrian Sociology* (2007) that in spite of Nietzsche's prescient views on society,

> Sociology . . . was an area where Nietzsche's influence was not particularly apparent, not at least when compared to that of Karl Marx: while Marx's impact on sociology is largely unquestioned, for many a "Nietzschean sociology" seems not to have existed. Only in recent years has there been . . . interest in developing such a notion. Yet although Marx and Nietzsche are by no means founders of sociology, their respective analyses inspired many of the crucial concerns of early sociology . . . they raised various important questions, which sociology aimed to answer later on. (2007, 3)[3]

An important consideration forwarded in my work is that Nietzsche's sociological imagination cannot be distilled without assistance from other sociologists. These additional thinkers and their contributions to a Nietzschean sociological imagination will be further discussed in the coming chapters. I will be revisiting in greater depth ideas from sociologists such as C. Wright Mills and his sociological imagination, a perspective that will be made operative with Nietzsche's critique of decadent society and culture. Jürgen Habermas and Erich Fromm will also be made to offer up their sociologies in ways that amalgamate with Nietzsche's sociological imagination. Contemporary Nietzsche thinkers and biographers will also be frequently invoked, notably Nietzsche scholars such Walter Kaufmann, Maudemarie Clark, Julian Young, and Franz Solms-Laubach, to name but a few. When in need of reflecting upon the legacies and dysfunctions of utopian energies in the evolution of modernity, insights by Zygmunt Bauman (2000) will be harnessed. As these scholars' arguments and concepts are introduced in the assembly of Nietzsche's sociological imagination, it is my hope that the conclusion of this work will reveal contours of a Nietzsche sociology, one that is informed by additional social thinkers of modernity, nihilism, democracy, and the human condition. Reflected in such an undertaking is that the lexicon that begins and ends my work will be different.

Echoing Nietzsche's concern for the individual to exhibit self-mastery in life struggle, in a context where God and Christianity are "dead," this work examines through a Nietzsche lens the next iteration of systemic dysfunction, the dysfunction of modernity and democracy as they enable totalitarianism and authoritarianism to police society, doing irreparable harm to the sovereignty and freedoms of people. One need not look far for such an exemplar: the current president of the United States at the time of this writing is the quintessential example of how a dysfunctional democracy accommodates authoritarianism and dictatorial dynamics.[4] Designed to function as a critical thought exercise writ large, my work attempts to highlight the eerie parallels between the contentions that god and democracy are dead: both are idealized sublimations of a people, both serve as idealized outcomes, both are designed to control and police human behavior, both need conjured enemies to exist, and both employ their ideals to admonish and punish non-conformists. Simply stated, the "worship" of democratism, along with other *isms* of modernity, is but the worship of a new "god," a new idol composed for a secular era, yet both systems exhibit acute hypocrisies and double standards that vacillate with political climate. Detwiler echoes Nietzsche's sentiments by noting how in modernity "all systematic thought becomes a precarious affair, fraught with passion and predicated upon self-serving suppositions" that ultimately leads one "into nihilism and beyond" (1990, 6). If it has not yet become evident, I am adding to the sequence of nihilism-generating crises already offered by Nietzsche, namely that the demise of the classical Greek state was later followed by the demise of Christianity (and religion in general), only to be followed by a decaying modernity exemplified by its scripted and enforced utopianisms, defeatist and herdish ideologies, identity politics, and political correctness.

The depth and implication of such an assertion is overall meant to be a critical thought exercise, but one that, it is hoped, will make visible a path toward self-praxian resistances to democratic systems under de facto control by corporatist states. By the second half of the twentieth century, contemporary sociologists such as Jürgen Habermas incisively argued that "colonizing" tendencies exist *inside* democracy between election cycles, even in ostensibly inclusive political systems where voters and competing elites elect their leaders, if one adopts political scientist Robert Dahl's views (1956, 1961, 1968, 1989). Yet the quality of the spaces between election cycles where all of us engage with daily living, what Habermas envisions as the lifeworld, is rarely considered in the process of questioning the merits and validity of democracy.

The lifeworld, a term popularized by turn-of-the-twentieth-century philosopher Edmund Husserl and a later contemporary sociologist Alfred Schutz, represents the frenetic world of everyday occurrences and social interactions. It is an epistemological and ontological environment where social interactions take place beyond the scripts dispensed to us by regulatory institutions serving as forces of domination. For Habermas who took the concept to a greater analytical depth, the lifeworld's significance is how it functions as a site of democratic production and activism that can ostensibly challenge authority systems. These dynamics take place in the lifeworld's public spheres, a historical category of sites of social life where deliberation and problem solving for the actor and community take place.

Defined as any social environment "open to all, in contrast to closed or exclusive" systems (1991, 1), Habermas's rendering of the public sphere has been reconceptualized by other scholars, with Eley defining the concept as that "realm of social life in which something approaching public opinion can be formed" and where "access is guaranteed to all citizens" (1994, 289). Eley emphasizes how a "portion of the public sphere comes into being in every conversation" where "private individuals assemble to form a public body" (1994, 289). What is crucial for understanding the concept from a Habermasian perspective is that its entire thesis posits that democracy remains an incomplete project if lifeworld dynamics in public spheres do not include bottom-to-top democratic deliberations by individuals or the community. However, Habermas is also aware of the challenges of completing democracy in such a social context since the lifeworld is a liquid, dynamic horizon that is "always . . . moving" (1987, 119), one where "communicative action relies on a cooperative process of interpretation in which participants relate simultaneously to something in the objective, the social, and the subjective worlds" (Habermas 1987, 120).

Within such a lifeworld, whatever freedoms exist are severely constrained by institutional regulations and technical language emanating from bureaucracies and institutions. Thus, Habermas sees a colonized lifeworld as a signifier for what he famously observed to be an incomplete democracy, a repository of numerous incomplete freedoms. My work interprets Habermas's rendering of the aforementioned scenario as leading actors toward experiences with legitimation crises and nihilism. This situation is further exacerbated by an identity politics that force many to walk on multicultural minefields, that force upon the actor self-policing for the sake of remaining politically correct. Such scripts have resulted in lessening freedoms for the autonomy-aspiring individual. Flooded by technical and legal-regulatory language and multicultural panopticons of cultural defense and offense, individuals are led to find comfort in a variety of socially engineered spaces where groupthink and the need to feel persecuted by the "other," as seen in some narratives of identity politics, become a new "morality" replete with reified and unresolved angst and indignations. In this regard, the expectations by social systems for individuals to conform is their raison d'etre. For Sokol, "all religious and pseudo-religious ideologies would lack their main ingredient—malleable human material," if freethinkers begin purposing their own existence beyond the demands and expectations of social systems (Bergmann et al. 2007, 29).

Employing Habermas to enhance Nietzsche's sociological imagination allows us to illuminate an alternative sociological imagination, one that attempts to locate agency in freethinkers confronting impaired social systems through Nietzsche's epithet of the *übermensch*, the superhuman, the overcomer. As one who through self-mastery has freed the self from scripted culture and morality, one who can overcome every instance of life struggle due to living by one's own rules, virtues, and belief systems, such a character is argued in my work to be a needed actor when society's state and corporatocratic apparatuses are decadent.[5] Nietzsche in *Thus Spoke Zarathustra* had high hopes for such an overcomer, described as a self-conquering sovereign of one's senses and virtues (2006b, 51). It is thus useful for us to conceptualize the overcomer as an ideal type able to contest and prevail against, among other things, Weberian iron cages put into place by various iterations of the machinery of modernity. I attempt to make operative such an overcomer by illuminating the social terrain where such a person's agency will be needed to contest a modern society replete with nihilistic systems designed to define and regulate, if not dictate, the life experience. And because these systems output nihilistic elements such as technical and regulatory language, ideologies that defer sovereign individuals to systems, illusory utopias, and social scripts, they are viewed as existing in a condition of degeneration.

Few ideals in the twentieth century have been more touted geopolitically and reworked domestically than the need for democracy and democratic practices. As a sacralized concept that has taken on mystical undertones if not simply for admonishing rogue countries and failed states that are bereft of freedom, whatever their nuances may be, democracy's effects upon the life-world as a variable and not teleology have rarely been addressed. Moreover, there is a dangerous assumption that democracy, good governance, and personal freedoms mean the same thing. However, democracy should never be celebrated simply because people are able to participate in elections. As noted in a 2006 *Foreign Policy* article on failed states, voting will certainly allow the disenfranchised to voice their grievances, but such a process cannot be seen to, by default, translate into good governance. My position, through the ideas of Nietzsche and contemporary sociologists like Jürgen Habermas, attempts to address these distinctions. That is, not all democracies are the same. Democracies are variables: different eras will see a rise or fall in the quality of a state's democracy in ways that affect one's personal freedoms. Similarly, some states also see democracies disappear, if momentarily, only to return full force with a new government.[6] Yet were one to condemn democracy its proponents will be aghast and holler their indignations, an eerie response paralleling the indignation religious pundits certainly felt with Nietzsche's declaration that god is dead. The promises of both universes have been so idealized that their tropes: charismatic leaders, pageantry of uniforms, rituals, symbols, freedoms, human rights, and iterations of the "promised land," will hopefully allow this work to segue readers from Nietzsche's critique of god to a critique of democracy, yet another false "idol" if one adopts a Nietzschean lens.

The intention of this work is to employ Nietzsche's sociological imagination so that it can express an actor's desire for freedom from dysfunctional systems, understood in this work to be regulated by political, market, and cultural scripts that demand a currency: conformity as members of a captive audience, an outcome best captured by Antonio Gramsci's notion of hegemony and the market's manufacturing of consent. In his time, Nietzsche was a courageous and daring thinker that called out the death of God and Christianity; my role is to make operative Nietzsche's thinking for examining the next system I posit to falter after god and religion, modernity's democratism and its other *isms*, as well as how its degeneration keeps open the floodgates of nihilism. It is hoped the tenets conveyed herein will inspire readers to carefully consider the emancipatory potential of individual existence beyond the de jure offerings of democracy, for beyond this horizon is the cauldron of the lifeworld where numerous unresolved sociological issues percolate, where their broken pieces fall upon the populace as regulatory legal language while a similar sacralization of multiculturalism has promoted voluntary segregation and sectarian tensions. Additionally, the ostensibly "free" media continues to forge ahead with its vulgarized and propagandistic biases while conveying to excess histrionics, melodrama, sensationalism, and shock value. These aforementioned dynamics all challenge individuals seeking empowerment as they navigate their colonized lifeworlds.

A critical approach toward democracy will also enable readers to appreciate Nietzsche's prescient ideas about other utopian *isms*, that is, socialism, capitalism, atheism, Darwinism, feminism, to name but a few. Nietzsche did not spare these *isms* from scathing critique. For example, he vehemently rejects pessimism, an idea that Arthur Schopenhauer courted with Nietzsche's inspiration. Additionally, in his major work *Beyond Good and Evil* (2002), Nietzsche critiques hedonism, utilitarianism, and eudaimonism as naive thinking, while asking those who believe in their own sense of power to transcend such *isms* with disdain "as well as pity"—not pity for the doctrines per se, but how the doctrines have become internalized by the people (VII, SEC. 225 / 2002, 116). Nietzsche laments how such adherents are responsible for withering the life-affirming expanses of the self *in* humanity, that such a self *in* humanity is dwindling, and that modernity's conformists of all persuasions, indoctrinated by their social systems, "are making it smaller!" (VII, SEC. 225 / 2002, 116).

More importantly, that Nietzsche addresses, analyzes, and critiques these themes throughout his writings reveals his acumen for political analyses, and that "antipolitical interpretations" of Nietzsche, according to Detwiler, "are ultimately unconvincing" (1990, 3). For Detwiler, Nietzsche's acknowledgement of other political themes beyond the Greek state as discussed in *The Birth of Tragedy*, such as the *Imperium Romanum*, the Russian empire, along with historical characters like Napoléon Bonaparte and Cesare Borgia (who inspired Machiavelli's *Prince*), along with Machiavelli himself (whose ideas Nietzsche viewed as "perfection in politics"), reveals the deep commitment Nietzsche had not only with one's will to power—his "theory of the soul" according to Clark and Dudrick (2012, 243)—but with the problematics outputted by systemic power (see Detwiler 1990, 3–4).

Nietzsche's ideas can thus also be appreciated as they identify new possibilities for reimagining the human condition in a twenty-first-century modernity through actors who maximize their sovereignty to purpose their own existence. It is thus not surprising that Nietzsche had a strong disdain for social movements that attempted to save what he perceived to be an enfeebled humanity through the *isms* of his day. He also concomitantly saw democratic institutions that meted out power from above as decadent, a symbol of degeneration, and he expended much energy condemning its practices alongside the aforementioned *isms*. Such a disdain, for Nietzsche, was justified because the *isms*, through public policy, conflated exceptional human beings with conformists, ensuring the latter's fanatical control of society in spite of their sloganeered pieties to liberate all humanity. Hannah Arendt would decades later argue in *The Origins of Totalitarianism* (1973) that such a system functioned to obliterate important elites in society—philosophers, artists, free spirits, educators, and/or warriors of self-mastery—all of whom can be seen as overcoming types that are so welcomed by Nietzsche. We can understandably see why Nietzsche was unabashed in sloganeering the preservation of great yet benevolent elites who saw the noble mindset as one with the self-mastery to overcome obstacles thrown the way of the individual, obstacles that include conditions stemming from when the *isms* of modernity have enabled their own contradictions that ultimately negate the self. Arendt hauntingly validates Nietzsche's prescience:

> Intellectual, spiritual, and artistic initiative is as dangerous to totalitarianism as the gangster initiative of the mob, and both are more dangerous than mere political opposition. The consistent persecution . . . by the new mass leaders springs from more than their natural resentment against everything they cannot understand. Total domination does not allow for free initiative in any field of life, for any activity that is not entirely predictable. Totalitarianism in power . . . replaces all first-rate talents, regardless of their sympathies, with those crackpots and fools whose lack of intelligence and creativity is still the best guarantee of their loyalty. (1973, 339)

It is important to emphasize at this juncture that Nietzsche's notion of being noble is not based on legitimating a historical class of elites, but more rather, points to the actor with agency who has a warrior and judicious mindset as well as a master plan for self-affirmation. Such an actor should be contrasted with those with less fortitude who conform to scripts and rely on others for direction and authority to navigate the lifeworld. For Nietzsche, nobility is a state of being. The "noble" types are, for philosopher Paul Patton, "defined by their power over themselves rather than by their power over others" (Bergmann et al. 2007, 23). Nietzsche opined, frequently through the proxy of Zarathustra, that the scripts are themselves the problem, are themselves instruments that have been used to colonize the lifeworld in a Habermasian sense, robbing the noble-mindset of its nascence. As a proponent for higher humans, Nietzsche believed that those who do not understand their world should defer to those that do, for the latter fought for their place in the life experience. The latter are authors of their own destiny, having overcome life's trials and tribulations. Such higher humans are the embodiment of courage and fortitude that need to be discerned from society's followers and conformists. Nietzsche writes in *Beyond Good and Evil* how developing the self toward greatness requires one who is simply unique, propelled by a self-authored value system that allows such a person to maintain resolute poise in the art of living and suffering. Such a master of virtues is filled with an abundance of will, according to Nietzsche, and only such a character should be seen as exhibiting "greatness" (VI, SEC. 212 / 2002, 107).

Because Nietzsche's ideas are dynamic and rich with foresight relevant to our current liquid modernity, understanding his sociological imagination becomes an experience toward a renewed, lived freedom, rather than an introspective or contemplative undertaking that espouses renunciation through an ascetic ideal, to be understood as "the belief that the best human life is one of self-denial" (Clark 1990, 160). Nietzsche's views force us into a renewed encounter with the discontents of twenty-first-century experiences with modernity. These experiences, along with lifeworld colonization, can actually be viewed by the actor as the process unfolds every hour of every day: personal freedoms are eroded by corporatocratic scripts disguised as culture, political malfeasance is exhibited by leaders, and grassroots policing is undertaken by identity groups who thrive in the insularities of academia, cultural provincialisms, and voluntary segregation.

The illumination of a Nietzsche sociological imagination is meant to celebrate the urgency with which he positioned the overcomer to confront social systems. In this manner, Nietzsche's celebration of the ideal type of the elevated noble individual that is the overcomer, one for whom a society in its dysfunctions can be overcome through the appropriation of suffering for reassembly into a life-affirming ethos, reminds us about the continuing importance of prevailing as actors in a liminal society. For Nietzsche, were such an overcomer realized, a shared humanity will tie them together in their sovereignty, while those unable to rise from their discontents will cravenly slog on as conformists and poseurs, destined to be but captive sycophants that defer to convention and its manufacturing of perfunctory scripts. Nietzsche's conceptualizations and renderings of the overcomer, the will to power, the cultural philistine, *ressentiment*, *amor fati*, the eternal recurrence, last human beings, the revaluation of values, the herd, the "true world," pity, the noble mind, and controversially, the noble and servant moralities, to name but a few of his concepts, will thus be treated as integral to his sociological imagination, one that develops an overcoming identity that is an antipode to a victim identity.

The task of making operative Nietzsche's sociological imagination to highlight oppressive dynamics within democracy today is more feasible than imagined. The twenty-first century continues to exhibit numerous inequalities that are experienced by those who have inherited the promises of modernities, democracies, and free markets as new utopias, which for Nietzsche are but new false "idols" to replace god. Societies in such a state are in constant flux due to their decentralization and disjunction from one another, a situation allowing for states and their insides to putrefy in ways where democracy can face legitimation crises, compelling the actor to flock toward experts, further reproducing alternative hierarchies in a lifeworld already consumed by rationalized institutions and their technical, regulatory, and legal language. As sociologists, we already approach the human condition and experience through its patinas and intersections of inequality, class struggle, cultural wars, and identity politics of different persuasions; sociologists are already fortuitously connected to these discontents of modernity, discontents that are our raison d'être. In this regard, Bauman's description of a liquid modernity is important not least because its thesis about sociological ambivalence and fluidity potentially makes visible the conditions that generate nihilism, allowing a point of entry for Nietzsche's sociological imagination to animate the overcomer to confront the discontents of not only our philosopher's modernity but the liquid modernity of the twenty-first century.

Employing a Nietzsche sociological imagination is not without some major challenges, however. Nietzsche disdained the earliest expression of the sociology and spewed vitriol against two contemporary sociologists of his era, Auguste Comte and Herbert Spencer. Nietzsche criticized the ideas of both Comte and Spencer for promoting views that entitle the collective aspirations of those Nietzsche perceived to be defeatists and conformists, those unable to overcome the trials and tribulations of the human condition exacerbated by social systems idealized by Comte and Spencer.[7] Nietzsche thus passionately sought a solution for the individual in systemic decay. As such, we can better appreciate Nietzsche's sociological imagination if we remain cognizant that Nietzsche valued agency as a means to confront a society unable to live up to its ideals.

Nietzsche's critique against defective social systems along with their institutions and bureaucracies is what makes his ideas surprisingly sociological. Sociologists such as Franz Solms-Laubach have devoted an entire monograph to assess whether Nietzsche was a sociologist, and whether there can be a Nietzschean sociology, which he ultimately affirmed. Philosophers such as Julian Young (2006), on the other hand, have convincingly presented Nietzsche's sociological emphasis for community, framing him as a committed communitarian as well as individualist. Young's discussion of Nietzsche as a communitarian is fortuitous for it provides many access points for sociology to amalgamate with Nietzsche's critical view of social systems. Kaufmann even argues that because Nietzsche focused on "the contrast of those who have power and those who lack it . . . he investigates it by contrasting not individuals but groups of people. The distinction therefore tends to become sociological as the consequences of oppression are considered" (1950, 297). Nietzsche not only envisioned an ideal community of life-affirming, noble-minded people, but he concerned himself with how such a community could ensure that narratives of greatness are reproduced for subsequent generations. In *Human, All Too Human*, Nietzsche chides the shortsighted for rupturing such a continuity, arguing how the end of a metaphysical outlook is evinced by individuals no longer preparing formulations for greatness and self-actualization that can be reproduced for posterity. The individual in such a *gesellschaft* mode is criticized for strategizing for opportunities on a short-term basis, neglecting the establishment of social institutions that can reproduce greatness to be bestowed upon members of subsequent generations.

Other scholars have conveyed their appreciation for what Nietzsche's sociological imaginations have uncovered. Patrik Aspers argues that Nietzsche's ideas are useful to sociology because

> he contributes to the sociological discussions on, for example, culture, theory, and being. Nietzsche's work is valuable because his ardent antisociology in fact highlights how much of human being is conditioned by the social . . . that both Nietzsche's critique of contemporary social thinking and his own ethical development reveal the social underpinning of human beings. A central theme of this sociological analysis is Nietzsche's discussion of what we today call "social constructivism," a viewpoint now well accepted in the social sciences. (2007, 474–475)

For Dominika Partyga, Nietzsche's readings of society, or more rather his reading of the entire human condition as it stands, "deprives us of the fake comfort of definitive answers" (2016, 416). In an American experience where the totalitarianism of identity groups has created petty provincialisms that halt dialog by invoking a persecuting "other" engaged in their perennial disenfranchisement, the scathing incisiveness that Nietzsche offers us for the sake of being liberated from such insular and defeatist identities informed by political correctness should be welcomed, especially in an age of cultural and political volatility—in an age where, especially in the United States, multicultural wars and voluntary segregation continue.

What Nietzsche articulates sociologically is that only by delinking the individual from impaired social systems can the actor then purpose their life path through what he terms as the "revaluation of all values," a process whereby the actor consciously and willfully disposes of or purges all previously-held belief systems. Nietzsche's criticism of sociologists like Comte and Spencer was based on how he believed they did not entertain the volatility and mortality of social systems and the values outputted by them, preferring instead to speak teleologically of laws that drive human and social development. Yet such a critique is but a foregone conclusion to contemporary sociologists: grand theories exhibit a too overarching explanatory scope upon the dynamics of actors, potentially denying them agency. Few sociologists today would ever seriously consider Comte's or Spencer's grand theories as relevant, let alone build their entire academic or research careers based on their suppositions. Nietzsche's prescience through his antisociology, one whose subversion of taken for granted values and systems, renders him not only a most radical and revolutionary sociological thinker, but one whose ideas embolden us to engage in a major paradigm shift toward developing ourselves in relation to very mortal and ephemeral societies.

Whether Nietzsche is a bona fide sociologist might actually be a misplaced question since the contemporary period he flourished in saw the birth of the discipline of sociology, one that was still exhibiting teething issues with its discourse. In this regard, mention needs to be made of how Nietzsche deeply influenced many German sociologists of his day. This influence was best illuminated by Solms-Laubach (2007) who highlighted how the philosopher's critiques influenced Max Weber, Alfred Weber, Ferdinand Tönnies, and Rosa Mayreder. For the members of the group, Nietzsche offered key themes for critiquing modernity's discontents and inequalities. For example, Solms-Laubach documented how Tönnies during his youth had an "existential experience" and "revelation" after reading Nietzsche's *Birth of Tragedy* but in later life became a critic of the philosopher (2007, 155).[8]

In my work, I view Nietzsche as an important figure through his existential sociological imagination. That is, Nietzsche's sociological imagination is where I hope to embed his existentialism into sociology in ways that reveal how actors can exhibit self-authored agency and sovereignty when the surrounding social order fails to fulfill its social contract. How such a self in society overcomes this situation offers up new conceptualizations of freedom forged by contestations against social systems within which they live. Yet for those less empowered, an escape from their own freedoms ensues as they flee from the responsibilities of decision-making needed to maintain their freedom, as so appropriately noted by the Frankfurt School's Erich Fromm. In this regard, my work examines how another group of social actors, those that prevail by not running away from freedom, can overcome democracy's contradictions by confronting its authoritarian and totalitarian tendencies as *the* act of freedom. It is an attempt to again introduce the importance of the individual as active agent within social systems, especially one that can overcome all iterations of systemic crises.

My work thus highlights the sociological and philosophical interplay of ideas in ways that illuminate the obstacles to be faced by the overcomer. Nietzsche is thus rendered a sociological thinker for a discipline that was also heavily informed by the discontents and meaninglessness of modern society, one that democracies are embedded in, one that provides numerous overlapping and conflicting contexts for the actor in search of defining the self in society. By ultimately exposing the vacillations of democracy and modernity's other *isms* as they appear to degenerate, my work envisions how systemic crises can serve as nodes for the overcomer's will to power to outmaneuver systemic dysfunctions. I must concede, however, that my work, envisioned as a big thought exercise, did not systematically operationalize many concepts, preferring instead to employ them in a dialogic manner. Thus, notions of systemic "dysfunction," or systemic "failure," or systemic "impairment," to name a few examples, should be seen at this juncture as rather synonymous and interchangeable terms. There are two main reasons for this approach. The first reason pertains to my wish to ensure that Nietzsche's ideas flow smoothly from one chapter to the next, as well as across all chapters in the work. For this to be achieved, I streamlined Nietzschean and sociological concepts by loosening them up for better breathability. The second reason is as I am still attempting to illuminate the usefulness of Nietzsche's philosophy for the discipline of sociology, many considerations remain rather fluid, considerations that will nonetheless try to articulate—if my work succeeds—that there is enough "propulsion" in Nietzsche's ideas to add to ongoing discourse about social contexts, ideologies, and other problematics that stifle individual agency today.

In chapter 1, C. Wright Mills's (1959) notion of the sociological imagination, the view that understanding the biography of the individual requires tying the person to history, social contexts, and social change, will be examined and woven into a reworking of Nietzsche as a sociological thinker. Additionally, the overcomer is discussed within the context of the sociological imagination, one that Mills believed allowed for a more accurate assessment of social and historical contexts affecting the self. Amalgamating the initiative that defines the overcomer within contexts critiqued by a Nietzsche sociological imagination thus readies the overcomer to be active in a variety of challenging social developments. That is, the process of reworking Mills's sociological imagination into a Nietzsche variant allows the sociological horizons of the latter to historically accommodate contexts of social duress, as when Nietzsche sequenced systemic crises beginning with the Dionysian Greek culture that was destroyed by Socratic reason, only to be followed by the death of God, Christianity, and soon, modernity itself.

Although Solms-Laubach's (2007) exegesis of Nietzsche and Kaufmann's (1950) and Clark's (1990, 2012, 2015) examinations of the philosopher's ideas are exponentially useful for deriving cues about an existential sociological imagination, the authors exhibited divergent trajectories in thought:

whereas Solms-Laubach convincingly explains why Nietzsche is an excellent sociologist, the latter two invite readers into a most thorough contextualization of Nietzsche's life, his notion of truth, and nuanced readings and applications of his most important concepts. However, the chapter also argues that an enhanced reading of Nietzsche requires the deployment of C. Wright Mills's penetrating mode of observation that is the sociological imagination, one that makes visible impaired social systems which the overcomer will confront. Chapter 1 thus begins the rendering of Nietzsche as a sociological thinker with a critical view of society, and how such a rendering shares affinities with Solms-Laubach's views that Nietzsche is a bona fide sociologist.

The overcomer, Nietzsche's *übermensch*, is also introduced in the first chapter to signify the importance of how such an actor will need to contest a variety of systemic crises to be discussed in the remaining chapters of this work. By making operative our overcomer at the outset as a praxian and sovereign being with agency, yet fully aware of its ideal type status, our elevated protagonist can thus be made to stare panoramically into the insides of society as the chapters unfold. The analogy and implication of someone at great heights gazing into society is deliberate for its symbolism, for Nietzsche believed that higher human beings and overcomers, with their elevated noble consciousness of self-mastery and self-authorship of life, would be the agents of change in a society he saw as failing, in a society "below" them. The importance of such a protagonist, introduced early in my work, will ideally allow readers to envision how a self-authoring agent can outmaneuver the paroxysms and nihilism of a modernity that Nietzsche illuminates and chastises.

Chapter 2 examines Nietzsche's publications employed in my work, their alternative titles, and how they will be referred to in shorthand. It begins, however, with a discussion of distortions that have been introduced in our understanding of Nietzsche due to the reworking of his ideas by his sister, Elisabeth Förster-Nietzsche. Due to her support for German nationalism, and later Hitler and Nazism, the "posthumously published" work by Nietzsche, *The Will to Power*, was actually Förster-Nietzsche's deleterious reassembly of her brother's notes where she appropriated the *übermensch* concept and reassembled it into an ideal type of the Aryan. This machination is the paramount reason that *The Will to Power*, a book that was not assembled by Nietzsche while he was still alive and in full possession of his mental faculties, will not be cited.

Nietzsche's writing style is also discussed in the chapter, especially his use of aphorisms, metaphors, and analogies as he writes about the modern human condition. Additionally, his idiosyncratic use of punctuation marks will also be discussed, especially Nietzsche's unconventional use of dashes, parentheses, ellipses, and colons, and how these are employed to make sentences pause for effect,[9] allowing readers to soak up his profundities, intensity, and rhythm. Nietzsche, as we shall see, is a very passionate, sometimes playful and humorous, but always very "vocal" writer, a politically-incorrect stentor. Nietzsche's charged and dynamic writing style, one that energetically reveals to readers his penetrating observations, substantiates the view that "no modern thinker of a like profundity has had at his command so flexible an instrument of expression," as describes the venerable Nietzsche biographer R. J. Hollingdale (1999, 16).

Nietzsche's penetrating writing style and insights have prompted philosophers such as Maudemarie Clark to offer praise, noting that Nietzsche "could do incredible things with language, things that most of us may be better off not even trying to imitate," as well as citing how such a dynamic style prompted Sigmund Freud to remark that Nietzsche has "greater self-knowledge than any man who ever lived, or is ever likely to live" (Clark 1990, ix–x). The conclusion of chapter 2 adopts a more serious tone regarding the importance of "learning" how to read Nietzsche: by reading his works in sequence of publication (Young 2006; Clark and Dudrick 2012) and in a manner that does not approach Nietzsche's writings "exoterically," that is, where we read him in an uncritical or careless manner based on, for example, mining for Nietzsche quotes without considering the historical contexts and life experiences that inspired the philosopher's ideas.

Chapters 3, 4, and 5 are divided according to the three publication periods that framed Nietzsche's life. The three publication periods span from his early writings (1872–1878) discussed in chapter 3, to his "nomadic" period (1879–1887) discussed in chapter 4. Chapter 5 discusses his last group of works before his mental collapse in 1889, the "1888 Texts," according to Aaron Ridley and Judith Norman, of *The Anti-Christ*, *Ecce Homo*, and *Twilight of the Idols* (cited in Nietzsche 2005). Whereas chapter 1 introduces Nietzsche's sociological imagination through C. Wright Mills, chapters 3, 4, and 5 will reveal its anatomy when seen throughout Nietzsche's different works. The task is at once manageable and difficult. It is manageable because Nietzsche was not the hyper-individualist many make him out to be, frequently expressing sociological concerns for a lack of overcoming characters that can attend to social systems in crises seen in, for example, the degeneration of Christianity and modern cultural and political ideologies. The difficulty of the task is to illuminate Nietzsche's sociological imaginations in a manner that will allow us to, in chapter 6, formulate some rudimentary assertions about the consequences of systemic crises and how these affect the self. As such, Nietzsche's works will be addressed in order of publication so that key sociological themes can be illuminated as they surface across a modernist era that Nietzsche felt to be increasingly decadent and nihilistic.

Nietzsche's autobiographical and reflective work, *Ecce Homo*, will receive a slightly different treatment, however. As one of his last major works in the 1888 period relevant to the sociological imagination, it will instead be employed throughout the summaries as a means for us to see how Nietzsche viewed his own arguments in hindsight. It thus will not be seen in the sequenced summaries of Nietzsche's works. Instead, two publications of *Ecce Homo* (2005, 2007b), the former from Cambridge University Press and the latter from Oxford University Press, will be employed to frame, reinforce, and summarize key arguments put forth by Nietzsche as we attend to his major works.

Chapter 6 examines Nietzsche's critical sociological imaginations toward a variety of systems, most notably the state, democratism, and by implication other political and social systems, and finally, the attributes in our population of conformists, or what Nietzsche pejoratively refers to as the herd. By titling chapter 6 with a "Motley Cow" reference, I highlight Nietzsche's observations in *Thus Spoke Zarathustra* of the cacophonous and conformist community caught up in the incessant rabble, melodrama, and dysfunctions of, in Habermas terms, a colonized lifeworld (1984, 1987). Chapter 6 is thus about making visible themes and processes that lead to systemic and legitimation crises of such societies and their effects upon the self, a process distinctly different than chapters 3, 4, and 5 which illuminate the flow of Nietzsche's concepts through his sociological imaginations, sequenced in order of his publications. In chapter 6, more sociological vocabulary is interwoven and amalgamated with many of Nietzsche's major ideas so that his critiques of the state, democratism, and other *isms* of modernity, along with their cultures of conformity, can be appreciated from a sociological perspective.

In undertaking the above tasks, I highlight for the overcomer ideal type the sociological terrain of social decay, one that stems from dysfunctions of religion, along with modern utopian ideologies and scripts that underpin state apparatuses. A listing of what could be considered critical propositions about the state and religion in regard to how they affect the self will thus be presented for consideration. From this set of propositions, I reinforce the view that the overcomer will need to be considered a praxian actor in light of modernity's failure to grant actors greater agency. Moreover, I also forward the view that the horizons of existential sociology begin where social systems can be seen to be in decline. In such a context, existential sociology can articulate and enable the person's agency and will to power to overcome the major consequence of impaired social systems: the creation of, or unmasking of, nihilism.

In chapter 7, I make visible Nietzsche's sociological views on how democratism and a market society enfeeble the population by rendering them a captive audience. How such a process takes place was never fully elaborated by

Nietzsche. Although Nietzsche's criticisms of democratic capitalism are pronounced, provocative, and incisive, it would be primarily Jürgen Habermas
and secondarily Erich Fromm, fellow associates of the Frankfurt School—
both of whom acknowledged the importance of existential views—that would
make visible the content of such institutionally configured conformity and
enfeeblement. Chapter 7 thus introduces Habermas's notion of the lifeworld
as colonized social and political environments. The colonization process,
undertaken through what he terms as juridification, is argued to be one of
the more tenacious constraining agents within democratism and capitalism's
lifeworlds. Indeed, chapter 7 aims to reveal that between the election cycles
of democracy, there exists numerous social contexts that enable totalitarian
dynamics to emanate from cultural spheres and apparatuses of the state. At
a time when American democracy is cheapened by a president exhibiting
authoritarian and nativist orientations toward minority populations and communities, concerns about lifeworld spaces thus validate Habermas's appre-
hension that an incomplete democracy manifests as a colonized lifeworld.
Habermas would likely affirm that such a context needs to be discerned from
the assumption that simply being able to vote in elections is enough to ensure
good governance.

In the chapter, I thus critique the assumption that democratic elections
can equate to good governance, and how such an assumption is the new
false idol of a mystified and sacralized democracy. I argue that such a dysfunctional democracy needs be framed by real political and cultural conditions as they unfurl in their social contexts, a process that I argue contains
totalitarian tendencies that demand citizen sycophancy to the outputs of the
state, whatever their diacritica may be. As such, a totalitarian democratism,
along with its political and cultural dynamics, will be seen to complement
one another through the symbiosis of different social institutions that underpin the state. I also hope to reveal that Nietzsche's view of a dysfunctional and decadent democracy makes visible how its totalitarian practices
may lay the foundations for a reified nihilism. The chapter will consider
how the top-to-bottom trajectory of bureaucratic and cultural colonization
of the lifeworld is further exacerbated by the indoctrination of the captive
citizen into a world of cultural and political scripts, and how the process of
establishing and purposing a sovereign existence is thus threatened by such
a totalitarian democratism.

Chapter 7 also intends to illuminate new terrains of praxis for our overcomer types, terrains that in spite of their unique sociological challenges, can
still be seen as fertile for the individual to flourish in ways that allow for sovereign control of how one can attend to their human condition. Contemporary

social scenarios offered by Michele Gelfand (2018), Ronald Inglehart (2018), and Nassim Nicholas Taleb (2010, 2012) are made visible for the overcoming type with a will to power to navigate. The chapter will attempt to ensure that Nietzsche's philosophy can somehow be made operative under different nuances of existing in society as illuminated by Gelfand, Inglehart, and Taleb. It introduces alternative vocabularies, and more importantly, alternative conceptualizations of social contexts and social forces that are still made to respond to Nietzsche's philosophy. The chapter concludes by considering the utility of Nietzsche's sociological imagination as an instrument for illuminating alternative paths for individual praxis, one that offers the self the empowerment needed to contest and prevail against the contradictions and dysfunctions of modernity's social systems.

A final note regarding how Nietzsche's works will be cited is in order before proceeding: Some of Nietzsche's works are identified with volumes, books (sometimes labeled essays or parts), and sections, while others have only books and sections. For his works with volumes, "Vol." will be employed to signify its number; if no volumes are employed by Nietzsche, a roman numeral will be employed for the book, essay, or part number, while "SEC." will be employed to indicate the section within the book. A forward slash "/" follows the section identifiers; following the "/" will be the edition year and page number of the specific work employed. For example, citing a Nietzsche passage in *Human, All Too Human* as "(Vol. 1, I, SEC. 22 / 1996, 23)" indicates the passage is located in the first volume of the work, in book I, and in section 22 across editions; however, the edition specifically employed in my work is signified by the year 1996 followed by page 23. The first method of citation can be employed for those who want to read across different Nietzsche editions of the same work to get a sense of variations in translation. Three of Nietzsche's works, *Thus Spoke Zarathustra, Twilight of the Idols,* and *Ecce Homo*, tend to give pride of place to titled sections rather than numbered ones; that said, *Twilight of the Idols* and *Ecce Homo*'s content headings are indeed cumbersome to cite, as sections are titled with subsections ordered numerically within them. To minimize citation confusion, visual clutter, and to save space, I will only cite the three works by identifying the year and page number in the author/date format per formatting requirements of the *Chicago Manual of Style*. For *Thus Spoke Zarathustra,* the citation year will be "2006b" as edited by Adrian Del Caro and Robert Pippin, for *Twilight of the Idols* the year will be "1997a" as edited by Tracy Strong, and *Ecce Homo* will be referenced by a "2005" and "2007b" designations as edited by Aaron Ridley and Judith Norman for the former and by Duncan Large for the latter.

NOTES

1. Judith Norman describes Nietzsche in "Nietzsche and Early Romanticism" as a "romantic in an uncapitalized manner," and that his ideas had little to do with nineteenth-century Romanticism (2002, 501). However, Norman argues that Nietzsche predates the late nineteenth-century Romanticists, belonging instead to Romanticism's earliest iteration, Jena Romanticism.

2. The Cambridge translation explains, according to Kaufmann's 1974 elaboration, that *gaya scienza* ("joyful, cheerful, or gay science") was a term used by the troubadours in the twelfth to fourteenth centuries to refer to the art of poetry. In *Ecce Homo* Nietzsche writes that he used the term *gaya scienza* to designate the specific "unity of *singer, knight,* and *free thinker* which distinguishes the marvelous culture of the Provençal people from all ambiguous cultures" (2007b, 123). Kaufmann's translation of *The Gay Science* (1974, 5–7) clarifies that the term "gay" as used by Nietzsche was not in reference to homosexuality. For Kaufmann, the title "*Gay Science*" evokes Nietzsche's "light-hearted defiance of convention," and that Nietzsche desired the title to convey how "serious thinking does not have to be stodgy, heavy, dusty, or in one word, Teutonic [German]." It is, for Kaufmann, an anti-academic and anti-professorial work that aims to usher in how knowledge should be able to proclaim its joy in embracing a new approach to life, one that shares an affinity with the free spirits, one that suggests that the self must be propelled by joy and lightness as expressed by Nietzsche in *Thus Spoke Zarathustra*. Kaufmann thus notes that *The Gay Science* should not be "misconstrued as implying Nietzsche was homosexual or that the book deals with homosexuality" (1974, 5).

3. Solms-Laubach also provides us a sense of chronology for situating Nietzsche among Germany's sociology theorists of the time, nothing that "Marx predates Nietzsche as a social thinker, while Max Weber, Ferdinand Tönnies, Rosa Mayreder and Alfred Weber . . . are sociologists and social thinkers after Nietzsche" (2007, 3).

4. A seminal work on this topic can be seen in Sheldon Wolin's *Democracy Incorporated: Managed Democracy and the Specter of Inverted Totalitarianism* (2008), a work we will discuss in this text. Also, see Henry Giroux's *American Nightmare: The Challenge of U.S. Authoritarianism* (2018a) and *The Public in Peril: Trump and the Menace of American Authoritarianism* (2018b).

5. Although the *übermensch* is translated to mean the "overman" or "superman," my essay prefers the concept's gender-neutral applicability and thus will employ the term "overcomer."

6. See Karl Marx's *18th Brumaire;* examine Thailand's modern "democracy," one shaped by numerous military coups, or the most populous democracy, India, internally colonizing the region of Jammu and Kashmir with over 10,000 troops, abrogating Article 370 that ensured its autonomy.

7. Because Solms-Laubach and Kaufmann have done an excellent job detailing Nietzsche's angst against classical sociology because it engages in validations of the collective and not the self, this work will not focus on any more tensions between Nietzsche's ideas and their compatibility with the trajectories of early sociology. It is already a foregone conclusion for your author that Nietzsche exhibits an incisive

sociological imagination that is rich in theoretical cues, one that is better suited for analyzing a future he saw arriving rather than for the period in which he lived.

8. Solms-Laubach (2007) and Hennis (1988) note that by the time Tönnies had become a scholar, he distanced himself from Nietzsche's writings, "from the demon of his youth" (Hennis 1988, 150). However, Tönnies's bravado was tempered when he tried to visit Nietzsche at Sils Maria on holiday, "but eventually did not dare to approach when he saw him across the street" (2007, 165).

9. Frequently overlooked in the literature is how Nietzsche's rhythmic writing style might well be influenced by his gifted background as a pianist and composer.

Chapter One

The Sociological Imagination

Nietzsche's sociologically oriented observations are rarely considered because of his iconic status as a philosopher. In this chapter, I hope to highlight Nietzsche's contribution to sociology, with assistance from American sociologist C. Wright Mills who originated the term "the sociological imagination." Through Mills, this chapter adopts the view that Nietzsche is an important social theorist with a prescient sociological imagination.

BRETHREN ACROSS TIME

Rendering Nietzsche as a social thinker with an insightful sociological imagination would not have been possible were it not for C. Wright Mills (1916–1962), American sociologist born 72 years after Nietzsche. Mills coined the term in his eponymous 1959 classic as a means for highlighting for sociology broader panoramas that tied the self to different contexts and periods of social life. By illuminating the actor's connections to these contexts, a biography tied to historical currents emerges to effectively frame the agency and human condition of the actor.

Mills, in many ways, paralleled Nietzsche in the way the former viewed knowledge production and agency. Although Nietzsche is well known for launching his critique against the grand sociologists of his day, specifically Auguste Comte and Herbert Spencer, Mills was similarly critical of his contemporaries, such as the important theorist Talcott Parsons, and of grand theories in general, all of which are "drunk on syntax, blind to semantics" (1959, 18). I am of the view that Mills's and Nietzsche's personae were quite similar as well. Both were provocative and subversive thinkers in their respective time periods. Like Nietzsche, Mills distilled social dynamics about power and empowerment in a highly critical manner. Both thinkers ceased knowledge production at approximately the same age: by age 45 in 1889, Nietzsche had suffered a mental collapse[1] that would relegate him a virtual invalid for the next eleven years until his death in 1900 at 55, enabling his sister, Elisabeth Förster-Nietzsche, as we shall elaborate later, to care for him, placing her close to his notes and unpublished materials. The available access allowed Elisabeth the capacity to transform her brother's philosophy into a narrative that promoted Nazi ideology. Mills himself died at the age of 45 after suffering complications from his alcoholism and fourth heart attack.

Up until his passing, Mills's professional life was turbulent and combative. He was "constantly at war" according to George Ritzer, having "fought with and against everyone and everything" (1992, 211). Irving Horowitz notes how contemporary sociology theorist Hans Gerth described the young Mills as "an excellent operator, whippersnapper," a "promising young man on the make," and a "Texas cowboy a la ride and shoot" (1983, 72). Mills's combativeness surfaced during his doctoral studies when he was in his mid-twenties, approximately the same time a disillusioned Nietzsche had served as chair of Classical Philology at the University of Basel. In the case of Mills:

> Beginning in graduate school, he attacked the professors in his department, and later in his career he took on senior theorists in that department (calling one a "real fool"), leaders of American sociological theory (such as Parsons), and the dominant survey research methods (and methodologists) in the field. Eventually he came to be estranged and isolated from his colleagues at Columbia University. Mills said of himself: "I am an outlander . . . down deep and good." (Ritzer and Stepnisky 2013, 94)

Ritzer was not too charitable toward Mills who he felt "was not a great neo-Marxian theorist (he made no original contributions of his own to the theory)" (2013, 94). However, Ritzer concedes that Mills was "a great critic of American society (and of American sociological theory, especially the theorizing of Talcott Parsons)" (2013, 94). Mills was not only intellectually radical but personally radical as well. Like Nietzsche, Mills "refused to play the academic game according to the 'gentlemanly' rules of the day" (Ritzer and Stepnisky 2013, 94). Another uncanny similarity between Mills's and Nietzsche's experiences within their respective lifetimes was how the former was always "at with odds with people; he was also at odds with American society and challenged it on a variety of fronts" (1992, 211), not unlike Nietzsche's view of the German culture of his day being reproduced by poseurs of learning, what he termed cultural philistines, against whom Nietzsche's philosophy agitated. And like Nietzsche, Mills took no prisoners and harbored no favoritism to creed:

Mills did not restrict his critiques to conservative and establishment elements in the United States. Late in his life, Mills was invited to the Soviet Union and honored as a major critic of American society. Instead of meekly accepting the award, Mills took the occasion to attack censorship in the Soviet Union with a toast to a Soviet leader who had been purged and murdered by the Stalinists, proclaiming, "To the day when the complete works of Leon Trotsky are published in the Soviet Union!" (Ritzer and Stepnisky 2013, 94)

That Nietzsche was hostile to sociology needs to be understood in the historical context of his time: sociology was still a new discipline in the nineteenth century, embracing positivism to predict group dynamics in society. At the time the discipline remained overarching in its theorization and employed large deterministic brushstrokes to read and predict society, perhaps to a teleological fault, not to mention that little agency was articulated for the self engaged in the contestation of society. Having somewhat wounded sociology, Solms-Laubach (2007), Antonio (1995), and Kaufmann (1950), to name but a few, have nonetheless convincingly highlighted Nietzsche's sociological foundations, suggesting how the philosopher would have been a sociological thinker were he to see the discourse of contemporary sociology emerge. Antonio even went as far as to note how Nietzsche's antisociology is, ironically, sociologically rich in its capacity to compel sociologists into a state of reflexivity and positionality, if not critique, of their own discipline. Antonio argues that because "Nietzsche equated rationalization with cultural homogenization . . . he saw 'decadence' where classical theorists saw progress. In his view, sociology drapes sweeping cultural domination, regimentation, and exhaustion with the appearance of legitimacy" (1995, 6). Like Mills's confrontation of fellow sociologists, Nietzsche's contestations against sociology should hardly be seen as justifying our philosopher's exclusion from the discipline of sociology. As Antonio convincingly notes, Nietzsche was simply critiquing his society like most sociologists critique society and their own discipline. As such:

Nietzsche's absence from sociology diminishes disciplinary resources for fully engaging some of the most important classical and contemporary social theories. Moreover, his antisociology opposes tendencies to over value rationalization, overestimate levels of consensus and integration, and mistake domination and coercion for social integration or solidarity. It also poses sharp critiques of the social self and mass regimentation. (Antonio 1995, 32)

Furthermore, often overlooked is how Nietzsche envisioned himself the most capable of psychologists, a "psychologist without equal" as noted in *Ecce Homo*. In fact, Nietzsche was not at all impressed with the psychology of his day. In

Beyond Good and Evil Nietzsche denounces psychology as a discipline that is still plagued by its own prejudices, prejudices that prevented the discipline from entering the abyss, the "depth" of the human condition made visible by his philosophy. Nietzsche remarks that "to grasp psychology as . . . *the doctrine of the development of the will to power*, which is what I have done—nobody has ever come close to this, not even in thought" (I, SEC. 23 / 2002, 23). Interestingly, Nietzsche may have attributed his self-proclaimed psychological insights to the Buddha. In *Ecce Homo*, Nietzsche described the spiritual teacher as a most "profound psychologist" upon whom he heaped admiration in spite of his critical views of all religions (Nietzsche saw both Buddhism and Christianity as decadent and nihilistic) (2005, 81). In the same work, Nietzsche described how Buddha's philosophy functioned as a needed *"hygiene"* (2005, 81). Nietzsche's dismissal of the psychology of his day thus points to how he sought a perfected discourse for personal praxis which he found lacking in modernity.

Like Nietzsche, Mills was critical and cynical of group dynamics that seek power in hopes of "saving" others. In *The Power Elite* (2000) Mills indicted political elites—that interwoven community of corporate executives, government officials, and military leaders—as the source of social oppression, forcing other cultural groupings from different walks of life to defer to their imperatives. Mills's observations of this tendency can be appreciated for their prescience in highlighting the stratification of American political culture:

> The power elite are not solitary rulers. Advisers and consultants, spokesmen and opinion-makers are often the captains of their higher thought and decision. Immediately below the elite are the professional politicians of the middle levels of power, in the Congress and in the pressure groups, as well as among the new and old upper classes of town and city and region. Mingling with them, in curious ways which we shall explore, are those professional celebrities who live by being continually displayed but are never, so long as they remain celebrities, displayed enough. (Mills 2000, 4)

In *The Sociological Imagination*, Mills's observations share an affinity with Gramsci on the theme of how consent is manufactured and hegemony established:

> Those in authority attempt to justify their rule over institutions by linking it, as if it were a necessary consequence, with widely believed-in moral symbols, sacred emblems, legal formulae. These central conceptions may refer to a god or gods, the "vote of the majority," "the will of the people," "the aristocracy of talent or wealth," to the "divine right of kings," or to the allegedly extraordinary endowment of the ruler himself. Social scientists, following Weber, call such conceptions "legitimations," or sometimes "symbols of justification." (1959, 36)

Nietzsche too condemned major groupings and their machinations that are seen to be dispersed throughout what he perceived to be a degenerate modernity. However, Nietzsche narrowed down the consequences of elite machinations as they affect the self, for these mainstream and scripted elites are conceptualized as nothing more than agents that stifle the sovereignty of the individual. Unlike Mills, Nietzsche saw agency and praxis through the *unscripted* elite individual, the overcomer who authors one's own path toward self-mastery in opposition to or beyond collective narratives and prescriptions offered by conforming elites. In *Untimely Meditations*, Nietzsche inspires the overcomer to forge ahead in life, to build—and this must be emphasized—on their own accord, bridges that can cross over life's streaming of trials and tribulations. This unique life trajectory belongs solely to the self-authoring overcomer that must embrace life's unknowns. Where such a path leads matters not to Nietzsche (and neither should it matter to the overcomer); as such, he urges us to ask no questions and that we simply embark on our journey (III, SEC. 1 / 1997b, 129). For both Mills and Nietzsche, collective elites stifled social change and praxis and this needed to be addressed: the former saw the comprehensive stifling of groups and their agency to confront power elites while the latter saw the stifling of the elite individual in relation to conformist power elites and groups that wallow in groupthink, unable to author their own life trajectories on their own terms. That said, Kaufmann arguably sums up the overcomer best as one who has transcended "his animal nature, organized the chaos of his passions, sublimated his impulses, and given style to his character" (1950, 316). The overcomer, then, is one who "disciplined himself to wholeness," is a person of tolerance "not from weakness but from strength"; such a person is a spirit "who has *become free*" (1950, 316).

In the post–World War II period in the United States, Mills saw the return of an agent with backing of the collective: the "warlord," one although formerly indoctrinated in the military and having earned one's mettle there, now surfaces as president of the United States, one accompanied by lesser warlords such as the "Secretary of Defense . . . his assistants" and "behind office walls . . . a military board of directors—the Joint Chiefs of Staff" (2000, 187). Mills continues to illuminate larger concentrics of influence, noting how "immediately below the Joint Chiefs there is a higher circle of generals and admirals which presides over the elaborate and far-flung land, sea, and air forces, as well as the economic and political liaisons held necessary to maintain them" (2000, 187). For Nietzsche, such kinds of power structures promoted the ideological *isms* of a degenerate society, most dangerous of which is nationalism. All *isms*, however, require a captive audience to engage in conformity to the state's manufacturing of culture and consent. In this regard, Mills and Nietzsche effectively inform each other: both considered how systemic flaws affect actors in society, with Nietzsche taking the consideration to the most intimate of all levels, the suffering yet triumphant human being, in flesh and in blood.

Given the similar challenges experienced by Mills and Nietzsche during their periods of intellectual production, amalgamating Mills's ideas with Nietzsche's should not be seen as a reckless undertaking. There exists an affinity of frustration, angst, and animus exhibited by both thinkers that bonds their respective historical epochs, allowing their polemics and tensions to function as a segue toward considering prospects for the self in today's liquid modernity. Both thinkers reveal how it is difficult to understand the self without tying them to institutions, where for Mills, one's "biography is enacted" (1959, 161). Both are skeptical of capitalism and socialism. Both echo each other across the ages as Nietzsche warned about the degeneration of social and political systems while Mills saw in their twentieth-century manifestations discontents, double standards, and hypocrisies. In Mills's view, Marxism had become a "dreary rhetoric of bureaucratic defense and abuse" while liberalism was presciently argued to have evolved into a "trivial and irrelevant way of masking social reality" (1959, 167). Mills further claims that social development cannot be understood "in terms of the liberal nor Marxian interpretation of politics and culture" (1959, 167), echoing Nietzsche's view that both systems are decadent and degenerate, as will be detailed in subsequent chapters. More boldly, both Nietzsche and Mills saw how increasing rationality did not provide existential meaning (Nietzsche) or increased freedoms (Mills).

UNDERSTANDING THE
SOCIOLOGICAL IMAGINATION

Although Nietzsche and Mills do not completely synchronize on all sociological views, what matters for this monograph is Mills's contribution of the sociological imagination, one which makes operative Nietzsche's antisystemic views. Mills's conceptualizes the sociological imagination as lucid awareness of the self's experiences seen within different contexts of society. Such contexts and complexities can be historical, as in the time period the self is alive in, or it can be structural, as in the self's relationship to bureaucracies and institutions of the day. For Mills, such a multiaxial sociological imagination "enables its possessor to understand the larger historical scene in terms of its *meaning* [emphasis added] for the inner life and the external career of a variety of individuals" (1959, 5). Enhancing meaning is crucial for understanding and improving the human condition, especially for existential thinkers such as Nietzsche. In *The Gay Science*, Nietzsche argues that a key human experience is when the actor, whether courageously or apprehensively, concedes that there is a desperate need to know "*why* he exists" (I, SEC. 1 / 2001, 29). The sociological imagination thus enables actors to understand how their search for meaning is inexplicably "bounded by the private orbits in which they live," and how frequently "their visions and their powers are limited to the close-up scenes of job, family, neighborhood" (Mills 1959, 3). Mills emphasizes how the self's sociological imagination thus "enables us to grasp history and biography and the relations between the two within society" (1959, 6). For Mills, the self's difficult epistemic and ontologic concerns in a context regulated by the power elite means that sociology's "intellectual journey" cannot be resolved—especially if the "problems of biography, history and of their intersections within a society" (insofar as meaning-generation is concerned)—are neglected (1959, 6).

Mills envisions how such actors empowered by their sociological imaginations can comprehend social structure, their essential institutions, their interrelationships with "other varieties of the social order," and their place within the historical conditions of society (1959, 6). Mills himself demonstrated his own sociological imagination at work, noting how

> when a society is industrialized, a peasant becomes a worker; a feudal lord is liquidated or becomes a businessman. When classes rise or fall, a man is employed or unemployed; when the rate of investment goes up or down, a man takes new heart or goes broke. . . . Neither the life of an individual nor the history of a society can be understood without understanding both. (1959, 3)

The sociological imagination, then, is a perspective that envisions how different concentrics of social contexts frame the individual, as well as serving as a lens for the individual to be situationally aware of those same social contexts. Such an orientation allows the individual with a sociological imagination to

> shift from one perspective to another—from the political to the psychological; from examination of a single family to comparative assessment of the national budgets of the world; from the theological school to the military establishment; from considerations of an oil industry to studies of contemporary poetry. It is the capacity to range from the most impersonal and remote transformations to the most intimate features of the human self—and to see the relations between the two. (Mills 1959, 7)

Perhaps most important for synchronizing Mills's ideas with Nietzsche's views is the former's concern about the type of actor reflected in society given the aforementioned contextual delimitations. Mills asks: "What varieties of men and women now prevail in this society and in this period? And what varieties are coming to prevail? In what ways are they selected and formed, liberated and repressed, made sensitive and blunted? What kinds of 'human nature' are revealed in the conduct and character we observe in this society in this period?" (1959, 6–7). It is at this juncture that my work introduces Nietzsche's ideal type, the *übermensch*: the overcomer—the superhuman *being*—as a praxian actor who can withstand and survive, even thrive, in modernity's systemic crises that regress others toward a conformist and captive condition. Furthermore, toward the closing sections of this chapter a discussion of the bane of Nietzsche's overcomer, the "herd" that is constituted by "last human beings," will also be examined.

Because the overcomer is the ultimate exemplar of Nietzsche's idealized being able to overcome the trials and tribulations of life, I introduce the overcomer at this early juncture for one key reason: by introducing such a character at the outset, subsequent chapters can then be presented as harboring the obstacles that mandate overcoming by overcoming types. Nietzsche envisioned the overcomer ideal type as a highly proactive, dynamic, and praxian being ready to confront the systemic and cultural impediments arrayed against the person's self-assembly of new moralities, new self-conceptualizations, and novel actions that reinforce one's sovereignty, (while those who conform are envisioned as sycophants who defer to, if not reify, the impediments). The overcomer as praxian agent enables the ideal type to be positioned to contest the many crises of modernity and its foment of decadence, conditions that stifle the development of the elevated and noble-minded being. Yet there is also a new community for the overcomer, consisting of those contesting the power of conformity and mediocrity, what Nietzsche describes as higher human beings, the great creative people with noble mindsets that underpin the essence of what the overcomer can be. Their focused trajectory of goal attainment, life enhancement, judicious use of their will to power, and their sense of awareness of the long chronology of history that birthed them, have highly sensitized them toward living life with tenacity, purpose, and self-authored meaning. In *Ecce Homo*, Nietzsche renders the great iconic artists and thinkers of the Renaissance as part and parcel of such a community. Its members respected their solitude and adopted a higher value system based on a noble mindset and life-affirmation, values that for our philosopher are "future-confirming," values that allow us to triumph "at the seat of the opposing values, the *values of decline*" (2007b, 84).

THE *ÜBERMENSCH*: THE OVERCOMER

Where Mills stopped short in rendering the sovereign actor as praxian and proactive, Nietzsche in *On the Genealogy of Morality* offered the ideal type that is the *übermensch*, the overcomer, as not only a sovereign being capable of self-mastery over the trials and tribulations of the lifeworld, but as a sovereign ideal type that will still prevail in spite of systemic dysfunctions, one with "his own independent, enduring will" informed by a candescent awareness of one's power and freedom (II, SEC. 2 / 2006a, 37). In *Ecce Homo*, Nietzsche describes the overcomer as one who is not alienated and able to connect to the harsh realities of life and living, one who makes the decision to stand against all of modernity's manufactured consents and sacralities (2005, 143–148). Nietzsche's prescription for the overcomer is essentially a total prescription for the actor desiring an emancipated and authentic existence. In *Human, All Too Human*, he chastises the person who is unable to exhibit self-mastery over their impulsive temperament, vindictiveness, and reckless impulses. Nietzsche describes such a person as inept, not unlike a farmer who continues to plant his crops near a river known to perennially flood. He also famously and understandably proclaims in *Thus Spoke Zarathustra* how such a human being is something that we, in search of a new and better humanity, must replace, must overcome. He passionately argues that it is time that humanity sets itself on such a trajectory through the overcomer, for in such a person is planted a better and more hopeful humanity for the future. The overcomer, then, is born dialectically—and this can hardly be emphasized enough in my work—through the courageous embrace of life struggle and suffering as a means for overcoming. Nietzsche deploys his metaphors and analogies to reinforce this position. Nietzsche notes how he himself had to descend into the depths of being and suffering like never before, and in this state of despair, in his darkest hours—hours of Nietzsche's "blackest flood"—was training that readied him for the vagaries of life and living again, since even the highest of mountains of earth emerged from the deepest depths of the ocean according to our philosopher (Nietzsche 2006b, 122). In *Beyond Good and Evil*, Nietzsche embraces the teachability of suffering and attributes to it an outcome of renewal, noting: "The discipline of suffering, of *great* suffering—don't you know that *this* discipline has been the sole cause of every enhancement in humanity so far? The tension that breeds strength into the unhappy soul . . .—weren't these the gifts of . . . great suffering?" (VII, SEC. 225 / 2002, 116–117).

In *Untimely Meditations*, Nietzsche again emphasizes the educational value of life hardship and struggle, even describing tragedy in positive terms because meaning from tragedy will counter the fears and anxieties that affect the individual confronting figurative and literal mortalities. The one salvation for humanity, then, according to Nietzsche, is for the actor to appreciate, respect, and embrace a "*sense for the tragic*," and how the "ennoblement" of humanity will be determined by this very "supreme" undertaking (IV, SEC. 4 / 1997b, 213). By the publication of *The Anti-Christ*, Nietzsche describes how people unable to confront tragedy become barbarians because "to the barbarians there is nothing respectable about suffering: they need an interpretation before they can admit to themselves *that* they suffer" (SEC. 23 / 2005, 19). It is thus not surprising that Nietzsche glorified pre-Socratic Greek society in *The Birth of Tragedy*, his first publication, for its use of tragedy in the arts to embrace life's trials and tribulations. By the publication of *Nietzsche contra Wagner*, Nietzsche matured the overcomer to be a brilliant dialectician, one who takes the extremism of society, of people, and of living, and tames it on their path to self-mastery. This revelation—a sort of *crescendo* in how he saw his ideal type of the self—is best captured in length:

> I have often asked myself whether I am not more deeply indebted to the hardest years of my life than to all the rest. What my innermost nature tells me is that . . . it should not just be tolerated, it should be *loved . . . Amor Fati* [the love of one's fate]: that is my innermost nature.—And as far as my long infirmity is concerned, isn't it the case that I am unspeakably more indebted to it than I am to my health? I owe a higher health to it, a health that becomes stronger from everything that does not kill it off! *I owe my philosophy to it as well . . .* Only great pain . . . that long, slow pain that takes its time and in which we are burned, as it were, over green wood—, forces us philosophers to descend into our ultimate depths and put aside all trust, everything good-natured, everything that veils, or is mild or average—things in which formerly we may have found our humanity. . . . one should not jump to the conclusion that this necessarily makes one gloomy. . . . Even love of life is still possible,—only one loves *differently.* ("Epilogue," *Nietzsche contra Wagner*, 2005, 280–281)

Providing more cues about the disposition of the overcomer, Nietzsche argues that the systemic death of god is a positive demystification, one that also "implies the end of all limitations for mankind" and thus there will be "no limit to what a strong-willed individual can achieve" (Solms-Laubach 2007, 87). I thus extend the notion of how the crises of democratism (along with other *isms*) present new possibilities for a twenty-first-century overcomer to contest. In the case of democratism, calling out democracy for its dysfunctions, which Mills forthrightly observed had benefitted only a "small portion of mankind historically" (1959, 4), is one of the key energies that drive Nietzsche's philosophy. Extrapolating from a dysfunctional democratic context thus still honors the integrity of Nietzsche's efforts to rigorously seek out freedom in the midst of his sociological imagination: in modernity's detritus. In *Anti-Christ*, Nietzsche declares that "*we ourselves*, we free spirits, already constitute a revaluation of all values, a *living* declaration of war on and victory over all old concepts of 'true' and 'untrue'" (2005, 11). In *Twilight of the Idols*, Nietzsche describes the free sovereign being as one with the courage and will to be responsible for oneself; for Nietzsche, this "free human be-ing is a *warrior*—[emphasis added]" (1997a, 75). Nietzsche was no idealist, however. He warns in *Thus Spoke Zarathustra* that a person pursuing such an ideal must realize that getting to know the self, let alone confronting it, is a fearsome process inherent in the act of overcoming, in the act of becoming an overcomer. Through his proxy Zarathustra, Nietzsche nonetheless reminds the self cast adrift in the tumultuous ocean of modernity's systemic defects that one must always engage in self-overcoming for the sake of purposing existence.

To the detriment of one's freedom, Mills similarly affirms how an actor unable to develop a sociological imagination encounters the impoverishment of meaning and purpose.

> Seldom aware of the intricate connection between the patterns of their own lives and the course of world history, ordinary men do not usually know what this connection means for the kinds of men they are becoming and for the kinds of history-making in which they might take part. They do not possess the quality of mind essential to grasp the interplay of man and society, of biography and history, of self and world. They cannot cope with their personal troubles in such ways as to control the structural transformations that usually lie behind them. (Mills 1959, 3–4)

The compelling observation by Mills illuminates, in my view, the conditions that unwittingly lead the actor toward nihilism. When actors are disjuncted from their social world, whether we are here dealing with Marx's alienation, Durkheim's notion of *anomie*, or Weber's warning about rational-legal bu-reaucracies trapping the actor in modern society's iron cages, the implication is rather clear: the human condition of modernity, even more so in a frenetic liquid modernity, is framed by defective systems that generate nihilism in its wake. For Mills, when one does not tie biography to history and social change there is a risk that conditions for an unfulfilled and unempowered life, a life without meaning, will be created. Yet Mills laments how most human beings "do not usually define the troubles they endure in terms of historical change and institutional contradiction" (1959, 3).

Nietzsche advocates that an actor in such a situation should completely reject their social systems, systems like Christianity and the ideological and cultural scripts derived from the *isms* of his day. It is a process the overcomer can employ to transform the self from a passive to active nihilist, the latter of which harnesses one's will to power to establish self-mastery for the sake of meaning-generation and purposing existence through overcoming. The over-comer's raison d'être can be seen in Zarathustra's proclamation of his life project: to appeal to all conformists to therefore break free from their herds.

He reassures all that the demolition of old "tablets of values" is a righteous act, a gesture that announces to the world that the overcomer must now be, through sheer will to power, the creative force in its own rebirth or renewal—and this is how one must confront decadence, according to Nietzsche (2006b, 14). In contrast, the passive nihilist is Nietzsche's "last man," the member of the conforming herd, one that is the antithesis of the active nihilist who, for political theorist Leslie Paul Thiele, is "life affirming" and "confronts worldly suffering without slandering worldly life" (Bergmann et al. 2007, 31).

Nietzsche believes that the process of confronting decadence and its accompanying social structures mandates a radical rejection of scripts, values, and conventional morality. Such a process requires an understanding of how decadence is tied to malfunctioning social structures in all their bureaucratic complexity and coldness, structures that are the subject of Nietzsche's critique against systems as will be seen in later chapters. It is in this context that Nietzsche's sociological imagination emerges, one that envisions a praxian overcomer and the person's will to power to embrace all suffering for the sake of overcoming and purposing one's existence in life. Nietzsche was serious about the emancipatory potential inherent in the overcomer. To get a sense of Nietzsche's expected outcomes for the overcomer, he asserts in *Thus Spoke Zarathustra* that a humanity in the deep time of a future society will judge our development through this new ideal type of the human being. He remarks: "What is the ape to the human? A laughing stock or a painful embarrassment. And that is precisely what the human shall be to the overman: a laughing stock or a painful embarrassment" (2006b, 6). Nietzsche biographer R. J. Hollingdale comments on how such an overcomer, such a super human, is one who "achieves . . . what nations once achieved when they raised themselves from the level of herds" (1999, 162).

To confront the daunting, almost life-threatening task of vanquishing decadence and nihilism, Nietzsche urges the audience in *Thus Spoke Zarathustra* to no longer escape from reality, for by doing so one escapes from creating meaning for the earth. Zarathustra, the character, continues to motivate his audience by noting that he will inspire humanity towards a new life-affirming will, a will to power that dares to embark on if not create new trajectories for those with less mettle and fortitude—what Nietzsche sees as the "sick"—to embrace, for such sick persons "despised the body and the earth," unfurling a nihilism that compelled them to invent the notion of heaven and its "redeeming drops of blood" (2006b, 21). Thus, Zarathustra was a proponent of overcoming for the sake of happiness as well, a state only attainable when one's will to power is made operative. Hollingdale claims that Nietzsche's formulation of the will to power gives great emphasis to the view that "the greatest increase of power brings the greatest happiness; that which demands the greatest power is the overcoming of oneself; the happiest man is the man who has overcome himself—the superhuman" (1999, 163). For Nietzsche, only such a self can withstand the nihilism that now permeates an age without god.

The will to power of the overcomer is thus about rejecting systemic imperatives because they are not life affirming for the person attempting to exhibit self-mastery and empowerment. Yet there will be consequences for those who adopt such a subversive stance, illuminated by Nietzsche's sociological imagination when he observes in *Human, All Too Human* how free-spirited thinkers who dare to think inimitably beyond their origin, environment, occupation, and social status will invariably be attacked by those who benefit from conforming to society's social systems and their demands. The conformist community will thus condemn such a free thinker and their ideas as offensive, shocking, and subversive. He warns in *Beyond Good and Evil* how an independent self with a tremendous will to walk one's own path will be seen as threatening to the mainstream, frightening the conformists and compelling them to henceforth judge the attributes that constitute the character of such a person as evil (Nietzsche V, SEC. 201 / 2002, 89). In spite of such social resistance, Nietzsche remains emphatically in favor of assembling an overcomer able to build strength and mettle as well as enhance one's sovereignty to author one's own values. In *The Gay Science* Nietzsche gives us insight into the covenants of sovereign, self-authoring overcomers as those who are engaged in the birthing of great new values that are self-authored, values that exclude "people's moral chatter about others" in ways that offend us (IV, SEC. 335 / 2001, 189). Nietzsche advises us to avoid such social dynamics because last humans have nothing better to do "but drag the past a few steps further through time" since they lack the wherewithal to live in the present—just like the "great majority!" (IV, SEC. 335 / 2001, 189).

Nietzsche thus asked of his readers in *Untimely Meditations* to work on the self in spite of social discontents, to take inventory, so to speak, on life, on one's hopes and dreams for affirming life in ways that uplift the soul (III, SEC. 1 / 1997b, 129). Unfazed by social admonishments, Nietzsche proclaims through the prophet in *Thus Spoke Zarathustra* how "in the desert" the truthful and free spirits have always dwelled, yet citizens in cities are but "draft animals" and remain "servants and harnessed, even if they gleam in golden harnesses" (2006b, 80).

It must be emphasized that Nietzsche's view of the overcomer should not be envisioned as a philosophy for proselytizing to a captive audience. Nietzsche expected all overcomers to live by their own vision of a sovereign, life-affirming philosophy. He felt we needed to respond when the universal frameworks of modernity, one that destroyed god and replaced it with institutional simulacra meant to acquire new loyalties and sycophants, are no longer tenable. Nietzsche did not render the overcomer an evangelist in search of a flock, yet overcomers are at least conceptually linked to higher humans who engage in their self-authoring and purposing of existence. He expected every individual to pursue a self-defined path, to accept all consequences of one's own actions, and to infuse one's own morality and meaning into life on one's own terms. In *Beyond Good and Evil*, Nietzsche declares how the noble-minded individual is self-authoring and does not depend on others for approval or for validating their dignity and sense of self-worth, and that such a person *"creates values"* and "honors everything he sees in himself" (IX, SEC. 260 / 2002, 154). In *Ecce Homo*, Nietzsche proclaims in hindsight through the character Zarathustra:

> Alone I go now, my disciples! You too must go away now, and alone! . . . Go away from me and guard yourselves against Zarathustra! . . . One repays a teacher poorly if one always remains only a student. . . . You are my believers, but what do any believers matter! . . . Now I bid you lose me and find your-selves; and only *when you have all denied me* will I return to you. (2007b, 5)

The "Nietzschean project," as observes Thiele, was to purpose the overcomer with a "passion for growth and greatness in a world without gods" (Bergmann et al. 2007, 31). Nietzsche was thus in search of great, sovereign human be-ings not only to satiate his advocacy for the overcomer, but most importantly for the orientation of this work, because these great human beings are agents of social change, as Nietzsche insightfully observed in *Twilight of the Idols*:

> Great human beings are necessary, the age in which they appear is accidental; the fact that they almost always become masters of their age is simply due to the fact that they are stronger, that they are older, that things have been gathered up longer for them. The relation of a genius to his age is like the relation between strong and weak, or between old and young: the age is always relatively much younger, thinner, more immature, less secure, more childish. (1997a, 79)

Nietzsche's overcomer is an iteration of Weber's charismatic leader with one key exception: this overcomer/charismatic leader will, ostensibly, never have their charisma routinized since they are always on a path of renewal and reassembly. For Thiele, the Nietzschean project requires sovereign actors to "engage in the art of judgement" for now there is an "absence of final adju-dicators sporting white beards. It requires judgement without the benefit of a god's-eye view from which our verdicts might be rendered with certainty" (Bergmann et al. 2007, 31). In *Untimely Meditations*, Nietzsche explains how this path requires the overcoming actor to engage in critical (for judging) and monumental (for identifying heroes and role models) confrontations with their history, one that must be undertaken for its rewriting and reassembly. The two aforementioned relationships to history need to be discerned from the third, the antiquarian (the detail-oriented yet *un*critical observer of history), who illuminates a past in all its textures and details.

As will be seen in later chapters, only by acknowledging these roles can the overcomer stave off the putrefaction of systems that have been embedded and reified in social life. Nietzsche thus advocates in *Untimely Meditations* for the quality, not quantity, of people as a function of social change, but only after the overcomer harnesses history in the correct monumental, antiquarian, and critical dosages. The overcomer critical of history will need to decolonize and reassemble certain chunks of history by carefully breaking up and dissolving a part of the past (Nietzsche II, SEC. 3 / 1997b, 75–76). Nietzsche also warns how seeking such a catharsis can be fraught with danger because some actors simply cannot or refuse to forget their pains in their critical relationship to history. Such persons obsess over the minutiae of history that have nothing to do with the empowerment of the individual, an antiquarian approach toward the past. They also knead the past with a victim identity that embraces their perennial sense of feeling persecuted. Nietzsche warns how defeatist characters thus view the past with heavy critical dosages, and that such persons who live by recklessly "judging and destroying a past are always dangerous and endangered men and ages" (II, SEC. 3 / 1997b, 76). As can be seen in the aforementioned excerpt, Nietzsche's advocacy for a careful approach toward history is meant to avoid its tendency to negate life. Nietzsche therefore offers an example of an overcoming, monumentalist orientation toward the past to contest the Germany of his time, one that can be set into motion by a devoted group of overcoming types. Thus, past greatness transplanted into modernity may therefore be realizable again and one should not be daunted by its prospects. Nietzsche reassures us, noting, "Supposing someone believed that it would require no more than a hundred men . . . to do away with the bogus form of culture which has just now become the fashion in Germany, how greatly it would strengthen him to realize that the culture of the Renaissance was raised on the shoulders of just such a band of a hundred men" (II, SEC. 2 / 1997b, 69).

Overcomers do not live in an irretrievable past. They take history and repurpose it into a self-affirming, life-affirming, action-oriented catalyst for one's will to power, unwilling to allow history to fester with life-negating content (as in, for example, how history can focus on wars as agents of social change). Not surprisingly, Nietzsche warns how conventional history contains excessive content of life-negation. In one's capacity as an antiquarian, critical, and monumentalist overcomer, the life-negating past should thus be scrutinized, broken up, and dissolved, for too much "human violence and weakness have always played a mighty role in them" (Nietzsche II, SEC. 3 / 1997b, 76). The key difference between the overcomer and non-overcomer, then, is that the latter exhibit so little empowerment that such a person perishes "from a single experience, from a single painful event . . . from a single subtle piece of injustice, like a man bleeding to death from a scratch" (Nietzsche II, SEC. 1 / 1997b, 62). In contrast, the overcomer exhibits "superlative health and vigour, a joy to all who see him" while the pretender "sickens and collapses because the lines of his horizon are always restlessly changing" (Nietzsche II, SEC. 1 / 1997b, 63).

THE CONFORMISTS WHO
CONSTITUTE THE HERD

For all that has been said about the merits of the overcomer, what then can one surmise about those who occupy the opposite end of a person authoring and purposing life on one's own terms? A variety of characters and/or sentiments define such members of what Nietzsche pejoratively referred to as the herd: those trapped in groupthink and a conformist mentality. As members of a captive audience, members of the herd are also fed on by the institutions, bureaucracies, and degenerate cultures of their day, with their hollow pretentions and dutiful sycophancy to cultural scripts generating nihilism in the process. People in such groups include those Nietzsche refers to as cultural philistines. Deriving his critique from the examination of citizens who participated in and benefitted from the German "high" culture of his day, Nietzsche considers such individuals as poseurs, enthusiastically supporting the mainstream in ways that feed their self-serving dispositions. In *Untimely Meditations*, Nietzsche describes such a poseur as one who dutifully follows the procedural details of their social and cultural institutions in ways that reinforce and reproduce the status quo (I, SEC. 2 / 1997b, 7). What exists outside this regulatory box is deemed subversive and countercultural. Conforming not because of humility but because of the lust to be festooned with the adornments of awards and recognitions, such a conformist dutifully internalizes conventionally accepted cultural and ideological scripts, keeps up appearances, and defers to a systemically defined sense of occasion for which the emancipated sovereign has no sense. In *Human, All Too Human*, Nietzsche asserts that when such poseurs are asked about culture they regurgitate a first opinion that is usually not their own, but one that legitimates their own social capital and what their community of peers deem as worthwhile problematics. Their own opinions remain suppressed so as to not challenge whatever sensibilities are subscribed to by the status quo (Nietzsche Vol. 1, IX, SEC. 571 / 1996, 187).

Those who see through this pretentiousness and disingenuousness are thus resented by the cultural philistine. The reason for their resentment is because even a proto-overcomer can readily call out the philistine for being an obstacle to anyone striving to be at their most sovereign, most creative, and most noble. For Nietzsche in *Untimely Meditations*, the German cultural philistine exhibits character attributes that impede one's desire for sovereign empowerment and full creative expression. Extrapolating from the German type, Nietzsche argues that such individuals fancy themselves as ambassadors and defenders of contemporary culture in spite of their pretensions. As such, Nietzsche denounces the cultural philistine and criticizes such a person for their hostility toward the empowered, simply because the latter refuse to "believe you when you say you have already found what it is seeking" (I, SEC. 2 / 1997b, 8).

In *Untimely Meditations*, the non-overcoming cultural philistine can also be seen as an antiquarian. Antiquarians find comfort and solace in a sort of frozen history that does not destroy their romanticized and self-serving packaging of the past. In this process, history becomes justification, and the justifications are "inserted" into the psyche of the individual, becoming a fortress too sacred to critique because doing so becomes a personalized attack upon the actor. The uncritical fusion of self with history is thus disingenuous in Nietzsche's view. Packaging the past by interweaving human experiences with particular details of history allows the antiquarian's veneration of bygone days to have great value when it offers contentment and pleasure on even the "wretched conditions in which a man or a nation lives" (Nietzsche II, SEC. 3 / 1997b, 73). No wonder Nietzsche felt the antiquarian perspective of the human experience enables a major distortion in how history could be understood since "everything old and past that enters one's field of vision . . . is in the end blandly taken to be equally worthy of reverence, while everything that does not approach this antiquity with reverence, that is to say everything new and evolving, is rejected and persecuted" (II, SEC. 3 / 1997b, 74).

Although Mills himself somewhat deviated from Nietzsche in how history is conceptualized, the former's rendering of the sociological imagination required history. However, Mills expected the sociological imagination to consider a past that frames the actor, not one that can be reduced or internalized within the actor. That is, for Mills, the sociological imagination requires us to take the past into consideration as context for empowering the individual and group vis-à-vis institutional changes over time, and in a manner where history is seen as being unable to structurally, only affectively, be reduced to the individual and group. Mills thus envisions history as an organized memory of all of humanity to "keep the human record straight," yet concedes how "memory, as written history, is enormously malleable" and "changes, often quite drastically, from one generation of historians to another" (1959,

144–145). In this regard, Mills's accommodations of subjectivist views of the past are able to consider the affective and inspirational forces of history that individuals internalize. One may surmise that because Nietzsche shares similar concerns, he urges us to forge ahead to confront such distortions of history, especially when antiquarian, critical, and monumentalist characters warp history to reinforce their own prejudices.

An example of Nietzsche's concern about antiquarian distortion is seen in his observation of the antiquarian who lives in the past, and that such a past weighs heavily on such an individual. As a result, antiquarian history degenerates when it cannot feed on the present in ways that allow it to be repackaged for the past (Nietzsche II, SEC. 3 / 1997b, 75). Nietzsche argues how an extreme antiquarian thus appropriates history in ways that are non-affirming, hostile, and dangerous to life and living. Their myopic readings of the past to derive cues for inferring about the present and future do not consider how although the past may predict the future it certainly cannot determine it. For Nietzsche, an oversaturation of uncritically accepted history therefore implants the harmful belief that one is a "latecomer" and "epigone" (II, SEC. 5 / 1997b, 83).

The aforementioned actors cripple the individual's personality and will to power. Individuals become entangled with systems that give them reassuring narratives to internalize as automatons soaking up formulations of past greatness. Already alluded to in *Human, All Too Human*, such peoples are considered modern-day primitives by Nietzsche as they dutifully follow laws and traditions they believe justify their own character and cultural dispositions. For Mills and Nietzsche, history is filled with its trials, tribulations, and epics, and must be treated with care. Nietzsche in *Untimely Meditations*, however, was less charitable toward antiquarians' views of history. Such actors are seen as being too timid because they find comfort and solace by hiding behind accepted traditions, values, and worldviews. Trapped and fearful of paradigm shifts, such actors only feel safe within the confines of nation and its manufactured cultures and customs. Guided by latent or explicit fears, they restrain themselves from a healthy wanderlust that searches for meaning and purpose beyond their comfort zones. Not surprisingly, Nietzsche therefore offers a more ideal discernment, namely that history should only be constructed by strong characters since those with less fortitude will be engulfed and extinguished by it (II, SEC. 5 / 1997b, 86).

NIETZSCHE'S SOCIOLOGICAL IMAGINATION AND THE SOVEREIGN BEING

In this chapter Nietzsche's overcomer, introduced through our philosopher's sociological imagination reworked from Mills's original rendering, is made operative in a variety of social contexts and situations. Mills's sociological imagination, interwoven with Nietzsche's sociological views, is an important amalgamation that will set this monograph's trajectory apart from other works envisioning Nietzsche as a sociologist. Nietzsche's sociological imagination will therefore allow us to "make sense of the wider sociocultural transformations" and "the ambiguities and paradoxes that characterised 'modernity'" (Solms-Laubach 2007, 27). Rendering Nietzsche a critical sociologist highlights how the self and society exist not only in terms of meaning, but crucially, how such meaning is derived from the material consequences of existence when systems like democracy, for example, no longer elevate the self in the lifeworld. More importantly, by tying our rendering of Nietzsche to the material consequences of the modern human condition, I avoid analyzing the self and society through the postmodern process of deconstruction, a process that renders social variables an aesthetic to be deconstructed to the nth degree. Life has material consequences. Nietzsche dove into them headfirst, something we should undertake as well.

Democracy during Nietzsche's era had already found traction and was slowly eroding away residual aristocracies of Europe; it already destroyed various iterations of the French monarchy a few generations previous. Not surprisingly, by the late nineteenth century, democracy and the industrializing free market were rendered a new idol in many parts of Western Europe, ushering a slow but inevitable reassembly of culture into a compilation of scripts that promote all permutations of material and non-material consumption, a vulgar process that continues unabated under globalization. Such processes, Nietzsche would likely argue, will overwhelm last human beings of the lifeworld, thus creating the birth pangs of, at the very least, a legitimation crisis felt toward their social systems. Yet, having falsely equated democracy with good governance, they remained highly dependent on its precarious and untenable yet still reified social systems to quell their angst and uncertainties.

The individual, no longer free, remains asleep and uncritical. Such persons have now become a piece of a puzzle complicit in the colonization of their own lifeworld. For Nietzsche, key scripts are thus created in the lifeworld that Habermas would later posit as promoting its own colonization: the belief that one can generate prosperity in unprecedented ways or allowing the orientation of *gesellschaft* to determine social and community life. Within this heavy modernity and its regulatory frameworks, actors are also expected to nourish its *isms*; that is, nationalism, socialism, democratism, capitalism, feminism, Darwinism, to name but a few. The process further entrenches the lifeworld's captive audiences into a state of uncritical reification of systems that can ultimately overpower the sovereign self, even when such systems may be illegitimate due to its propagation of double standards and hypocrisies.

Nietzsche, however, was no proponent of providing fish for the needy. His philosophy would rather prefer to teach the person how to fish, so to speak. This stance should not be seen as one of cruelty and abandonment, however, for Nietzsche sincerely believed that systemic demands for acquiescence sapped the will of the individual, ultimately positioning the individual at the precipice of nihilism, one that conformists will descend into when systemic resources and ideologies are depleted and exhausted. The overcomer will need to realize that in such conditions, as emphasized by Nietzsche in *Dawn of Day*, one's strength must be harnessed not for external outcome, not "upon works but upon himself as a work, that is, his own self-control, the purifying of his own imagination, the order and selection in his inspirations and tasks" (V., SEC. 548 / 2007a, 380). Not surprisingly for Nietzsche, suffering and tragedy become teachable experiences that inform us about the human condition. In *The Gay Science*, published five years after *Untimely Meditations*, Nietzsche again returns to this important theme central to his philosophy: how individuals can appropriate corporeal and emotional challenges for renewal. Nietzsche claims that for such developing and elevating individuals "pain itself gives them their greatest moments!" (IV, SEC. 318 / 2001, 179). In *Ecce Homo* he proclaims, "I have never been so happy with myself as in my life's periods of greatest illness and pain" (2007b, 58). From one who worshipped inner strength, systems in failure thus became catalysts for Nietzsche's formulation of how the overcomer can exist, excel, and triumph, yet still author one's own process of becoming and being without surrendering to systemic imperatives articulated by social institutions. Not surprisingly, Solms-Laubach observes how "Nietzsche does not hold the current state of 'culture,' 'education' and 'civilisation' of his own society in high esteem," since none of these spheres of life "have helped to enhance 'life'" (2007, 139) nor allow people to be "self-creative beings" that can be "responsible for their own destinies" (2007, 141).

The ingredients of teaching the sovereign actor how to fish in a tumultuous ocean, to reassemble the self in the process, will be how Nietzsche's major works will be approached. Here is where my rendering of Nietzsche is not unlike Solms-Laubach's view, namely that Nietzsche embodies the role of educator/activist, one whose aim it was to teach "men how to live and, more specifically, how to live as man" (Murphy 1984, 3). Yet should we not succeed in this undertaking, we can find comfort in Nietzsche's own absolution when he noted in *Ecce Homo*, "All my writings are fish-hooks: perhaps I am as good as anyone fishing? . . . If nothing was *caught,* then I am not to blame. *There weren't any fish . . .*" (2007b, 77).

For Nietzsche, when systemic forces fail society, how the self overcomes dysfunctions to usher in a new society becomes a chief concern, and in my view, where existential sociology can contribute knowledge about where meaning of existence surfaces when social contexts are constituted by impaired social systems. Nietzsche believed that even with stable functioning systems, the best outcome had been to create a populace existing in conformity and deference, if not sycophancy, a pattern that can be seen among local elites of the now defunct Third World who, during the nineteenth and twentieth centuries, sold themselves out to colonial enterprises that proselytized civilization and human rights, yet transformed large swathes of the globe into graveyards of imperialism replete with numerous unresolved inequalities that still affect the human condition today. As such, the material consequences of death and poverty that afflicted so many subalterns were, for twentieth-century Marxist philosopher Antonio Gramsci, due to how they had been left out of representative forces and institutions that could directly affect their lives, a result of the standard colonial practice of embedding a politics of exclusion into their imperialist enterprises. Solms-Laubach concludes that Nietzsche is thus "very pessimistic about . . . social institutions that determine . . . the modern 'state'" (2007, 141), especially when they enable individuals to become appropriated by capitalist and/or imperialist hegemonies that manufacture their consent.

Nietzsche was, in essence, "done" with modernity and sought a new *Volk* of overcomers—a new people, a new nation—to lay the foundations for establishing communities with tremendous autonomy for its individuals to excel and self-actualize (Young 2006).[2] Nietzsche was thus concerned about how actors will lack the courage, initiative, and agency to overcome the aforementioned factors. These same actors are most vulnerable to modernity's systemic and ideological decay, resulting in their crisis of meaning. And it is through such legitimation and systemic crises and its output of nihilistic worldviews that inspire the proactive overcomer, an actor with agency, sovereignty, and self-mastery to prevail in spite of systemic dysfunctions. The trials and tribulations human beings must go through when their systems relegate them to dystopia, destitution, and death are real challenges for the overcomer that Nietzsche saw sociologically, conveyed in a uniquely romantic, sociologically-penetrating, yet frenetic fashion. Solms-Laubach's summary of Nietzsche is appropriate at this juncture:

Even if they do not regard Nietzsche as a social thinker of the first rank, most of his commentators would, however, agree that his writings provided a radical critique of modern society in general. . . . His views were both ruthless and original to such a degree, that they sparked off an unprecedented reaction in many academic and non-academic disciplines, as well as among the educated public. (2007, 5)

Solms-Laubach continues:

> Nietzsche's attempt to undermine traditional values and to question the authoritative claims made by scientific rhetoric, makes him a very dynamic and at the same time potentially dangerous ally for sociology. The "dynamic" capacity of Nietzsche's contribution to sociology lies in his ability to function as a creative and radical critic of both the insincerity and hypocrisy that modern men live by, as well as of the general decadence that characterised his society. (2007, 6–7)

For us to appreciate Nietzsche's uniquely esoteric means of communicating his thoughts, chapter 2 will discuss his writing style before proceeding to chapters 3, 4, and 5. As will be conveyed in chapter 2, Nietzsche requested his readers to learn how to read him. By obliging, we will thus be better prepared for the next three chapters that examine, in sequence, Nietzsche's major publications that exhibit anti-systemic analyses. With the overcomer already fashioned as an actor with agency and self-mastery in this chapter, readers will do well to transplant such an actor to confront the problematics to be elaborated in the following chapters.

NOTES

1. An impressive 2008 study on the later Nietzsche's mental health in *Acta Neurol Belg* titled "The Neurological Illness of Friedrich Nietzsche" was published by researchers at the Department of Neurology at Ghent University, Belgium. Exploring historical accounts with original German sources, as well as letters from friends and kin, and from Nietzsche himself, the researchers point to the philosopher as having suffered from cerebral autosomal dominant arteriopathy with subcortical infarcts and leukoencephalopathy (CADASIL). Symptoms such as "migraine, psychiatric disturbance, cognitive decline with dementia and stroke" characterize those with CADASIL (Hemelsoet, Hemelsoet, and Devreese 2008). Such a finding counters the conventional view that Nietzsche's descent into cognitive decline was a result of neurosyphilitic infection (syphilis) acquired during his youth. The current findings will certainly add to more vigorous debate about the physical illnesses suffered by Nietzsche throughout his adult life.

2. Daniel Breazeale, editor of *Meditations*, notes how Nietzsche employed the term to refer to a new people, a new nation. A cryptic equivalent exists in the English language in the form of "folk-story," yet Breazeale concedes that the word "by itself is now archaic in English" (cited in Nietzsche 1997b, 229).

Chapter Two

How to Approach
Nietzsche's Works

Friedrich Nietzsche's most sociologically relevant works span eleven texts, with publication dates from 1872 until 1888. In chronological order, *The Birth of Tragedy* was published in 1872, followed by the different "meditations" of *Untimely Meditations* published between 1873 and 1876. *Human, All Too Human: A Book for Free Spirits* was published by 1878, *The Dawn of Day*, alternatively referred to as *Daybreak*, was completed by 1881, while *The Gay Science*, alternatively referred to as *Joyful Wisdom,* was published by 1882. The perennial favorite of many, the four parts of *Thus Spoke Zarathustra, A Book for All and None* were published separately between 1883 and 1892, while *Beyond Good and Evil: Prelude to a Philosophy of the Future* was released in 1886. *On the Genealogy of Morality* was published a year later. In a prolific period of writing from 1888 onward until his mental collapse in 1889, Nietzsche ultimately published *Twilight of the Idols, or, How to Philosophize with a Hammer* and the controversial *The Anti-Christ: A Curse on Christianity.* His final work, *Ecce Homo: How One Becomes What One Is* was completed in 1888 but was published posthumously in 1908, eight years after Nietzsche's passing. Nine of the titles, due to their length, will henceforth be referred to in shorthand, as seen in the table on the next page.

Nietzsche's works that are least sociological, or those for which their veracity cannot be confirmed, will not be included in the discussion of a Nietzsche sociological imagination. In this category, his least relevant but not inconsequential works include *Dionysian Dithyrambs* (2004), a collection of poetry first published in 1891, as well as writings where Nietzsche critiques and ultimately rejects the German composer Richard Wagner, to whom he had once been a mentee, a close friend, and admirer. In this regard, *The Case of Wagner,* published in 1888, as well as a critical essay titled *Nietzsche contra Wagner* in 1889 will not be explored, with the exception of two passages

The Birth of Tragedy	Birth
Untimely Meditations	Meditations
Human, All Too Human: A Book for Free Spirits	Human
The Dawn of Day	Dawn
The Gay Science	Science
Thus Spoke Zarathustra	Zarathustra
Beyond Good and Evil: Prelude to a Philosophy of the Future	Beyond
On the Genealogy of Morality	Genealogy
Twilight of the Idols, or, How to Philosophize with a Hammer	Twilight
The Anti-Christ: A Curse on Christianity	Anti-Christ
Ecce Homo: How to Become What You Are	Ecce Homo

from the latter. One had already been cited in chapter 1 to further enhance our understanding of the overcomer; the other mention will shortly be referenced to serve as an account of Nietzsche's cessation of friendship with his mentor, Richard Wagner, due to the latter's growing anti-Semitism.

The main reason for the aforementioned exclusions is due to how Nietzsche primarily adopted a music critic role in these writings, one that critiqued Richard Wagner's evolution as a composer as well as his increasing anti-Semitism, character attributes that later resulted in the end of their friendship. The core of these works is thus personal; it appears to be the most thematically "distant" work from Nietzsche's aforementioned publications and exhibits the least relevant sociological imaginations. That said, one key observation can be made in *Nietzsche contra Wagner*, if only briefly, about Nietzsche's rejection of Wagner that compelled the former to put his thoughts into words, a task we need to address at the outset because it establishes the position that Nietzsche is far from being the anti-Semite those who carelessly misunderstand his ideas interpret him to be. In the section titled "How I Broke Away From Wagner," Nietzsche recalls:

> In the summer of 1876, right in the middle of the first *Festspiel*,[1] I took leave of Wagner. I cannot stand ambiguities: since coming to Germany, Wagner had acceded step by step to everything that I hate—even to anti-Semitism . . . At that time it was indeed high time *to take my leave*: and I immediately received a confirmation of the fact. Richard Wagner, seemingly the all-conquering, actually a decaying, despairing decadent, suddenly sank down helpless and shattered before the Christian cross . . . Was there no German with eyes in his head, empathy in his conscience, for this dreadful spectacle? Was I the only one who—*suffered* from it?— (2005, 276)

Nietzsche's words clearly counter the view that he had proto-nationalist tendencies due to his emphasis on excellence, a noble predisposition, and self-mastery as a sovereign overcomer—attributes that would later be distorted by his sister to render the ideal Aryan. According to Nietzsche, Wagner had grown to become a nationalist—the bane of the former's ideas—since the *ism* of nationalism is but one of many types of authority systems that demands a captive and thus unfree audience. This collective of conformists, what Nietzsche terms the herd, is ripe for exploitation by political entrepreneurs and political malcontents as they influence their conformists to replace their love of a Christian God with the glorification of the German nation. The above passage underscores one of the major currents energizing Nietzsche's thoughts, and although *Nietzsche contra Wagner* will not be further discussed in this work, its mention here remains useful if not for simply pointing out that our philosopher lived his beliefs and accepted their consequences, a tendency that will be seen in many of his works.

THE *NACHLASS*

Other works that will partially be harnessed for the assembly of Nietzsche's sociological imagination include the many fragmentary notes, letters to friends and associates, and incomplete essays referred to as the *Nachlass*.[2] The large body of notes and writings left by Nietzsche in a motley state has generated a healthy discussion as to whether these materials are worthy of consideration. For some, the contents of the *Nachlass* can be divided into two major groups. Kaufmann envisions Nietzsche's *Nachlass* in this manner, seeing its contents as constituted by "the material that never found its way into a published work and . . . the notes that were eventually put to use and developed in his later works" (1950, 77). Other scholars like Linda Williams (1996) sees three distinct categories in the *Nachlass*. For Williams, the first category primarily refers to the works Nietzsche had already published or were in the process of being published at the time he descended into insanity. These include *Ecce Homo*, *Nietzsche contra Wagner*, *Anti-Christ*, and *Twilight*. Another category of the *Nachlass* includes his lecture notes prepared during his employment at the University of Basel, while the final category pertains to Nietzsche's notes "which vary from simple fragments or single sentences to sketchy outlines of various projects to several long paragraphs in essay form" (Williams 1996, 448).[3]

In terms of how the *Nachlass* has been received, Stefan L. Sorgner observes of Nietzsche's readership in *Metaphysics without Truth*:

> One can distinguish three main camps which the principal Nietzsche interpreters have taken: Firstly, there are the interpreters like Maudemarie Clark who rely

almost exclusively on Nietzsche's published work. Secondly, there are the ones who agree with Derrida's position which accords an equality of value between the published, and unpublished work. Thirdly, there are the followers of Heidegger who regard the unpublished work to be of superior value in comparison to the published work. (2007, 17)

Solms-Laubach (2007) describes how many scholars tend to only validate Nietzsche's published writings as confirmation of his resolve. Kaufmann argues how such sentiments about Nietzsche's published writings reveal these scholars' desires to confront the philosopher's ideas in a manner where the latter "would be willing to stand up for it" (1950, 77). Those who are more speculative consider his unpublished materials as deserving pride of place since they "seem to hold the key to Nietzsche's true legacy," while progressive thinkers advocate for balancing what is epistemic and ontologic from both contexts (Solms-Laubach 2007, xx).

Kaufmann exhibits a progressive approach toward Nietzsche thought. He points to the usefulness of Nietzsche's ideas dispersed throughout his unpublished or unfinished writings. Kaufmann remarks how these notes, along with those contained in *The Will to Power*, "are of great interest, frequently very suggestive, and distinctly helpful as background material for a better understanding of the finished books" (1950, 77). Solms-Laubach also approaches Nietzsche's works progressively, noting that "Nietzsche's published writings clearly benefits from a comparison with the material Nietzsche wrote around that time, but which he did not see fit for publication or which he just delivered in public lectures" (2007, xxi). Clark's approach, however, focuses on vetting Nietzsche through his publications, one that for Solms-Laubach is "obviously easiest to defend" (2007, xxii). Clark's more nuanced rationale for focusing on the published materials is based on her view that "where Nietzsche's notes suggest a position different from that suggested by the published writings, it is usually a philosophically weaker one" (1990, 26). Clark therefore assigns the *Nachlass* "a very secondary status" (1990, 26). In Young's exegesis of Nietzsche as a communitarian, the *Nachlass* was "only very discretely" referred to since even "Nietzsche wanted the *Nachlass* destroyed at his death—understandably since it contains a great deal of weak material" (2006, 7). The orientation of my work adopts Williams's, Clark's, and Young's approaches, one that gives pride of place to published materials, a process that will skirt into the *Nachlass* only insofar as the materials are sociologically relevant and can be attributed to Nietzsche alone. That said, the letters written by Nietzsche that constitute the *Nachlass*, many of which were compiled by philosopher Christopher Middleton, are "like aerial photography of a subterranean labyrinth" (2007, xi).

Finally, it should also be noted that the orientations of Nietzsche's views did change throughout his life. Although uncritical readers have highlighted the changes as betraying contradictions in Nietzsche's line of thinking, Clark (1990, 2015) and Young (2006) argue more convincingly that changes in some areas of Nietzsche's philosophy reflect, instead, a maturation in his thinking. Moreover, they also indicate how unresolved matters in Nietzsche's early writings were resolved in his later works. These resolutions can be seen in sociologically-related topics that pertain to empiricism, the state, social class, praxis, and self and society. Where views of Nietzsche differ between his earlier and later works, highlights will be made about his conceptual evolution. It is with these parameters of concerns that I summarize Nietzsche's works in a manner that illuminates his sociological imagination. That said, *Nachlass* or otherwise, Nietzsche never waivered from his style, one that has always exhibited a "delicate orchestration of his deep intuitions" (Middleton 2007, xiii).

THE WILL TO POWER

Regardless of how one sets the parameters of the *Nachlass*, what remains clear is that *The Will to Power* was not a work completed by Nietzsche. An irresponsible compilation of Nietzsche's notes that would become *The Will to Power* was undertaken by Nietzsche's sister, Elisabeth Förster-Nietzsche, who, during her capacity as her brother's caretaker after his mental collapse, forwarded the work to promote Aryan supremacy, German nationalism, and favorable views toward the Third Reich. Philosopher Alan D. Schrift comments:

> Nietzsche chose to write in a style that invites misunderstanding—his use of metaphor, dissimulation, and hyperbole in particular, all make it easier for his words to be taken to mean something other than what he might have intended (assuming that one can know what he intended in any definitive way, which I think is not the case). That said, there is no question in my mind that the Nazis willfully misappropriated Nietzsche's language and engaged in a level of textual and editorial corruption to allow Nietzsche to apparently say anti-Semitic comments that he never in fact said. (Bergmann et al. 2007, 15)

Such an approach to writing rendered Nietzsche vulnerable to Förster-Nietzsche's exploitation of her brother toward the end of his life, his most vulnerable period, allowing her to cohere his thoughts posthumously into *The Will to Power*. In this treatment by Förster-Nietzsche, Nietzsche's *übermensch* became an epithet not for an elite self-affirming human being, but for the perfect Aryan/German. Yet, it is well known that Nietzsche detested nationalism and considered himself a European, and, toward the end of his life, was even stateless.[4] At this juncture in our discussion, it suffices to say that even as an adolescent Nietzsche's view of a shared humanity was revealed in his short story of twenty chapters titled *Capri and Heligoland*. In it Nietzsche proclaims through his character, "We are pilgrims in this world—we are citizens of the world" (Hollingdale 1999, 23).

The damage to Nietzsche's legacy caused by his sister is well known, but it would be Walter Kaufmann's detailed elaboration of Förster-Nietzsche's machinations that allowed the West to absolve Nietzsche from being seen as a fascist. Solms-Laubach is more forthright, detailing how *The Will to Power* published posthumously after Nietzsche's death was a product that "was falsified to a large, and in many cases irreversible, extent . . . [and that] any passage from this book should, therefore, be treated with some suspicion" (2007, 14). Solms-Laubach, thus emphasizes how "there is no such book as *Der Wille zur Macht* [*The Will to Power*], at least not one that can be genuinely ascribed to Friedrich Nietzsche" (2007, xxii). Williams of *Science* reminds readers that *The Will to Power* is not a Nietzsche work published by the philosopher himself, but is instead a work with content rather recklessly compiled by his sister (cited in Nietzsche 2001, xvi). Even Anthony M. Ludovici's translation of *The Will to Power* (2010) acknowledges the state of affairs:

> Unfortunately, *The Will to Power* was never completed by its author. The text from which this translation was made is a posthumous publication, and it suffers from all the disadvantages that a book must suffer from which has been arranged and ordered by foster hands . . . [and] it was . . . little more than a vast collection of notes and rough drafts, set down by Nietzsche . . . as the material for his chief work . . . which Nietzsche must have had the intention of elaborating at some future time. (cited in Nietzsche 2010, 5)

Although Nietzsche's themes on self-empowerment are dispersed throughout the text—this is incontrovertible—the manufactured messages and narratives by Förster-Nietzsche are not bona fide Nietzsche, but function as a distorted rendering of Nietzsche's ideas and tenets recklessly assembled. This sad state of affairs, however, did at least organize into one textual exposition the thematic cues that Nietzsche had contemplated for many years as he formulated his notion of the *übermensch*. Fortunately, the kernels of the overcomer are alluded to if not explicitly addressed in Nietzsche's other published works as can be seen in the quotes cited in the previous chapter. That is, an assembly of *übermensch* themes dispersed through Nietzsche's texts outside the Förster-Nietzsche-inspired *Will to Power* is just as able to point readers to what Nietzsche expected from the ideal type. My efforts have been to focus on reassembling the overcomer from readings of Nietzsche's published works, a process that will in no way include distortions of existential ideas constructed by Förster-Nietzsche. Such a reassembly is not only possible, but necessary, to situate the overcomer within the scope of our examination: systemic crises born from contradictions inherent in modernity's *isms*.

It is comforting to know that the overwhelming majority of thinkers today do not consider Nietzsche responsible for the appropriation of his ideas by the Nazis. In an important article titled "What Does Nietzsche Mean to Philosophers Today?" published in the journal *Kritika & Kontext* (2007, 13–19), contemporary scholars shared similar views that absolved Nietzsche from Nazism. Even philosopher Richard Rorty, arguably the most critical of Nietzsche in the discussion, acknowledges that Nietzsche is "guiltless of encouraging the Nazis," further adding that "no thinker can afford to worry about what use will be made of his ideas in the future." Philosophers Paul Patton and Teodor Münz share similar sentiments, with the former noting, "I do not believe Nietzsche bears any responsibility for the appropriation of his ideas by Nazism," while the latter explained that Nietzsche "only proclaimed his philosophy"; Frantisek Novosád is most laudatory, arguing that Nietzsche is even able to "interpret fascism and, actually, communism," and that both Nietzsche and Marx presciently knew that "Europe was really a powder keg and one spark was enough to bring a series of catastrophes to humanity." Fellow philosopher Jan Sokol echoes similar sentiments, arguing that "Nietzsche . . . perhaps similar to Marx," had no way of anticipating "what damage radical philosophical views could cause if implemented into real politics and tailored accordingly" (Bergmann et al. 2007, 17).

THE NIETZSCHE STYLE

Nietzsche's writing style, even for his day, was considered unique due to its interweaving of prose and aphorisms that are configured mostly in labeled and unlabeled sections, parts, essays, and/or volumes. Even though Nietzsche frequently conveys his contemplations in sections rather than chapters, he was able to make a variety of entries that had enough girth to be critically incisive, even though some of these propositions did not exhibit full elaborations needed to extend his ideas into full-length chapters. However, this idiosyncrasy can be attributed to how Nietzsche frequently wrote: as a consequence of experiencing episodes of total inspiration and realization, a state of being that sociologist Kurt Wolff describes as "surrender and catch" (1962, 1976). I am of the view that Nietzsche's concept of the eternal recurrence to be elaborated in the next chapter—envisioned as a

thought exercise that tests whether one has the mettle to be an overcomer—
was inspired into existence during a surrender and catch moment from one
of his walks at Sils Maria in Switzerland. Even during Nietzsche's later
years when he moves away from heavy aphoristic expressions, the spirit of
the aphorism, "the summation of a lengthy process of thought in a single
striking sentence," would intermittently surface in the philosopher's writings inspired by his sojourns into nature (Hollingdale 1999, 170), sojourns
that likely birthed many surrender and catch episodes for Nietzsche. These
thoughts became the *staccato* for Nietzsche's favorite themes, frequently
drafted in mountain ecosystems that he felt would be ideal for minimizing
the many physical ailments that plagued him for much of his life. Nietzsche
thus captured important philosophical realizations in a notebook that accompanied him on many hikes. In one of his more famous proclamations from
Ecce Homo, Nietzsche notes that his philosophy is about willingly living "in
ice and high mountains—seeking out everything alien and questionable in
existence, everything that has hitherto been excluded by morality" (2007b,
4). Nietzsche writes about how such mountain air was the pristine "air of
the heights," where "the ice is near" and the "solitude is immense—but how
peacefully everything lies in the light" (2007b, 4).

As for Nietzsche's aphoristic style, the aphorisms range from one sentence
to large paragraphs that, according to Keith Ansell-Pearson of *Genealogy*,
still manage to coalesce into key themes that serve as building blocks upon
which Nietzsche harvested his penetrating critiques against all diacritica of
morality (cited in Nietzsche 2006a, xv). Nietzsche's aphoristic-heavy writings can be seen in *Human, Dawn, Science,* and *Beyond*, while more con-
tinuous text can be seen in *Zarathustra, Genealogy, Anti-Christ*, and *Ecce
Homo.* However, even in this latter group of works, Hollingdale notes that the
aphorisms make their appearances again (1999, 118). W. G. Runciman argues
that Nietzsche's handling of aphorisms is valuable because it can only emerge
when "both the aphorist and the reader can agree to be accurate" (2000, 7).
Nietzsche's use of aphorisms injects tremendous "vitality and liveliness" in
his critiques (Solms-Laubach 2007, 51) unless one has read only *Genealogy*
where Nietzsche expresses his thoughts with enough girth to manifest his
text as lengthier paragraphs. Although Nietzsche's colorful style may obscure the operationalizations of a variety of sociological themes seen in his
writings, disentangling them from his penetrating observations, especially if
they exhibit useful social views, would detract from the richness and passion
of his sociological imagination. That said, Novosád accuses Nietzsche for
exhibiting an "adolescent taste for provoking people, for striking at what we
usually consider obvious"; yet he also rightfully credits many Nietzsche passages that bring "to the surface long hidden truths, or breaks age-old taboos

of thought" (Bergmann et al. 2007, 11). Thiele echoes Novosád, noting how "ruffling feathers—and occasionally plucking them out—became an art form with Nietzsche" (Bergmann et al. 2007, 13).

During the late 1980s, the classic BBC series *The Great Philosophers* saw its host Bryan Magee discuss with German literature scholar Joseph Peter Stern the particularities of Nietzsche's writing style. In the conversation Magee highlights Stern's comments about Nietzsche's use of metaphors. Stern notes:

> You spoke earlier about his style, and I think it is an extraordinary powerful, effective style. If I ask myself where it derives from, I think it derives from a strange invention or discovery he seems to have made of how to place his discourse somewhere half-way between metaphor and literal meaning. And this is something which very few people, certainly very few German writers, have done before him. As far as thinking is concerned, he stands entirely on his own. . . . This style, which is pitched half-way between metaphor and literal state-ment, is something quite extraordinary. And I think unless we understand it for what it is we are going to misread him. (Magee 2001, 248)

Stern then offers a passage that is indicative of such a Nietzsche style:

> When he talked about the terrible deprivation that nineteenth-century people experienced through what he called luridly "the death of God," he wrote as fol-lows: "Rather than cope with the unbearable loneliness of their condition, many will continue to seek their shattered God, and for His sake they will love the very serpents that dwell among His ruins." Now you see this mixture of, on the one hand, conceptual thinking—"loneliness" and "condition" are abstract terms belonging to conceptual thought, and the entire argument is part of a historical generalisation—with, on the other hand, serpents glistening through the ruins of the shattered God. Well that, and the refusal to go beyond that—the refusal to write out the theory behind the metaphors—essentially constitutes what he's about. (Magee 2001, 248)

Adding to Magee's example, Nietzsche writes in *Science*, "Our visible moral qualities . . . take their course; and the invisible ones . . . also take their course: probably a totally different one, with lines and subtleties and sculptures that might amuse a god with a divine microscope" (I, SEC. 8 / 2001, 35). In *Genealogy*, Nietzsche observes that when a "tree actually bears fruit . . . we then find the *sovereign individual* as the ripest fruit on its tree" (II, SEC. 2 / 2006a, 36–37). In the seminal *Zarathustra* he snidely questions, "You lived in your solitude as if in the sea, and the sea carried you. Alas, you want to climb ashore?" (2006b, 4). In Nietzsche's autobiographical *Ecce Homo*, the philosopher reflects how "on this perfect day, when everything is ripening and not only the grapes are turning brown, a shaft of sunlight has just fallen on my life" (2007b, 6).

However, I view Stern's claim that Nietzsche's refusal to offer up textual exposition for a potential social theory to be misplaced. The alacrity with which Nietzsche conveyed his ideas, his discussion of Greek tragedy, his reprimand of certain thinkers, his view of overcoming, and his pronouncements through the proxy Zarathustra, are indeed manifested through his employment of metaphors. Yet as we shall see in chapter 6 when Nietzsche concentrates on critiquing social institutions and their operators, the metaphors and analogies are noticeably tempered, allowing more disciplined theoretical assertions to surface. Whatever remaining metaphors that do coexist with these theoretical assertions fortunately add greatly to the intensity of Nietzsche's foci. That many readers and some scholars have not considered this attribute of Nietzsche's polemical style is likely due to them never having approached Nietzsche's writing in a manner that searched for sociological horizons. In his more sociological observations, Nietzsche's ideas are conveyed with a greater degree of candor and seriousness. The joyful, euphoric proclamations, and the occasional drawn-out banter or polemics against whom he once admired (Schopenhauer, Wagner) and those on his hit list (Comte, Spencer, Darwin, to name but a few), are comparatively subdued. In this regard, Nietzsche's sociological imaginations, laded with theoretical cues, remain rich, incisive, and critical.

Nietzsche also frequently emphasized his thoughts tautologically, a rhetorical style of writing that incorporates repetition in different iterations as a means of maintaining emphasis and rhythm. The sentence in *Beyond*, "They are people without solitude, without their own solitude . . . [ellipsis added]," is an example (Nietzsche II, SEC. 44 / 2002, 40). As one who appreciates their deployment, Nietzsche's use of tautology should be seen as his enthusiastic desire to convey, through the rhythm that tautological writing offers, urgency and definitiveness of assertions and proclamations. Observations about Nietzsche's writing style should also include mention about the visually frenetic attributes of how his text is presented. By this I mean Nietzsche's frequent use of exclamation marks, Latin phrases, unique placement of punctuation marks—what Duncan Large of *Ecce Homo* describes as Nietzsche's "idiosyncratic punctuation" (cited in Nietzsche 2007b, xxviv). Nietzsche also frequently employs semi-colons to slightly shift the trajectory of his long sentences without digressing so as to maintain its momentum. Careless readers of Nietzsche will lose their rhythm and pace if they are not mindful. This situation is somewhat exacerbated when Nietzsche's tone is taken into consideration. Nietzsche himself acknowledges in *Ecce Homo* how his tone under certain circumstances can be "harsh and mocking" (2007b, 55). Furthermore, although there is always some meaning that is lost to translation, translators of Nietzsche's works from its original German have faithfully transplanted Nietzsche's frequent use of italicized passages. I will be mindful in allowing those passages italicized by Nietzsche to remain as is in my quotes of his passages, while those italics I employ for my own emphases will be identified.

Additionally, Nietzsche often begins sentences with a dash and similarly draws it to a close with another dash, and sometimes two dashes—the latter of which Rainer J. Hanshe (2010) describes as Nietzsche's "emblem"—an employment that might precede, of all things, a colon or semi-colon. Nietzsche also frequently ends sentences with ellipses. For example, in *Ecce Homo*, Nietzsche notes of his fate that "nobody before me knew the right way, the way *up*: only starting with me did hopes, tasks, prescribed paths for culture exist again—*I am the bearer of these glad tidings* . . . This also makes me a destiny.— —" (2005, 137). Nietzsche dares to leave his thoughts open-ended, perhaps a justified style since Nietzsche, according to Middleton, "seldom takes us down the darker galleries of his labyrinth, and the periods may end in cryptic dots when he is doing just that," and in this regard he is a "master of a kind of definitive silence" (1996, xiv). Moreover, Nietzsche combines punctuation marks that should be stand-alone symbols to further accent his thoughts. The following passage in *Human* illustrates this tendency: "—The believer in magic and miracles reflects on how to impose a law on nature—: and, in brief, the religious cult is the outcome of this reflection" (Nietzsche Vol. 1, III, SEC. 111 / 1996, 64).[5]

Nietzsche's employment of dashes deserves more mention as many translations of his works omit them in quoted passages. A stimulating examination of Nietzsche's use of dashes can be found in Hanshe's discussion of their employment (2010, 9). Hanshe describes how Nietzsche embraced the use of dashes, seeing in them a significance that transcends communicated thought. Nietzsche even noted in an 1884 letter written to his sister, Elisabeth, that proclaimed, "Everything I have written hitherto is foreground; for me the real thing begins only with the dashes" (Middleton 1996, 241). Hanshe argues that "although it is well known that Nietzsche's use of dashes is astonishingly manifold, they are still largely ignored, that is, rarely read or interpreted, and it is clear how negligible this has been and remains" (2010, 10). For Hanshe, Nietzsche's use of the dash "is no mere sign. . . . It is not only employed to conceal certain thoughts and to keep others silent, but to refrain from pronouncing some thoughts" (2010, 11–12). Hanshe cites a variety of scholars who also appreciate this aspect of Nietzsche's expression. For example, Loeb interprets the dash as a form of deduction (2006, 174). Some see Nietzsche's use of dashes as an announcement of a break in thought (Löwith 1997) while others such as Klein view them as a "transitional force" (1997, 64) and warn that there will be a misreading and misunderstanding of Nietzsche when readers ignore the significance of the dash. Others see Nietzsche's employment of the dash as having "many intentional functions," and that Nietzsche "writes in several published notes that he likes in his books the dashes more than everything that is expressed with words" (Van Tongeren 2000, 94). Regardless of the differing viewpoints on Nietzsche's use of dashes, Hanshe implores readers to "attend to them with the greatest care," for they will enable us to "decipher his visual riddle, a riddle that for over 100 years has remained an unheard and unseen enigma"; he implores us to thus "smash our ears in order to hear with our eyes" (2010, 12).

Mention also needs to be made about how I will present Nietzsche's works as we highlight his sociological imaginations: in a chronological manner suggested by Young (2006). Young offers four prudent reasons, followed by a fifth and six justification of my own. An exception will be made, however, for how *Ecce Homo*—completed only weeks before Nietzsche's mental collapse—will be employed. Since the work was structured by Nietzsche as primarily an autobiography of our philosopher reflecting upon his past works, it will be harnessed to "excavate" from hindsight Nietzsche's views on key themes as they appear across his publishing periods.

The first reason for adopting a chronological approach is to ensure that one can follow the development of Nietzsche's ideas in a manner that is similar to how Nietzsche reads himself, as in the autobiographical *Ecce Homo*. Secondly, Young finds that a chronological approach is important for illuminating "strong continuities in his [Nietzsche's] thinking" that allow readers to "interpret with confidence passages that are unclear or whose meaning is in dispute" (2006, 6). The third justification for adopting a chronological approach is to set a positive example on how one should not read Nietzsche: by recklessly mining quotes from Nietzsche's works in a manner that is out of sequence. For Strong, there is indeed a "great temptation to succumb to Nietzsche's quotability" (1997a, xiv). Clark and Dudrick (2012) also warn that reading Nietzsche casually risks his ideas being understood exoterically.

In many instances Nietzsche emphasized that he wrote for the very few of society, for the esoteric as it were. In *Dawn*, Nietzsche beseeches his readers: "My patient friends, this book appeals only to perfect readers and philologists: *learn* to read me well!" (Preface, SEC. 5 / 2007a, 9). In *Zarathustra*, the prophet describes his ideal readers as "bold searchers" that dare to "put to terrible seas with cunning sails," as those who allow their souls to be "lured by flutes to every maelstrom" (Nietzsche 2006b, 124). A more poignant and prescient proclamation can be seen in *Anti-Christ*'s first paragraph: "This book belongs to the very few. Perhaps none of them are even alive yet. Maybe they are the ones who will understand my *Zarathustra*. . . .—My day won't come until the day after tomorrow. Some people are born posthumously" (Nietzsche, Preface / 2005, 3). Nietzsche was correct. Nietzsche never wavered on the high standards he had for those who dared to read his writings. Even late in his life, near his mental collapse, Nietzsche was discerning about his ideal type of reader. In *Ecce Homo*, Nietzsche even remarks that such an ideal reader is one who is courageous and curious, one who is also "supple, cunning, cautious, a born adventurer and discoverer" (2007b, 40).

Young's fourth reason is shared by Clark (1990): a chronological reading of Nietzsche allows thinkers to see the maturation and evolution of Nietzsche's ideas. Young comments that watching "the birth, growth and refinement of a great thinker's thought is . . . much more exciting than receiving the finished product in one neatly packaged lump" (2006, 7). The fifth reason for adopting a chronological analysis of Nietzsche pertains to Alexander Nehamas's (1988) excellent suggestion that we see each of Nietzsche's works as monologues that have longitudinal value. Clark is similarly nuanced in her approach to Nietzsche, noting that "unlike a single sentence cut off from any connection to others, each section of Nietzsche's published works is embedded in a very rich context constituted by other sections of the same work, and, usually by earlier and later works" (1990, 18).

Hollingdale observes how Nietzsche's thinking process and writing style are but examples of the philosopher *"talking to oneself"* (1999, 116). Refined, if not developed during his long solitary walks, Nietzsche's note-taking of his thoughts were captured in but a small notebook that accompanied him, one that for Hollingdale likely included words "spoken aloud, with gesticulations" as this style is "implicit in the whole tenor of his writings" (1999, 116). One sees these writing attributes quite vividly through the protagonist Zarathustra where his raison d'être was based on his numerous proclamations and emphases. "Hearing" and reading Nietzsche in such a manner reveals nodes of Nietzsche's emphases and concerns that are always being assembled, maintained, and sometimes disassembled for the reader; one can see this quite explicitly in *Ecce Homo* when Nietzsche revisits the merits of his previous writings. To fully appreciate Nietzsche's writing style, it is best to consider Hollingdale's understanding of Nietzsche's tenor as one that is intimate yet still based on "heightened conversation" (1999, 117), one that gradually reveals a philosophy that will open our eyes and illuminate how a "new world has been discovered" (1999, 116).

Nehamas notes how a "train of thought," if one approaches Nietzsche's philosophy as a series of monologues, connects similar themes, a style most pronounced in *Beyond* and *Science*. However, Nehamas's approach focuses on thematic atavisms that surface within a book. My approach adopts a more expansive panorama, to visit atavisms of similar themes as they emerge, rise, and ebb across Nietzsche's published works. From this process, a key set of foundational monologues will facilitate the process of cautiously extrapolating a Nietzsche sociological imagination about the self experiencing the crises of social systems. For example, in my efforts to make operative Nietzsche's critique of the state, Nietzsche's views of the state will be anchored back to *Birth.* Doing so allows us to envision how Nietzsche viewed the degeneration of the state and social systems since the collapse of ancient Greece. It also allows us to approach Nietzsche's critical sociological imagination on impaired social systems with a longer chronology, beyond the collapse of ancient Greece, toward the collapse of Christianity/religion, and toward a sociological view that a putrefaction of modernity and its *isms* remain ongoing. That the Greek state collapsed into decadence, only to have Christianity, its metaphysics, and theodicies follow the same path, points us to important implications for a renewed understanding of the self and society during the latter's dysfunctions.

The sixth and final reason for adopting a chronological reading of Nietzsche is because his sociological critiques against the dysfunctions of social systems express much profundities about existence in society over time. Given the hegemonic and frequently reified entity that is society, understanding its social changes requires a long chronology for its tales to unfold. Nietzsche gives us a chronology from the Greeks toward the discontents of modernity where a new biography of the self in a decaying society urgently requires the self-authoring overcomer to emerge. Moreover, we can also situate Nietzsche through our sociological imaginations, into a rapidly changing Germany that had in tow cultural, political, and economic dynamics that dislocated communities and individuals. How these contexts shaped Nietzsche in his short life point to the importance of seeing a Nietzsche evolving with, and ultimately, distancing himself from, a variety of socially-constructed norms and values to finally go it alone philosophically.

So how does one read Nietzsche overall? Horstmann of *Beyond,* suggests that we approach Nietzsche's writing with three considerations in mind: The first consideration is that we should approach Nietzsche's views not as readers anticipating some absolutist truth to be birthed, for he was unabashedly making his own observations and proclamations. Secondly, we also should be patient with Nietzsche's candidly blunt and politically incorrect views that try to cut through the clutter of society's disingenuousness and superficialities—the indignant philosopher was ready to brawl and his language reflects his impatient desire to confront society's most cherished pieties and moralities. Finally, Horstmann reminds readers to not forget that Nietzsche saw through "us," the "insensitive academic" types, and purposely configured social distance to ensure that his impact from remote and secret horizons was an expression of self-authored uniqueness (cited in Nietzsche 2002, xiv).

Karzai, however, offers the best and most practical advice on how to read our philosopher, suggesting that we "read him while sitting down quietly and calmly, with patience" (2019, xxiv).

From a sociological perspective, we need to appreciate Nietzsche's deeply felt disappointments about modern society. We also need to be patient with his assertions, for these he built over time, and thus, the importance of us reading his works chronologically. We can also appreciate his notion of the praxian human being, the overcomer, as a sociologically relevant ideal type that had to be born for the sake of critiquing and overcoming the discontents and dysfunctions of modernity. We can also seriously consider his critical assessment of modernity, its tendencies, and its institutions of power and culture insofar as they affect the self when such systems no longer provide freedom, community, and meaning for the individual. Finally, we need to enjoy Nietzsche's conversational and polemical style of writing, interwoven with metaphors, analogies, poetry, and his famous aphorisms, as argues philosopher Robert Crease:

> Polemics, especially by authors who are well known for their use of metaphor, irony and hyperbole, cannot be read as if they were conventional journal articles. As the philosopher Robert Scharff likes to say, one might just as well cite the famous beginning of *The Social Contract* ("Man is born free . . .") to mock Jean-Jacques Rousseau for believing that everyone is walking around wearing chains. (Crease 2018)

The next three chapters' summaries of Nietzsche's works begin the process by which I convey his discussion of the social, one that reveals sociological insights into the crises of social systems and its consequences for the self. In this regard, we can appreciate Horstmann's view that Nietzsche's ability to captivate thinkers is due to how the latter's ideas act as a "mental tonic," one that will inspire readers to dare confront their most basic (and cherished) assumptions about self and society—a process that should be undertaken in a manner that offers the individual a dignified strategy of renewal to contest social systems that become impaired (cited in Nietzsche 2002, xxviii). That Nietzsche made it his life project to empower himself and others on how to overcome the decadence of modernity therefore offers us important lessons on the art and brutal truth of living.

NOTES

1. The term *Festspiel* denotes more than just "festival." It refers to a series of festivities centered around important symphonic and orchestral concerts and events, a sort of gala-like ceremony for classical music.

2. *Nachlass* refers to the unfinished and unpublished notes and works of a scholar, often seen as part and parcel to the person's literary estate.

3. Christopher Middleton's excellent *Selected Letters of Friedrich Nietzsche* (1996) contains over two hundred letters our philosopher had written to family, friends, and associates.

4. Nietzsche forfeited his Prussian citizenship in 1869 in hopes of becoming a Swiss national. However, because Nietzsche did not fulfill the qualifications needed to become a Swiss citizen, the philosopher remained stateless until his death (Hollingdale 1999), thus embodying the European identity he so celebrated.

5. I am personally of the view that Martin Speckter's unique yet rarely employed punctuation mark introduced in 1962 to capture an indignant query, the interrobang ("‽"), should have been conventionally employed by translators to capture Nietzsche's writing style, one that often conflates an indignant question with amplified excitability and intensity kneaded into the sentence.

Chapter Three

Nietzsche's Sociological Imaginations
The Early Years (1872–1878)

Summarizing Nietzsche in a manner that harnesses his sociological concepts for explanatory purposes is daunting. I attempt it in hopes of grounding Nietzsche's philosophy in summaries that reveal his sociological imaginations in greater detail than what was briefly introduced in chapter 1. Whereas chapter 1 reveals the protagonist that is the overcomer, chapters 3, 4, and 5 attempt to illuminate the depth of Nietzsche's sociological imaginations: through summaries of his most sociologically-relevant publications across different periods of the philosopher's life, a process distinct from chapter 6 where we specifically examine the nuanced dysfunctions as well as the consequences Nietzsche saw in one's existence within modern social systems. These approaches with their different trajectories should, ideally, make visible how one can understand the self's authoring of sovereignty as one epoch informed by religiosity yields to an industrialized and technocratic age.

Chapter 3 highlights works that have relevance for illuminating Nietzsche's sociological imaginations during his early years. This period of Nietzsche's life culminated with his resignation as professor of philology at Switzerland's University of Basel in 1879 due to chronic health problems. In spite of early life travails that affected Nietzsche, he published a variety of works from which we draw three that are most sociologically significant: *The Birth of Tragedy*, *Untimely Meditations*, and *Human, All Too Human*, with the last of the three, *Human,* published at a time when Nietzsche terminated his friendship with the increasingly nationalistic Richard Wagner in what Strong of *Twilight* described as a "public rupture" (cited in Nietzsche 1997a, viii). No longer an intimate to the Wagner clan and its inner circle or fettered to the scripted and regulatory world of an academia that would later be ridiculed, Nietzsche's wanderlust would take him to Switzerland, Italy, and

France, signaling other phases in Nietzsche's writing period, one that we will discuss in chapters 4 and 5.

THE BIRTH OF TRAGEDY (1872/1999)

The Birth of Tragedy[1] introduces Nietzsche's first major examination of how a community sublimates its experiences of suffering and crisis. In the work, Nietzsche examines the ancient Greeks and their coping mechanism for the trials and tribulations of life: by creating the tragic opera, or tragedy. Nietzsche argues that Athenian tragedy inspired the ancient Greeks to deal with pessimism, suffering, and nihilism through the medium of art. This orientation would be destroyed with Socrates's epistemology based on reason and logic. Interestingly, "modernity" for Nietzsche began with Socrates whose orientations toward theory and knowledge was credited (or implicated) for ultimately birthing the sciences in Nietzsche's time. Yet for Nietzsche, Greek tragedy gave meaning and purpose to a people through their confrontations and acceptance of suffering, creating the conditions for a society of self-affirming people with exceptional mental fortitude.

For Raymond Geuss of *Birth*, Nietzsche felt tragedy could be made to have life-enhancing effects (1999). Nietzsche thus welcomed a "tragic culture" that can be employed to inspire an affirmation for life. Nietzsche made some daring extrapolations, namely that the ancient Greek state harnessed artistic and musical expression as repositories for individual and communal strength, fashioned atop the anvil of the human condition. The return to hardness that can be transformed into life affirmation, even as far back as the ancient Hellenic period, did not thwart Nietzsche from rendering pre-Socratic Greece as an ideal type (Karzai 2019). Nietzsche describes in *Ecce Homo* that *Birth* conceptualizes tragedy as the highest and most daring art form for affirming life in all its manifestations, but "*without suffering from it*," for such a process injects meaning and purpose into its hardships (2005, 110). This ethos would later be destroyed by Socrates and his injection of methodical reasoning as a means for resolving life and social dilemmas, prompting Nietzsche to view Socrates's legacy as one that accommodated the arrival of the sciences. Yet Nietzsche was not impressed:

> And science itself, our science—what indeed is the meaning of all science, viewed as a symptom of life? What is the purpose, and, worse still, what is the origin of all science? What? Is the scientific method perhaps no more than fear of and flight from pessimism? A subtle defence against—truth? Or, to put it in moral terms, is it something like cowardice and insincerity? (An Attempt at Self-Criticism, SEC. 1 / 1999, 4)

Elsewhere, Nietzsche continues his disdain of the sciences, condemning positivism because it is

> spurred on by its powerful delusion . . . hurrying unstoppably to its limits, where the optimism hidden in the essence of logic will founder and break up. . . . When, to his horror, he sees how logic curls up around itself at these limits and finally bites its own tail, then a new form of knowledge breaks through, *tragic knowledge* [emphasis added], which . . . needs art for protection and as medicine. (SEC. 15 / 1999, 75)

Nietzsche idealized the pre-Socratic Greek state through its tragedy because it captured the trials and tribulations of a people through song, dance, theater, and activities that inject affirmation and vitality into life. The Dionysian free spirits of pre-Socratic Greece, symbol of a people liberated from the constraints of suffering and pain, indeed became the ideal type of community for Nietzsche. For Nietzsche, however, Socrates destroyed tragedy by forwarding rationality and reason—not suffering—as epistemic and ontologic paths (Young 2006). Nietzsche was not fazed by emotional or spiritual "pain," noting in *Ecce Homo* that pain should not be an anomaly of life, going as far as valuing it as a source of strength-generation (2005, 124). He exclaims in *Ecce Homo*: "If you do not have any more happiness to give me, well then! *You still have pain*" (2005, 124). For Nietzsche, appreciating Greek tragedy allows wisdoms born from anguish to be celebrated in ways that are no longer distorted by the "seductive distractions of the sciences"; instead Greek tragedy "turns its unmoved gaze on the total image of the world, and in this image it seeks to embrace eternal suffering with sympathetic feelings of love, acknowledging that suffering to be its own" (SEC. 18 / 1999, 87–88).

By examining the Dionysian spirit in *Birth* that celebrated and affirmed life, Nietzsche juxtaposed its social implications against the counterpoint, the Apollonian approach of envisioning order and stability in a universe bereft of emotion. In *Birth*, Apollo and Socrates were analogs for the sciences. The forces between culture and civilization, then, can be seen in the tensions between the Dionysian and the Apollonian forces at play in ancient Greece, forces that nonetheless allow social tensions to bring forth "cultural advance" (Solms-Laubach 2007, 133). Not surprisingly, Nietzsche treats *Birth* as an exercise in romanticism. Echoing Young's (2006) view that Nietzsche was not a hyper-individualist, but a philosopher bent on establishing a new and idealized community, Geuss argues that *Birth*

> is concerned with the description of a highly idealized past which is analysed so as to highlight its contrast with and superiority to the "modern" world, and it ends with a peroration which calls for the utopian construction of a form of

society and culture which will break radically with the present and re-embody
the positively valued features of the past. (cited in Nietzsche 1999, xiii)

The capacity for the ancient Greeks to not be fazed by pessimism was
ensured by a Greek tragedy that sublimated their pain and suffering into the
genre. Rather than fall into nihilism as passive nihilists who accept their suffering in a defeatist manner, the ancient Greeks transformed their anguish
into art that affirmed their overcoming heroes, establishing community in the
process. Such an act of active nihilism, according to Thiele, "arises out of a
gratitude for life" (Bergmann at al. 2007, 31). Nietzsche reminds readers to
respect how community strength is ensconced through the example offered
us by the ancient Greeks, and to appreciate therefore how they were able to
employ the "enormous power of tragedy to stimulate, purify, and discharge
the entire life of the people" (SEC. 21 / 1999, 99). Nietzsche continues on
how "we shall never comprehend the supreme value of tragedy until, *like the
Greeks* [emphasis added], we experience it as the essence of all . . . healing
energies, as a mediator between the strongest and inherently most fateful
qualities of a people" (SEC. 21, 1999, 99). Within this context, Nietzsche
was most explicit about his acceptance of community and nation, countering
Nietzsche scholars such as Kaufmann who preferred to view the philosopher
as a hyper-individualist. Young emphasizes that Nietzsche's celebration of
community is reflected in the philosopher's admiration of the *Volk* and its
Volkish traditions, one that turn-of-the-twentieth-century sociologist Ferdinand Tönnies describes as a community operating under *gemeinschaft* values.
Young explains the importance of the *Volk* for Nietzsche:

> Nietzsche's proximity to the Volkish tradition, in his later as much as his early
> work, is something I shall be concerned to argue at length. . . . however, I shall
> mention now: the interesting linguistic fact that though Nietzsche has . . . a num-
> ber of highly abusive terms for social collectivities—"*Pöbel* (mob or rabble),"
> "*Gesindel* (mob or rabble)" and to a lesser degree "*Herde* (herd)"—there is
> nowhere in the published works where he uses "*Volk*" (in the sense of ethnic
> unity) except as a term of utmost respect. (Young 2006, 5)[2]

Nietzsche's *Birth* provides an ideal type for society excavated from a romanticized past, one that Young describes as a "festival-centered society, a
society with a metaphysical ethos that permeates and unifies the total life of
the 'people'" for the sake of establishing a "healthy society" (2006, 44). Nietzsche also warns in an early rendering of what would later be his "improvers of humanity" explicated in *Twilight* the need to be mindful of any "shep-
herd" of modern times proclaiming their mastery over the natural or natural
inclinations of humanity, for such a person "is merely a counterfeit" (SEC.

8 / 1999, 42). Model ourselves after the ancient Greeks, so goes Nietzsche's philosophy, for they wanted to experience the truth of nature and *about* our natures "at full strength" (SEC. 8 / 1999, 42). The younger Nietzsche, then, can be seen as a communitarian—albeit an idealistic one—that draws inspiration for empowerment not only from the music of Dionysian Greece, but more importantly, from its tragic mythos as well.

In *Birth*, Nietzsche expected culture to create the conditions for great people and individuals to emerge. These conditions found their release through art, the passions, and the creative spirit. The celebration of the ancient, pre-Socratic Greeks, then, was an elegiac necessity that served as an antipode to the modernity against which Nietzsche laboriously confronted in his subsequent works. Surprisingly, Christianity—the bane of much of Nietzsche's philosophy—was treated rather charitably in *Birth*. Young notes how although Nietzsche still harbored a "hostile attitude to the content of Christian morality . . . the medieval Church" was nonetheless "a unifying institution" for which Nietzsche retained an "intense admiration" (2006, 44). I am of the view that the foundations of the overcomer's dawn can be seen in *Birth* as well, one that had yet to explicitly emerge in full charismatic form even though the decadence of Nietzsche's modernity calls out for such an individual: a figure who is able to employ new self-authored cues to assemble greatness in human beings through some form of historical stratigraphy, with its earliest layers exemplified by the culture, art forms, and the state in pre-Socratic Greece, a culture of "ancient strength" that "only stirs powerfully in momentous times and then returns to dreaming of some future awakening" (Nietzsche SEC. 23 / 1999, 109). Until then, however, pundits of culture, education, civilization will still have to appear "before the judge Dionysos whom no man can deceive" (Nietzsche SEC. 19 / 1999, 94). Solms-Laubach summarizes such a position effectively:

> In this context it is interesting to note that both Marx and Nietzsche shared the view of Greek antiquity as representing the highest embodiment of art, and hence both shared an almost metaphysical notion of an idealised past age. . . . The cultural realm of the Western world is, according to Nietzsche, basically an extension of the cultural realm of ancient Greece. And since the "original" cultural realm had experienced a steady decline and even an eventual collapse, Nietzsche believed that the seeds for a similar development soon to take place in modern Western societies had already been implanted in their cultural foundations. (2007, 134)

Nietzsche's fascination with how systemic decay negatively affects the individual will remain a continuing concern in his philosophy. My work forwards the view that the overcomer, the *übermensch*, is an epithet for a new human being that can emerge from modernity's systemic decay, with self-made values, culture, and morality. Because Nietzsche saw modernist culture as putrefied, *Birth* is employed to inspire us toward creating culture outside the framework of modernity and its very mortal institutions (Jurist 2000). Nietzsche thus felt that the German culture of his day ought to inspire individuals to self-cultivate their intellectual development "outside the social order" (Jurist 2000, 62). This can be achieved if we excavate from a more glorious epoch where the ideals of empowerment and triumph, of release from the hardships of simply living, are born from the paroxysms of a tough life of struggle, something the pre-Socratic and creative Greeks were able to realize, according to Nietzsche. Enthusiastically desiring the integration of Greek tragedy into the *faux* German culture that Nietzsche saw in his day represented his first major philosophical proclamation of the importance of the arts, especially in their embrace of the most trying aspects of the human condition for cultural renewal. The center of gravity in *Birth,* particularly its focus on how culture can promote great human beings such as philosophers, artists, and saints, finds another iteration in a Nietzsche work we have already referenced thus far, *Untimely Meditations* (Hollingdale 1999, 82).

UNTIMELY MEDITATIONS (1873–1876/1997B)

In *Untimely Meditations*, Nietzsche tackles a variety of diverse topics that addresses his views on theologian David Strauss, how history is lived and experienced, the philosopher Arthur Schopenhauer, and the composer Richard Wagner. Although such a wide panorama of interests might appear as if Nietzsche is unable to cohere his philosophy into a sociological imagination, Daniel Breazeale of *Meditations* observes that this is not the case given that prototypical themes that surface in this work will be further amplified by Nietzsche in his later works. *Meditations* thus contains important Nietzschean themes that address the "relationship between life, art and philosophy; the character and cultivation of the 'true self'; education" and the "difference between genuine wisdom and mere knowledge (or 'science')" (cited in Nietzsche 1997b, vii).

   Nietzsche's most sociological ideas in *Meditations*, however, stem from his critique of Western culture. Nietzsche begins this critique by condemning the nationalism born from Germany's victory over France in the Franco-Prussian War, one which Nietzsche took part in as a medical orderly. Taking umbrage with how the German state conflated civilization with culture following their victory over the French, Nietzsche downplays Germany's ostensible greatness since German culture was never adopted by the defeated French during the post-war period. French cultural life continued unabated, one which was in no way excised from the bosom of the French nation in spite of the tragic war that cost almost a million lives, a quarter of which were civilian casualties. For Nietzsche, the German narrative of nation from the period, compared to the French, left much to be desired. Jingoism had taken root and the German state was becoming bloated with its own self-aggrandizement, further enabled and placated by the nascent German middle class and intelligentsia.

As the modern German state began to take form in the post-Franco-Prussian War, Nietzsche illuminates an inherent tension between its culture and civilization. Sensing how nascent German nationalism was becoming uncritically embedded in the German worldview, a disappointed Nietzsche reminds readers that *Meditations* was not written for everyone. Nietzsche's disappointment with the mass populace and its scripted conventional moralities prompted him toward similar caveats in later works. His reminders to readers that he is writing for the very few can be seen in *Human*, *Science*, and *Anti-Christ*. Yet it would be in *Meditations* where Nietzsche first revealed his concerns for how German nationalism had intoxicated the majority of its citizens into an uncritical deference to the state.

Nietzsche also criticizes the hubris and bureaucratic tendencies of Western and German modernity, awash with institutions that exist to render industrial "civilized" society decadent, destroying community in the process, while creating pretentious individuals consumed with "petty, atomistic egoism" (Young 2006, 44). Now held as a captive audience of modernity, systems dominate social life as most of the citizenry operate only within conventional scripts and regulations meted out by the status quo. The contemporary version of the herd, the conformists, is born. As a result, modernity has become decadent and has lost its purpose. Nietzsche argues that its operators do not realize their need to evolve culture toward the creation of excellent beings and as such hinder what should be the goal of nature: the procreation of the genius with a noble mindset (III, SEC. 3 / 1997b, 142). Culture and its humanity then, should aspire toward one goal, to "work continually at the production of individual great men—that and nothing else is its task" (Nietzsche III, SEC. 6 / 1997b, 161). For Nietzsche, the modernist culture of his day, as seen through the German example, is in an ossified state and is unable to attain "true saintliness" (III, SEC. 3 / 1997b, 142). Nietzsche thus outlines in *Meditations* the importance of self-affirming human beings that can reassemble greatness in themselves through their self-authored relationship to history. For a culture to enable such a task requires a nuanced understanding of how great human beings can effectively navigate the history of its people, of the *Volk*, in ways that are cultural rather than political. Nietzsche, then, desires that we employ history, ideally without "occidental prejudice" and for the "purpose of *life!*" (II, SEC. 1 / 1997b, 66).

Nietzsche warns us in *Meditations* that conditions by which proto-nationalisms form are based on the misappropriation of history. He thus focuses on how one can relate to monumental, antiquarian, and critical history anew, in ways that provide cues for the overcomer to self-actualize. For the monumental historian, praxis includes a reworking of history—done out of time, in an *untimely* manner—a process that enables newer and elevated beings to emerge. Such a new being then reappropriates history in a manner where its heroes and self-affirming individuals become role models for those who desire to become sovereign. Such figures have to be superb beings with excellent character worthy of being imitated (Nietzsche II, SEC. 2 / 1997b, 70). According to Young (2006), the monumentalists that harness excellence and life affirmation dispersed in history express dynamic and creative possibilities.

Through his notion of the antiquarian historian Nietzsche highlights another means by which one relates to history (II, SEC. 2 & SEC. 3 / 1997b, 72–76): the antiquarian historian views history in all its textures yet fails to harness its diacritica for uplifting the individual to a higher elevation of existence. Instead, safety is found in a yesteryear or bygone eras within which the antiquarian hides, having embedded themselves into history, transforming it into a womb bloated by a safe and idealized past (Nietzsche II, SEC. 3 / 1997b, 73). Yet the antiquarian has a redeeming quality in that such persons can check on monumentalists who commit errors, such as when they serve the state in generating epic narratives that inform nationalist nation construction and cultural production. Young argues that such an "antiquarian spirit" serves as a bulwark against the "worship of false 'idols'" but paralyzes creative energies and creation (2006, 38–39).

Nietzsche's view of the critical historian is that such a character is one who assesses and passes judgment on past diacritica (II, SEC. 2 / 1997b, 72). Such critical historians, according to Young, "must possess . . . from time to time . . . the strength to break up and dissolve a part of the past" in the process of cultural production and production of the great human being (2006, 39). Therefore, in spite of Nietzsche's celebration of the monumentalist historian, he nonetheless was concerned about a cultural production carelessly derived from the past, a repository with content constituted by human-generated violence and exemplars of human frailty, both of which influenced history in unpredictable ways. Nietzsche provocatively argues that critical historians are therefore aware of the multifold manufactured inequalities that still pockmark society with problematics that are ignored by an uncritical employment of monumental and antiquarian views. Such narratives should never be used to frame one's life experience, for since we are the outcome of earlier generations, we are also the outcome of their aberrations, passions and errors, and indeed of their crimes. . . . The best we can do is to confront . . . through a new, stern discipline . . . our inborn heritage and implant in ourselves a new habit, a new instinct, a second nature, so that our first nature withers away. (II, SEC. 3 / 1997b, 76)

For Young (2006, 39), the interaction of the three historical approaches, "provided they interact the right way," can be harnessed by the overcomer to set into motion social change:

Monumental history inspires cultural change, change which, ideally, through continuity with the past, preserves the identity of a culture. The antiquarian spirit, on the other hand, by placing a brake on the wilder uses of the "monument," helps to ensure that cultural change is identity-preserving, that it takes the shape of reform rather than "revolution". . . . The critical spirit, by contrast, counteracts the ossifying effects of pure antiquarianism, creates the ground on which alone effective monuments can be constructed. (2006, 39)

With the above passage, one can envision how Nietzsche is establishing the foundations for his anti-systemic views against Western modernity, and in a manner that most in the twenty-first century would find familiar: Nietzsche highlights how the German state appropriates the authoring of culture in ways that provide scripts, morality, and regulations for the conformist, the antithesis of the overcomer, what Nietzsche terms the cultural philistine, a poseur who

fancies that he is himself a son of the muses and man of culture. . . . and since he everywhere discovers cultivated people of his own kind, and finds all public institutions, schools and cultural and artistic bodies organized in accordance with his kind of cultivation and in the service of his requirements. (I, SEC. 2 / 1997b, 7)

Nietzsche thus illuminates systemic tendencies that repress the rise of liberating knowledge for emancipation and self-actualization. By making visible systemic tendencies that constrain people from becoming excellent human beings able to overcome life struggle, Nietzsche also provides insights into the need for enlightened elites to return culture to its task of creating a great humanity for the sake of establishing an authentic, apolitical *Volk*. Such a task of culture is needed to overcome modernity's distortions of culture's purpose, one that in the Germany of Nietzsche's time resulted in a decadence characterized by a vulgarized hodgepodge of expressions and aesthetics masquerading as social problems or trends (I, SEC. 1 / 1997b, 6). Even in reflection during his later years as conveyed in *Ecce Homo*, Nietzsche remained steadfast in his criticism of German culture, one which he viewed with contempt because the modern new nation is all form, but no content; it was meaningless and insubstantial—it had no real life-affirming goals for cultural production, consisting of only public opinion (2005, 112).

HUMAN, ALL TOO HUMAN:
A BOOK FOR FREE SPIRITS (1878/1996)

Human, All Too Human is considered Nietzsche's more psychological work, written in his famous aphoristic style. However, Nietzsche's sociological observations of systemic dysfunctions are apparent as well, especially in how he perceives their effects upon the praxian free spirit, understood in *Ecce Homo* as one who resolutely reassembles and reconstitutes the self again. Proclaiming how *Human* is meant for free spirits, albeit ones that have yet to arrive, Nietzsche nonetheless conveys his readiness for their arrival. Nietzsche argues that Europe will soon field such excellent individuals, noting with anticipation, "I see them already *coming*, slowly, slowly; and perhaps I shall do something to speed their coming" (Vol. 1, Preface, SEC. 2 / 1996, 6). The urgency one senses from this view reflects the growing concern Nietzsche had for the exhaustion of Enlightenment ideals and its effects upon cultural production, seen in his discussion of other topics ranging from Voltaire to Darwin, to the end of his friendship with Richard Wagner. In *Human*, Nietzsche also launches his first "sustained critique of Christianity" as the progenitor of our aforementioned discontents (Young 2006, 62).

Whereas in *Meditations* Nietzsche wrote in-depth and without what might appear to be digressions, in *Human* Nietzsche appears to digress, but only for those who read Nietzsche exoterically as warns Clark and Dudrick (2012). Many Nietzschean themes from earlier works continue to find extrapolations in *Human* in ways that allow the architecture of themes from previous writings to adequately frame what appears, on the surface of the work, to be disjuncted views. In this regard, Nietzsche still offers up sociological imaginations, for example, in his discussion of high and low culture, his criticism of Christian views of good and evil, and his disagreements toward Darwinism. However, Nietzsche's response to Darwinism reveals the subversive brilliance and optimism—and arguably compassion—of his dialectical reasoning on strong and weak characters. For Nietzsche, progress and regress are intimately connected: progress is for Nietzsche, dare I say, caused by regress. In their social manifestations, those with fortitude were shaped by their exposure to and survival of life's travails. Those deemed as enfeebled could be made stronger from their experiences with degeneration—be it from physical mutilations or even from character attributes that point to one's reprehensible disposition. Nietzsche observes how "rarely is a degeneration, a mutilation . . . without an advantage in some other direction" (Vol. 1, V, SEC. 224 / 1996, 107). In a penetrating and poignant passage in *Human*, Nietzsche describes how the physically ill—even if they come from a warlike martial race—can still fulfill a significant social role by dispensing wisdoms and profundities on life and death, an individual who is sight-impaired in one eye will invariably strengthen their remaining eye, while the blind will be able to experience deeper introspections and "see more deeply within themselves and in any event possess sharper hearing" (Vol. 1, V. SEC. 224 / 1996, 107). Culture, then, must school us with resolve so that we can continue on our path of overcoming life challenges without being deflected by any struggles that stifle our sovereignty (Nietzsche Vol. 1, V. SEC. 224 / 1996, 108).

The sociology in *Human* thus lies in its presentation of social obstacles that impede the free spirit, the proto-*übermensch* for Young (2006), from overcoming. That the overcoming person has to vanquish life obstacles means that in *Human* nothing of social importance is seen to be too sacred to be confronted and criticized. Nietzsche harbors such a view because he is urgently grappling with the dynamics for the free spirit's nascence, for the terrain such a free spirit navigates is precarious if only for its tendency to be a repository of scripts, manufactured stratifications, and regulations that the uncritical, the captive audience of modernity, the conformists (what Nietzsche referred to as the herd in *Science* and "last man" in *Zarathustra*) thrive under. Nietzsche was willing to entertain the consequences of this frenetic educational project, conceding that his "writings have been called a schooling in suspicion . . . but fortunately also in courage, indeed in audacity" (Vol. 1, Preface, SEC. 1 / 1996, 5). Yet such schooling in suspicion also validates those lacking fortitude to find avenues toward greatness, a sentiment that again hints at Nietzsche's expectation that the one-eyed, the sickly, the blind can all become active nihilists, self-authored praxian beings, and free spirits; that is, even those disadvantaged can all become overcomers.

Perhaps most relevant for my work, Nietzsche's position on science became tempered in *Human,* a shift in his orientation toward a system he initially felt to be decadent. Recall in *Birth* that Nietzsche condemns the proto-scientist Socrates for ruining the legacy of pre-Socratic Greek culture and its acceptance of life struggle through the sensual and creative energies of art, dance, and song. For Nietzsche, the rational and reasonable mindset championed by Socrates only debased Greek culture toward decadence and life negation. Socrates is implicated for generating the mindset that surrendered the Greeks to Apollo, symbol of reason and rationality, the counterpoint to Nietzsche's Dionysus. By *Human*, however, Nietzsche's tone welcomed the possibilities of the scientific enterprise and its potentially liberating role. Nietzsche even argues how a healthy culture informed by the sciences can offer "unpretentious truths" of existence rather than being blissfully deceived by "metaphysical and artistic ages and men," all of whom render us ignorant in our bliss (Vol. 1, I, SEC. 3 / 1996, 13). He further asserts that religiosity, artistic expression, and moralizations all fail to address "the 'nature of the world in itself'" (Vol. 1, I, SEC. 10 / 1996, 16). Indeed, should the self be trapped in the realm of metaphysical ideas and teleologies, Nietzsche argues that epistemological and ontological intuitions in such a context will reach a dead end and fail to further develop the self (Vol. 1, I, SEC. 10 / 1996, 16). In this regard, Young comments that *Human* seems to "represent a 180 degree turn, a 'paradigm shift,' in Nietzsche thinking" and that "something close to 'Socratism,' the position of 'theoretical man,' deplored in *The Birth*, has now become Nietzsche's own position" (2006, 60). He continues:

> Nietzsche's position now seems to be that we should give up "narcoticizing" human ills with art and religion since science is well on the way to "abolishing" the causes of those ills. . . . Scientific "optimism," deplored in the romantic period, now seems to have become the order of the day. It is no wonder, then, that most of Nietzsche's friends were stunned and appalled when the work appeared. . . . It was as though the pope, or at least a cardinal, had declared himself an atheist. (Young 2006, 60)

Clark notes that Nietzsche's views in *Human* envision the world of representation as erroneous because it failed to "correspond to the world disclosed by science" (1990, 96). Clark also highlights Nietzsche's paradigm shift toward a more favorable view of the sciences, especially its provision of empirical truths to be distinguished from the metaphysical "truths" that uncritically accommodate teleological reifications. For Clark, Nietzsche's disdain of the metaphysical world is based on the philosopher's view that to "believe in a metaphysical world is to believe that our best empirical theory is not merely false, but radically false" (Clark 1990, 98). We get a better understanding through Clark's assessment why Nietzsche so fervently rejects religion and religiosity, a rejection that for Young (2006, 58) ushered in our philosopher's positivist period.

More important for a sociological discussion of Nietzsche are his views of democracy, a topic that will in the remaining chapters allow us to examine Nietzsche's anti-systemic views. These views underpin a theory of social systems in crisis and how the overcomer can prevail in spite of systemic dysfunctions, since Nietzsche viewed democratism as an explicit symptom of the state's putrefaction (Vol. I, VIII, SEC. 472 / 1996, 173). That said, non-sociologically informed readers overlook such a critique by citing, instead,

Nietzsche's claim that the "democratization of Europe is irresistible" (Vol. 2, II, SEC. 275 / 1996, 376). A closer examination of this apparent contradiction actually reveals Nietzsche's lingering suspicions and ambivalence toward democracy, and the notion that Europeans are seen to irresistibly embrace democracy needs to be seen as their enthusiasm, not necessarily Nietzsche's. Thus, although Nietzsche expresses the sentiment that democratization is irresistible, he also describes the process as "desolate and monotonous," one that is nonetheless needed to "separate ourselves from the Middle Ages" (Vol. 2, II, SEC. 275 / 1996, 376). Nietzsche's pessimism about the democratic actor should be seen as valid, according to Schrift:

> The fact that Hitler was popularly elected in Germany, or the fact that George W. Bush was reelected in 2004 after having arguably lost and then stolen the election in 2000, and after having engaged in a series of policy decisions that were unwise, indeed largely "un-American," and also to a great extent known to have been based on lies and ideological commitments that had little connection with the geo-political realities of the day, points to the fact that Nietzsche's pessimism about "democratic man" might be more than justified. (Bergmann et al. 2007, 39)

Where Nietzsche counters Weber on how authority systems unfold can be seen in the former's view that envisions an interplay between democratic dynamics and monarchism in modernity. Queens and kings are needed, with each serving as a "splendid ornament on the simple and practical garment of democracy," one that is a "symbol of history itself" (Nietzsche Vol. 2, II, SEC. 281 / 1996, 379). Although seeing modernity's craving for a transcending mythos of state and *Volk*, Nietzsche nonetheless desires offices serving royalism to be, and this is significant, "correctly *positioned*" (Vol. 2, II, SEC. 281 / 1996, 379). Clark thus convincingly argues that Nietzsche's embrace of elite human beings in no way conflicts with his acceptance of democratic institutions that in themselves are already and ideally about elevating different categories of political actors. Nietzsche tolerates certain kinds of inequality so that great noble-minded human beings can emerge to function as leaders and agents of social change. Clark asserts that "Nietzsche's problem with democracy [presumably without a higher elite] is not that it destroys the appreciation of our desire for success or excellence . . . but that it *debases our standards for what constitutes success and excellence*, making them crude, plebian, and even barbaric" (2015, 176). The constitutional queen and king, the duchesses and lords, *if they have a noble mindset*—that is, to be correctly positioned—can serve as counterpoints to the crude, plebian, and barbaric. It is in this context that Clark reminds us how the decay of the state Nietzsche tied to democratic dynamics is also what the philosopher felt was an opportunity for social renewal, allowing higher forms of excellence in the human being to surface. Clark argues that Nietzsche's problem with democracy is how it rejects this part of the aristocratic belief system, and "thereby undermines the craving for higher states of the soul" (2015, 176). It should be emphasized at this juncture, however, that Nietzsche's references to aristocratic and noble beings are for the most part figurative and not about advocating for a particular social stratum. As we shall see in later sections of my work, Nietzsche frequently employed these terms to denote a state of being where a higher mindfulness for excellence and greatness, a sense of self-affirmation and passion for overcoming, constitute the character of the overcomer. Conversely, he will also employ royalist titles for lambasting what he perceives to be the degenerates of modernity.

Further evidence that Nietzsche was not anti-democratic, but concerned primarily about how systemic dysfunctions constrain the full expression of those who desire to overcome, can be seen in his discussion of socialism, a system that for Nietzsche hid last humans' desires for power under the guise of seeking justice for the oppressed. He even appears to have indirectly challenged Marx when he snidely questioned the socialist historical view of class oppression, remarking that "assuming it is *really* the rebellion of those who have been oppressed and held down for millennia against their oppressors" (Vol. 1, VIII, SEC. 446 / 1996, 163).[3] Nietzsche presciently warns us about states that acquire too much power, arguing that even socialist-aspiring societies will be taxed so immoderately that its people will "assail the capitalists, the merchants and the princes of the stock exchange with a progressive tax and slowly create in fact a middle class which will be in a position to *forget* socialism like an illness it has recovered from" (Vol. 2, II, SEC. 292 / 1996, 383–384). Nonetheless, Nietzsche concedes that socialism deserved some respect because it is a "mighty" lever that requires humanity to, "under certain circumstances . . . strengthen it" (Vol. 1, VIII, SEC. 446 / 1996, 163), even though he warns how a socialism that has become despotic exclusively expresses its powers through collective rather than individual ideals.

Nietzsche is hardly the radical anti-democratist as popular culture renders him. Nor is Nietzsche apolitical or antipolitical, a position taken by Kaufmann who believes that Nietzsche was more "concerned with the individual and not the group" (Clark 2015, 164). This position Young (2006) emphatically disagrees with given his attempts to illuminate Nietzsche's deep commitment to community. Nietzsche's position on democracy is complex; if one were to read his statements on democracy in *Human*, he welcomes democracy with cautious enthusiasm, sprinkled with a sense of suspicion about its potential, yet ready for its decay and its ability to generate meaninglessness, thus creating space for the return of the aristocratic and noble mindsets and their affirmation of a higher state of being.

Nietzsche's anti-systemic observations continue throughout *Human* as he conveys his early critiques of Christianity, saints, religious life, the state, politicians, solitude, and culture, among other things. Although the sections that address these topics do not occupy large swathes of *Human*, Nietzsche approaches democracy and socialism with an insightful sociological imagination, illuminating a dysfunctional life terrain where impediments to the free spirit are many. Perhaps it is not surprising that in *Ecce Homo*, Nietzsche would refer to *Human* as a monumental work that should be seen as a tribute to crisis, one that nonetheless and practically in "every sentence . . . expresses a victory" (2007b, 55). Nietzsche proclaims in *Ecce Homo* that *Human* was written to free himself from things that did not accurately express his true nature, especially in his confrontations with all forms of social and existential crises. Thus, the free spirit in *Human* is given the early task of overcoming modernity's institutional constraints even though, for Hollingdale, the work is still filled with undeveloped ideas that give Nietzsche's writings an "air of compendia rather than of individual works" (1999, 132). This would change by the time *Dawn* was released, the first of many works from Nietzsche's "nomadic" period to be discussed in the next chapter, for by then our philosopher had relinquished his role as a professor while commencing his new role as a free spirit.

NOTES

1. When Nietzsche's works are displayed with two or more years, the first year refers to the year of its original publication while the latter refer to the year/years of other editions employed for my work. This treatment will be seen in the section heading for *Twilight of the Idols*, for example.

2. Young (2006, 5) presents important knowledge on the term *Volk*: "As the Volkish movement progressed many of its adherents became viciously nationalistic, militaristic and anti-Semitic. A great many (conspicuously Martin Heidegger) became Nazis. And a great deal of the vocabulary of Nazism—'*Volksgemeinschaft*,' '*Volksgenossenschaft*,' '*Volkskörper*,' '*Volk-i-seinem-Staat*' and so on—was drawn from the Volkish Tradition." He further adds: "By no means all who, in the 1920s and 1930s, thought in Volkish ways became Nazis. Oswald Spengler, Ernst Jünger and Stefan George did not. And, moreover, many Volkish thinkers who had initially supported Hitler became appalled when it became clear just *what* they had supported . . . there is no essential connexion between Volkish thinking as such and Nazism, no essential connexion, that is to say, between German communitarianism on the one hand and nationalism or fascism or totalitarianism or anti-Semitism on the other" (2006, 6).

3. Nietzsche's *Human* was published when Marx was 60 years of age and Nietzsche was 34. By *Human*'s publication, Marx's *Communist Manifesto* had already been distributed around Europe. Both leviathans died stateless.

Chapter Four

Nietzsche's Sociological Imaginations

The Nomadic Years (1879–1887)

Nietzsche's formal departure from the University of Basel in 1879 enabled his wanderlust across Italy, France, and Switzerland. Along the way Nietzsche spent time at the Mediterranean as well as hiked trails of the Swiss Alps, a period where he was able to devote full attention to his writings. A prolific period in Nietzsche's life, key works such as *Dawn of Day*, *The Gay Science*, *Thus Spoke Zarathustra*, *Beyond Good and Evil*, and *On the Genealogy of Morality* were all published. J. M. Kennedy of *Dawn* notes how this period of Nietzsche's life is significant because our philosopher is finally unfettered, released from the demands and pressures of a previous incarnation of himself. For Kennedy, our philosopher is reassembled in this period of life, like a "Genoese spring" that just as well signifies "the dawn" of a "new Nietzsche" (cited in Nietzsche 2007, v).

THE DAWN OF DAY (1881/2007A)

In the opening passage of *Ecce Homo*'s reflective discussion of the *Dawn of Day*, Nietzsche emphasizes how his "campaign against *morality* begins" with the latter work (2007b, 61). For Kennedy, *Dawn* shows a tighter formulation of Nietzsche's philosophy in that he is "trying to stand on his own legs" so as to "regain his spiritual freedom; he is feeling his way to his own philosophy" (cited in Nietzsche 2007a, v). Having released himself from the doctrines of those he admired, that is, philosopher Arthur Schopenhauer and composer Richard Wagner, *Dawn* thus reflects a new path in Nietzsche's thinking, one that includes a continuing critical assessment of Christianity and prescriptions for overcoming its tenets. Readers can also see additional observations by Nietzsche where he discusses how scripts emanate from social institutions of the state in ways that are moralized, a reflection of community expectations for actors to defer to conventional norms and value systems.

Examining morality as it is embedded in religious institutions, Nietzsche highlights its regulatory nature and how it demands obedience from an audience that has been rendered captive. Nietzsche posits that morality has staying power due to where it is embedded: in the all-encompassing framework of society's traditions, which further ensnare the actor into a web of rituals and cultural prescriptions, that is, into its forms and scripts. This framework, when combined with a collective sense of belonging born from a long chronology of its adherents' experiences with struggle, requires traditional institutions to be rooted in society. When such scripts are consumed through the "front" of culture, reproduced by the institutions and scripted back for society, different outcomes befall the population. This is the case because the consumption of such scripts, a variable, hints at one's degree of legitimation of that culture, the intimation being that in such contexts conformists will in varying degrees maintain their subscription to scripts through reification, sycophancy, and repetition. In contrast, Nietzsche's preferred variant of human beings (the free-spirited overcomer, for example) contests institutionalized culture for the sake of assembling a new variant of actors who do not seek their validation and sense of self-worth from contemporary social systems.

Modernity's manufacturing of race and culture, along with its diacritica of scripts, regulations, traditions, and morality, should not be seen as sacralized diacritica that constitute a people, according to Nietzsche. Insofar as his view on race is concerned, Nietzsche makes an early pronouncement that hints at his anti-nationalist stance to come, claiming that "it is probable that there are no pure races" (IV, SEC. 272 / 2007a, 253). By the time *Genealogy* was published a few years later, Nietzsche still maintained his criticism against German nationalism, describing it as: "the alcoholic-poisoning of Europe, which has strictly kept pace so far with the political and racial predominance of the Germans (—where they injected their blood, they injected their vice as well).—Third in line would be syphilis" (III, SEC. 21 / 2006, 107).

Because custom and tradition had to be imposed upon the populace, their moralities cannot be celebrated as a source of individualized social construction. Instead, Nietzsche argues that morality was not always employed by an ambitious individual for self-mastery; it was the desire for power, the person's will to power, that required the actor to first "make himself a kind of lawgiver and medicine-man, a sort of demi-god—in other words, he had to create customs, a dangerous and fearful thing to do!" (I, SEC. 9 / 2007a, 15). Nietzsche thus expected a similarly strong being to dismantle modern cultural institutions so as to prevent a reproduction of their decadence. This observation points to Nietzsche's ongoing development of the will to power thesis that, through *Dawn,* which does not "contain any mention of the will to power by that name," still nonetheless presents itself as a "dress rehearsal" before the will to power "is proclaimed as Nietzsche's basic principle" (Kaufmann 1950, 188). Again, the discontents and undesirable consequences of institutional and systemic decay are of concern to Nietzsche, yet such consequences are seen to simultaneously harbor opportunities for a rebirth of the overcoming self:

> Let us recall institutions and customs which, out of the fiery devotion of a moment, have created eternal fidelity; out of the pleasure of anger, eternal vengeance; out of despair, eternal mourning; out of a single hasty word, eternal obligation. A great deal of hypocrisy and falsehood came into the world as the result of such transformations; but each time, too, at the cost of such disadvantages, a new kind of *superhuman* conception which elevates mankind. (I, SEC. 27 / 2007a, 34)

It is not surprising, then, that Nietzsche did not spare the state from criticism. In some instances, rather than attack its structure, Nietzsche expresses concerns for the consequences of a state removed from the Greek ideal: it is populated by unscrupulous people that seek out a captive audience to transform into conformists. In *Dawn*, we thus see more material that counters certain popular renderings of Nietzsche as entirely anarchistic, one who, as a hyper-individualist, saw no need for a state, a position that Kaufmann forwards. Returning to a recurring theme seen in Nietzsche thought, specifically his view that modernity and its institutions have produced decadent individuals with debased standards, Nietzsche is also concerned about the cultural consequences that befall a community when it is led by those who are crude, plebian, and even barbaric: when allowed to enter the political system they reproduce their reactive, negative, and decadent values and feed them back to the community. Nietzsche laments in a manner that hints at why he sees a legitimation crisis in the institutions of modernity, noting that "it is by no means astonishing to find statesmen without principles, but with dominant instincts; a versatile mind, actuated by these dominant and violent instincts, and hence without principles—these qualities are looked upon as reasonable and natural in a statesman" (III, SEC. 167 / 2007a, 170).

Nietzsche is critical about one who blindly conforms to such aforementioned actors, for this person's "master" now reinforces the prejudice of the person with what Nietzsche would later term in *Genealogy* as *ressentiment*: revanchist values employed by different individuals and/or collectives trapped in, yet working from their defeatist groupthink so as to dislodge higher humans from legitimacy and power. Nietzsche's incisive observation of the culture of state politics can thus be appreciated from his warning in

Dawn that a "young man can be most surely corrupted when he is taught to value the like-minded more highly than the differently minded" (IV, SEC. 297 / 2007a, 262). Moreover, Nietzsche's perspective remains consistent when criticizing Christian morality which he sees as contributing to a herd or conformist mentality as it "assimilated the entire spirituality of an incalculable number of men who were by nature submissive, all those enthusiasts of humiliation and reverence, both refined and coarse" (I, SEC. 60 / 2007a, 61).

Although it would be in *Anti-Christ* where Nietzsche criticizes Christianity as a religion of pity, a condemnation that was also seen in *Twilight*, his most significant condition for approaching pity must first be visited in *Dawn*. Because most Nietzsche readers associate the philosopher's discussion of pity to be most pronounced in *Anti-Christ*, an unfortunate misunderstanding has arisen in the general readership about how Nietzsche sees pity: that is, because it is an attribute of morality, pity is, in essence, unnecessary. If one were to approach Nietzsche's view of pity from only *Anti-Christ*, his discussion and rejection of pity makes him seem utterly inhumane, for what could conceivably be contentious about pity when it is advocated by, say, good Samaritans and/or the religious faithful? Nietzsche had a response: aside from pity being rendered a script to be enacted upon the destitute, it injects a great degree of metaphysical and corporeal suffering into the dispenser of pity, with the person inevitably becoming "melancholy and ill" (II, SEC. 134 / 2007a, 145). Moreover, beyond the individual, the process of pitying through culturally generated scripts injects suffering back into the world; that is, Nietzsche is advocating that we employ intelligent pity that does not harm the self yet can still be humanitarian to the dispossessed. Nietzsche offers an example through the physician's role and how pity can, if the physician is not mindful, cloud the person's judgement. Thus, if the physician "wished in any sense of the word to serve humanity as a physician, he would have to take many precautions with respect to this feeling, as otherwise it would paralyse him at all critical moments, undermine the foundations of his knowledge, and unnerve his helpful and delicate hand" (II, SEC. 134 / 2007a, 145). Nietzsche shares a personal account as an example:

> Not long ago at 11 o'clock in the morning a man suddenly collapsed and fell down in front of me as if struck by lightning. All . . . at once gave . . . cries of horror, while I set the man on his feet again and waited until he recovered his speech. During this time no muscle of my face moved and I experienced no sensation of fear or pity; I simply did what was most urgent and reasonable and calmly proceeded on my way. (II, SEC. 114 / 2007a, 128)

Emphasis needs to be made that in *Dawn* one sees Nietzsche's pragmatic approach toward pity, an approach obscured in later works when he applies only critiques about pity without highlighting the conditions from which they stem. What Nietzsche is provocatively advocating is for the strength of the overcomer to be developed without obstructions, and how pity endorsed by institutions such as religion and Christianity actually erodes away such strength while increasing suffering in the world. Nietzsche crucially asserts in *Dawn,* and not in the later works *Twilight* and *Anti-Christ,* that pity, if it "gives rise to suffering—*and this must be our only point of view here* [emphasis added]—is a weakness, like every other indulgence in an injurious emotion" (II, SEC. 134 / 2007a, 144). Nietzsche continues, "And although . . . a certain amount of suffering may be indirectly diminished or removed . . . as a consequence of pity, we must not bring forward these occasional consequences . . . to justify the nature of pity which . . . is *prejudicial* [emphasis added]" (II, SEC. 134 / 2007a, 144). Pitying, if it causes the actor unbearable suffering, certainly functions as an "antidote to suicide," yet it also hubristically "enables us to taste superiority in small doses" (Nietzsche II, SEC. 136/ 2007a, 146).

Does this mean there is no room for compassion in Nietzsche's ideas? No room for empathy or even *verstehen* for that matter? Not if one finds a key qualification that absolves Nietzsche from being described as a ruthless philosopher obsessed with only indifferent enhancements of one's will to power. In *Dawn*, we find the absolution in Nietzsche's view that pity is an important expression toward humanity only if it does not impair one's will to power. Nietzsche, in my understanding, is first and foremost concerned with the actor's need for strength when systems are seen to be breaking down. Seen in this light, the consistency of Nietzsche's warning against pitying should be seen as a sentiment in defense of the strength needed to be preserved in the overcomer, and not as a theory on how ruthless the overcomer should be. Although Nietzsche scathingly criticizes pitying as a form of life negation, he does so in a manner that explicitly does not promote an inhumanity. His approach toward the sick validates such an assertion:

> Let us not forget also, however, that the injury caused to society and to the individual by the criminal is of the same species as that caused by the sick: for the sick spread cares and ill-humour; they are non-productive, consume the earnings of others, and at the same time require attendance, doctors, and support, and they really live on the time and strength of the healthy. In spite of this, however, we should designate as inhuman anyone who, for this reason, would wish to wreak vengeance on the sick. (III, SEC. 202 / 2007a, 207)

Nietzsche's discussion in *Dawn* is rarely appreciated for its subtext: to make visible the institutional impediments and its outputs (for example, Christianity and morality, the debased political leader and its conformist constituency) that stand in the way of the overcomer. That Nietzsche expresses sentiments imploring the overcomer to reject, if not transcend, institutional control is significant. The sentiments reinforce the overcomer as a most praxian being activating their agency. Nietzsche embraces such overcomers and their self-authoring of the life path, undertaken without the baggage of social scripts that are the bane of his ideas. Nietzsche thus offers a response to the question of what overcomers must do to outmaneuver a system no longer deemed as legitimate: forge ahead on one's own and not Nietzsche's terms.

> Think not that I will urge you to run the same perilous risk! or that I will urge you on even to the same solitude! For whoever proceeds on his own path meets nobody: this is the feature of one's "own path." No one comes to help him in his task: he must face everything quite alone—danger, bad luck, wickedness, foul weather. (Preface, SEC. 2 / 2007a, 2)

Nietzsche is perhaps aware that such an undertaking is a fearsome process, reminding readers about how he also undertook such a path to dismantle the continuing constraints of old morality:

> At that time I had undertaken something which could not have been done by everybody: I went down into the deepest depths; I tunneled to the very bottom; I started to investigate and unearth an old *faith* which for thousands of years we philosophers used to build on as the safest of all foundations . . . although every previous structure fell in: I began to undermine our *faith in morals.* (Preface, SEC. 2 / 2007a, 2)

All of the cues of what will later be a more clearly explicated will to power can be seen in *Dawn*. That there are a variety of social institutions being subjected to critique by Nietzsche in *Dawn* allows us to conveniently pit its decadence against the will to power of the overcomer. Yet the sacrifices the overcomer will need to make point to the seriousness with which Nietzsche envisions the deeply personal process by which a person becomes a super-human *being*. Thus, in *Dawn*, we see an often-overlooked symbiosis between Nietzsche's macro-sociological discussion of decaying social systems and the psychological conditions needed by the overcomer to prevail in nihilism. I thus disagree with Kaufmann's view that *Dawn* showed Nietzsche as less prescient because he "investigated his problems without any clear notion of possible systematic implications" (1950, 188). From the perspective of sociology where our practitioners employ many lenses to ascertain how institutions and social change are related, the systematic implications are not only clear, but explicitly so, judging by what has been conveyed thus far in *Dawn*.

THE GAY SCIENCE (1882/2001)

By the time Nietzsche publishes *The Gay Science*, his philosophy edges closer toward its confrontation with Christianity, to fully become explicit two works later in *Beyond*. Containing some of Nietzsche's most important tenets, Williams cites *Science* as yet another exemplar of Nietzsche's aphoristic style, one which he concedes contains many disjuncted passages (cited in Nietzsche 2001, vii–viii). The work consists of paragraphs, long sentences, and much poetry that for Williams shows Nietzsche gathering "thoughts which will . . . circle in on some central theme or problem" (cited in Nietzsche 1999, viii). Important themes do surface in *Science*, namely Nietzsche's views on the implications of the death of god, as well as his introduction of the doctrine of eternal recurrence, which as discussed earlier, is envisioned as a thought exercise designed for the overcomer, a self-test to confirm that such a person remains committed to an unending path of renewal, empowerment, and emancipation. Finally, Nietzsche examines how science can be transformed to promote life-affirmation and joy. Hollingdale describes *Science* as a Nietzsche work that still employed reason and logic in spite of their perceived exhaustion in modernity (cited in Nietzsche 1999, 138).

In *Science,* Nietzsche famously made proclamations that God is dead. Yet, less known to many fans of Nietzsche was that the first pronouncement was in reference to Buddha, whose death and subsequent sacralization, observed a critical Nietzsche, resurrected "his shadow in a cave for centuries—a tremendous, gruesome shadow" (III, SEC. 108 / 2001, 109). Only later does Nietzsche infamously proclaim through his proto-Zarathustra and proto-immoralist proxy, the madman, that "God is dead! God remains dead! And we have killed him!" (III, SEC. 125 / 2001, 120). In a scenario analogous to a revolutionary engaged in the overthrow of the old order, the madman "yells" the aforementioned message at townspeople gathered at a marketplace; he lectures them for being complicit in God's demise, stunning the crowd into silence. One can appreciate the motif and irony of the madman, that this individual with tremendous if not cantankerous clarity, deemed mentally unfit by the conformist herd, is in the eyes of Nietzsche, a stentor proclaiming a truth. The madman warns the town's inhabitants of a human condition in nihilism saturated with *ennui* and meaningless predicaments. He expresses disappointment and frustration when listeners ridicule his views. The madman then hurls his lantern to the ground, shattering it, and laments how his "time is not yet" and that such a "tremendous event is still on its way" (Nietzsche III, SEC. 125 / 2001, 120). Such a madman then barges into a variety of churches during the day, exemplifying for the townspeople how a rejection of the pieties of Christianity (and by implication those of Buddhism and all religions) should begin in what is already littering modernity, the tombs and sepulchres of God, the churches that in spite of their degeneration continue to be reified (Nietzsche III, SEC. 125 / 2001, 120).

Nietzsche believes we must respond to this isomorphic conformity because "given the way people are, there may still for millennia be caves in which they show his [Buddha or God's] shadow.—And we—we must still defeat his shadow as well!" (III, SEC. 108 / 2001, 109). Not surprisingly, we are warned of "soul doctors," the preachers of morals, and theologians, all of whom practice one bad habit: they convince adherents of their supposed faults by offering them a final radical cure, thus qualifying them for a spiritual reworking of their sorry souls (Nietzsche IV, SEC. 326 / 2001, 181). By laying the conditions for overcoming the vestiges of Christianity and religion in a nihilistic modernity, Nietzsche arguably prepared the idea of the eternal recurrence to test the mettle of the overcomer. Such a task is an urgent one since Nietzsche believed Christianity exacted a toll on humanity by punishment and critical judgment of others, an imprudent deployment of interpersonal and systemic power. We thus see a more compassionate and noble mindset of Nietzsche in *Science*, one that encourages people to focus on their own lives and to not change and punish people who do not abide by mainstream values.[1] Moreover, Nietzsche emphasizes that those with power who hurt others have failed to understand the nature of empowerment. Power for Nietzsche is about dispersion and magnanimity. A power employed in a life-negating manner, in contrast, enables us to hurt and injure others, a scenario Nietzsche deplores because such "power" is actually a form of disempowerment, a pathology that endangers us by clouding "our horizons with the prospect of revenge, scorn, punishment, failure" (I, SEC. 13 / 2001, 39).

True to form, Nietzsche embraces any undesirable outcome as a context for the self's renewal, rebirth, and empowerment. He lays out the conditions that are opportune for the overcomer's will to power to contest and vanquish the old self, old values, old societies, and old epochs—although it should be noted that in *Science*, as in *Dawn*, Nietzsche still had yet to refer to the will to power by name (Young 2006). Nonetheless, Nietzsche envisions such an active nihilist to prevail in spite of a decadent modernity. The overcomer's sheer determination to persevere, now amplified and fortified by the death of god and faith, will thus be seen in a person that has elevated the self to a higher state of being, beyond nihilism's deleterious effects. Nietzsche celebrates such a historical window of opportunity, one that gushes prospects for personal and historical empowerment, but on the condition that we dare to frame ourselves with some sacrality, for after all, "Do we not ourselves have to become gods merely to appear worthy of it?" (III, SEC. 125 / 2001, 120). Nietzsche anticipates how "there was never a greater deed—and whoever is born after us will on account of this deed belong to a higher history than all history up to now!" (III, SEC. 125 / 2001, 120). Later in the work Nietzsche inspires us further, emphasizing how our post-god modernity offers a pathway for the overcomer's existential wanderlust:

> We philosophers and "free spirits" feel illuminated by a new dawn; our heart overflows with gratitude, amazement, forebodings, expectation—finally the horizon seems clear again, even if not bright; finally our ships may set out again, set out to face any danger; every daring of the lover of knowledge is allowed again; the sea, our sea, lies open again; maybe there has never been such an "open sea." (V, SEC. 343 / 2001, 199)

So that those inspired to become overcomers do not remain complacent with their personal project of reassembly, renewal, and empowerment, Nietzsche offers us the doctrine of the eternal recurrence. The interpretation I hold, and arguably so, is that the eternal recurrence is a filtering thought exercise designed by Nietzsche to discern whether one's mettle is sufficient to be an overcomer. The key question posed by the doctrine of eternal recurrence is simply whether the self would enthusiastically live life with every single euphoric and tragic experience repeated for perpetuity. Derived from a surrender and catch experience at Lake Silvaplana in the Upper Engadine region of the eastern Swiss Alps, Nietzsche recounts in *Ecce Homo*: "The basic conception of the work, *the thought of eternal return*, this highest attainable formula of affirmation—belongs to August of 1881. . . . On that day I was walking through the woods by Lake of Silvaplana; not far from Surlei I stopped next to a massive block of stone that towered up in the shape of a pyramid. Then this thought came to me—" (2007b, 65). Nietzsche offers up a more colorful rendering in *Science* when he shares an account of his surreal epiphany through, of all exemplars, an instrumental demon that confronts a passerby with a riddle, a thought exercise, one that will bear upon the actor as a "heaviest weight" (IV, SEC. 341 / 2001, 194). Such a demon asks whether one would relive life again—with all its ecstasies and tragedies—repeated for perpetuity through an "eternal hourglass of existence," churning over and over again with us as but specks of dust (Nietzsche IV, SEC. 341 / 2001, 194). Hinting to readers that the self-evident answer is "no," that is, one would not want to engage with this cyclicity *ad infinitum* if only to avoid life's hardships, struggles, and tragedies, Nietzsche instead offers us a twist in his response: that he would embrace such a demon and proclaim it a god, with the lesson that living life over and over again, armed to the teeth with an overcoming *amor fati* deployed to embrace even those reprehensible and vile episodes of reliving, can become a sublime experience.

Lomax (2000) argues that although Nietzsche's eternal recurrence lacks "any empirical warrant," it nonetheless is effective in committing the elevated consciousness of the overcomer to an eternity of victorious struggle and despondent suffering, both of which need to be overcome. For Williams the important "theory" of eternal recurrence again surfaces in Nietzsche's later works such as *Zarathustra*, *Twilight*, and *Ecce Homo*, pointing to the motif's importance to our philosopher. Williams notes, however, that there are "some places in which it is treated as a theoretical idea, but they are largely confined to his unpublished notes (his *Nachlass*)" (cited in Nietzsche 2001, xvi). First mentioned in *Science*, Nietzsche envisioned through the eternal recurrence a scenario of repeated life challenges and suffering that underpin the human condition, a human condition where the actor experiences no inner peace, according to Williams (cited in Nietzsche 2001, xv). I am personally more optimistic than Williams and view Nietzsche's figurative embrace of war and peace as a binary with an inherent symbiosis that actually responds effectively to the inner conflicts percolating in the developing overcomer, inner conflicts that have to do with a person's acceptance of chaos in life struggle. Because Nietzsche was forthright about anticipating the formidable conditions of nihilistic existence, the eternal recurrence is deployed to render the overcomer an extremist active nihilist able to attend to any eternal discontents. Life's incessant discontents are, as we are now aware, embraced by Nietzsche as a means to emphasize the importance of fortitude and greatness needed by the overcomer to prevail. Such an overcomer, then, will forever *will* the "eternal recurrence of war and peace" (IV, SEC. 285 / 2001, 162). Embracing the eternal recurrence, then, constitutes the lyrics of the overcomer's anthem.

That Nietzsche conveys such an important ethos points to the urgent seriousness to which the philosopher juxtaposes the overcoming actor to social crises. Not surprisingly, the will to power is the instrument the bona fide overcomer must employ to accept one's eternal recurrence. Nietzsche was predictably enthusiastic about the possibilities, however, even sloganeering the importance of *amor fati*—the love of one's life, the love of one's fate— before the first textual exposition of eternal recurrence as a means toward accepting this cyclicity. The overcomer's *amor fati* thus prepares and prevents our actor from being fazed and stifled by life's challenges and struggles. Clearly, Nietzsche was inspired and excited about such a prospect, one based on enhancing the self's will to power to be able to accept difficult and trying experiences of the human condition with alacrity. He therefore invokes his doctrine to celebrate loving and living life in spite of its travails, proclaiming: "I will be one of those who make things beautiful. *Amor fati*: let that be my love from now on! . . . I want only to be a Yes-sayer!" (Nietzsche IV, SEC. 276 / 2001, 157).

For Nietzsche, the death of god meant institutionally-dispensed morality is no longer relevant for an emergent overcomer. For Rorty, in rejecting religiously-inspired metaphysics, Nietzsche believed there would be "greater human happiness if we all believed that we owe respect to nothing except our fellow humans" (Bergmann et al. 2007, 27). Having become anachronistic in the universe of the overcomer who dares to eternally sur-mount, morality reveals its true historical *im*permanence. Nietzsche thus cheers on the overcomer's new freedom and passion to renew, to reas-semble, provocatively arguing for a new morality to replace the older forms appropriated by religion and tradition. He argues that those seeking sover-eignty and freedom must embark on this project on one's own, and that such freedom "does not fall into anyone's lap as a wonderous gift" (Nietzsche II, SEC. 99 / 2001, 98). Advocating for a new self-authorship based on new modes of thinking, being, and becoming, Nietzsche cheers overcoming types to not obsess over morality and reminds them that they need to be able to "stand *above* morality—and not just stand with the anxious stiffness of someone who is afraid of slipping and falling . . . but also to float and play above it!" (II, SEC. 107 / 2001, 104–105).

Clearly for Nietzsche, the life-negating morality of religion and tradition, along with its herding tendencies, are major impediments for the overcomer. Celebrating what Nietzsche felt was the epochal event of modernity, the death of the Christian "God" and therefore god more generally, behooves us to entertain Young's (2006) view that Nietzsche saw old morality as propa-ganda. Moreover, Nietzsche audaciously argues that morality could just as well be an egregious error committed by evolving societies, and that we must finally confront, interrogate, and discard it completely. In *Science*, Nietzsche sociologically (and unflatteringly) chastises those who defer to a system of hitherto morality as conformists, ideal members of the herd. Their scripted morality, one of many in a panoply of diverse moralities, is therefore the "herd-instinct" in the individual (Nietzsche III, SEC. 116 / 2001, 115).

Nietzsche's sociological imagination, critical of cultural production and the manufacturing of consent, treats morality as a stratification system that promotes inequality, and that a new community in the wake of a post-moral world will need to shun this older iteration of rights and wrongs so that we can delink ourselves from herds and their moralities as a means of reform-ing society (III, SEC. 149 / 2001, 130).[2] A newer being is needed, a noble being who dares to contest mainstream values so that the creation of new selves will result in evolved human beings. Such people formulate their own laws and standards as a means of self-creation so that we can *"become who we are*—human beings who are new, unique, incomparable" (Nietzsche IV, SEC. 335 / 2001, 189).

The scientific establishment and their enterprises are also systems the sovereign, nobler being will need to confront. In *Science*, however, Nietzsche continues to express his cautious optimism about the scientific enterprise. In a godless age and its accompanying nihilism, science will need to be confronted surgically by the active nihilist so that its new role could be made to focus on promoting the vitality of life. As it stood for Nietzsche, the sciences of his day were deficient and decadent. For one, after becoming hegemonic within modernity, the scientific enterprise had to be seen as functioning to improve the modern human condition. The scientific enterprise thus required its adherents to approach it as an ethos and not as a passion. Its hegemonic status in society means that to preserve the system, one has to be a herded warrior, a character able to withstand a severe service that demanded careful adjudication in all matters great and small. For the scientific ethos, results are all that matters, and like the experience of being a soldier, what researchers encounter in their undertakings are primarily "reproaches and sharp reprimands" (Nietzsche IV, SEC. 293 / 2001, 166).

Nietzsche was ultimately charitable toward the false promises of our modern mystics, seeing the scientific enterprise as epistemologically iterative, noting how the scientific "ethos" owes itself to a previously more ignoble epoch where magicians, alchemists, astrologers, and witches "who with their promises and false claims created a thirst, hunger and taste for *hidden and forbidden powers*" (IV, SEC. 300 / 2001, 170). The demands and prescriptions of the scientific ethos are in themselves catalysts for generating a belief that through the sciences society will possess the wherewithal to unlock hidden and forbidden powers. In this regard, Nietzsche argues that science exhibits its own religiosity, even functioning as a sort of metaphysical faith. It is clear for Nietzsche, then, that science too has its own morality, namely that "*nothing* is *more* necessary than truth" and that "everything else has only secondary value" (V, SEC. 344 / 2001, 200). Nietzsche thus condemns the scientific establishment and their pursuit of truth for rendering and cheapening existence through "counting, calculating, weighing, seeing, grasping, and nothing else" (V, SEC. 373 / 2001, 239). The scientific enterprise and its ethos, then, had transformed the fundamentally good-natured person into a sinister and incessant skeptic.[3] Not surprisingly, Nietzsche attacks Herbert Spencer, seemingly unconvinced about how the latter's grand theories of society could, even through scientific rigor, be made operative in practice through human reason alone (V, SEC. 373 / 2001, 238).

Nietzsche is asking his readers to see the entirety of the scientific enterprise, in all its promises and failings. In his cautious optimism, however, Nietzsche sees a renewed life-affirming science, not unlike sentiments expressed in *Human*. The free spirit in the overcomer thus needs to harness the self's sovereignty to contest a science that can rob people of their joys and ecstasies by transforming them into cold automatons, even though science's goal is to maximize pleasure while minimizing displeasure (Nietzsche I, SEC. 12 / 2001, 38). Science should thus be harnessed as a positive, even a happy force of emancipation, but only if the actor can see the interwoven dynamics of meaning production in pleasure and pain. However, with the flaw of science being its clinical and technocratic approach toward the natural world, Nietzsche condemns how scientific interpretations are but the most undesirable interpretations since an explicitly mechanical view of the world would render it devoid of meaning. Yet recall that for Nietzsche, pain and meaninglessness can be instructive, functioning as catalysts for the actor's new assembly of self.

Desiring the pain and suffering of nihilism as teachable experiences for securing joy, Nietzsche—active nihilist *par excellence*—envisions how a new science can function as a *"great giver of pain!"* for in its previous iteration science decreased and diminished people's tolerance toward pain, creating conditions that also decreased people's ability to viscerally experience the joy that follows the conquering of such pain (I, SEC. 12 / 2001, 38). Here Nietzsche dialectically constructs an uplifting view of pain for the overcomer, since it is one's confrontation and acceptance of suffering and pain that generate the conditions for enabling "new galaxies of joy" to "flare up!" (I, SEC. 12 / 2001, 38). In this regard, *Science* makes visible conditions for the overcomer to surmount. The ideal type exhibits certain distinctive traits that prompted Hollingdale to observe that "Nietzsche is feeling his way towards an 'image of man' which embodies the power-impulse and somehow employs it as a creative force" (1999, 143). Such a force has uplifting energy, prompting the stentor in Nietzsche to urge us to live dangerously with no fear, daring us to build our cities on the slopes of Mt. Vesuvius as well as send our ships into uncharted seas to celebrate how we, as a new people, are engaged in the process of courageously being and becoming, no longer "living hidden in forests like shy deer!" (IV, SEC. 283 / 2001, 161).

THUS SPOKE ZARATHUSTRA (1883–1892/2006B)

Nietzsche's solitary summers in the small Swiss village of Sils Maria ultimately produced classic works such as *Thus Spoke Zarathustra* (1883/2006b), *Beyond Good and Evil* (1886/2002), and *Twilight of the Idols* (1888/1997a). However, it would be Nietzsche's *Zarathustra* that has often been cited as one of his most important works. The book is unique in that a tale is told through its protagonist Zarathustra, presented by Nietzsche as a proto-*übermensch*, who, after ten years holed up in the mountains engaged in contemplation, decides it is time to reenter society. A story about a prophet with a great concern and deep love for humanity who emerges from his ten-year period of contemplation, bloated with urgent wisdoms that must be conveyed, the book highlights how Zarathustra engages in a campaign to sloganeer the merits of the overcomer as well as criticize the attributes and the superficial travails of the herd.

The character Zarathustra conveys key tenets of the philosopher's previous writings into an epic monologue that essentially calls on people experiencing the putrefaction of Christianity to assemble a new reality. Zarathustra's proclamations need to be seen as "a consequence of the critical experiments of *Human, All Too Human, Daybreak* and *The Gay Science*, and not a contradiction of them" (Hollingdale 1999, 138). Vicariously fulfilling his role as a stentor through Zarathustra, an "ancient Persian prophet" who was "Nietzsche's surrogate" according to Adrian Del Caro and Robert B. Pippin (cited in Nietzsche 2006b, xii), one sees Nietzsche proclaiming the core energy required of humanity without god—the will to power—as well as continuing his address of the theme of eternal recurrence, the view that every human being's experientials exist in an endless, repetitive cyclicity.

The eternal recurrence is again revisited by Nietzsche in *Zarathustra*. That Nietzsche revisits this theme is indicative of the seriousness in which the philosopher views the development of internal strength to repeatedly overcome life struggles. Living, then, requires the needed but painful excavation of every morsel of will for an empowerment that can withstand an eternity of recurring struggle, for "only where life is, is there also will; but not will to life, instead—thus I teach you—will to power!" (Nietzsche 2006b, 90). Hollingdale provides an excellent summary of Nietzsche's overcomer:

> Nietzsche envisages the universe as a kaleidoscope of changes. . . . The superman, therefore, as the man whose will to power has increased the most by overcoming the most, is the most joyful man. . . . Such a man will affirm life, love life and say Yes even to misery and pain, because he realizes that the joy he has known would not have been possible apart from the pain he has known; and he will not be dismayed at the idea that the joy of his life will be repeated endlessly, neither will he flinch from the knowledge that its pain must be repeated too. (1999, 167)

Nietzsche himself asks: "Have you ever said Yes to one joy? Oh my friends, then you also said Yes to *all* pain" (2006b, 263). Hollingdale echoes Nietzsche, adding that the sensation one gets with increases in power, that is, the sensation of joy born from overcoming life pain, "is itself the strongest advocate of the eternal recurrence" (1999, 167).

Nietzsche's proclamation of the will to power should be seen as an internalized fortress that can withstand onslaughts from the lifeworlds of the herd, cultural philistines, and last human beings who follow life scripts and regulations with little fanfare, passion, or purpose—contexts of people who can no longer exhibit self-mastery. Thus, the will to power is not only about the power to confront mainstream values but also about one's power over oneself (Hollingdale 1999, 158). Nietzsche describes the last human being as one who is engaged in the diminishing of the self as well as the minimizing of the dynamic aspects of life and living. Nietzsche's welcome of danger and proximity to death is designed to demonstrate how both are important catalysts that lead to renewal, rebirth, and revitalized passions. Last human beings, however, cannot bear hardship and hide in the safety of their conformist cocoons and experience a long life of *ennui* where "each wants the same, each is the same, and whoever feels differently goes voluntarily into the insane asylum" (Nietzsche 2006b, 10). For Nietzsche, our rootedness in safety is decadent, for we have thus given up knowing what love, longing, creation, and becoming an overcomer means. That is, the bar set by last human beings is low: to experience comfort and predictability. For Del Caro and Pippin, last human beings can no longer overcome and master themselves and live in herd-like complacency. Last human beings are thus those who exist in society as followers preoccupied with their mundane minutiae.

Less observed and appreciated about Zarathustra is where he launches his efforts to teach about the overcomer, a town named "Motley Cow," an analog for the human experience within the garrulous cacophony of modernity. As community, Motley Cow exhibits a volatile mixture of those seeking, listening, conforming, and challenging Zarathustra's ideas. For Young, "'Motley' signifies the semi-'barbarism' we have repeatedly seen ascribed to modernity" (2010, 368). It is also the world of the herd, as signified by the "cow" reference. Zarathustra thus seeks different audiences in his travels to be enlightened to the fact that god is dead and that the epoch of the overcomer and the will to power has arrived. A much more evolved character than which first appeared in the form of the nameless madman in *Science*, the gadfly and stentor that is now Zarathustra debates his teachings with men, women, townsfolk, and anthropomorphized animal characters, all of whom exhibit a variety of ideological persuasions and roles. As such, his teachings are rejected by some people while others become his disciples. The work ends with Zarathustra continuing his journey to spread his teachings about the overcomer.

Bloated with knowledge and insight prior to his descent to Motley Cow, Zarathustra proclaims, "Behold! I am weary of my wisdom, like a bee that has gathered too much honey. I need hands that reach out" (Nietzsche 2006b, 3). As he pronounces the importance of the overcomer for humanity, the characters Zarathustra encounters include people and animals as aforementioned, with the latter enthusiastically proclaiming for Zarathustra what they see as his path, proclaiming that *"you are the teacher of eternal recurrence—that now is your destiny!"* (Nietzsche 2006b, 177). Perhaps most important for our understanding of *Zarathustra* is that Nietzsche proclaims through the protagonist how the *übermensch* must be the goal humanity sets for itself, echoing what had been presented about the role of culture in *Meditations*. Like *Meditations*, Nietzsche's view in *Zarathustra* is that our modern cultural terrain is littered with unnecessary ideological impediments and scripts that block the aspirations of those who desire to overcome. In this regard, all social systems in *Zarathustra* are seen as flawed in some dramatic way, thus behooving the need for overcomers and great human beings. Nietzsche's frequent concerns with the failure of modernist culture to produce great human beings, already earlier explicated in *Meditations'* discussion of the cultural philistine, is given new urgency through Zarathustra's condemnations of the herd mentality and its pretentious "rabble," the language of Motley Cow.

Nietzsche argues through Zarathustra that there is tremendous dignity walking one's own path. Although the journey might be solitary, it is nonetheless a dignified one that allows us to exist beyond "our gilded, fake, makeup wearing rabble—even if it calls itself 'good society,'—even if it calls itself 'nobility'" (Nietzsche 2006b, 197). Nietzsche criticizes the rabble and its dysfunctional communicative content that enable vile emotions and fallacies to surface into the public, for it "does not know what is great, what is small, what is straight and honest: it is innocently crooked, it always lies" (2006b, 235). Unable to or erroneously harnessing history to create their interpretation of the new human being, the modern self is disenfranchised when compared to the emancipated, that is, those able to adopt a judicious monumental, antiquarian, and critical understanding of their location in history to create themselves. Not surprisingly, Nietzsche accuses despotic leaders and their vulgarization of history for reproducing such rabble. Such a process takes place with hopes the captive audience will exhibit short memories, compelling Nietzsche to proclaim, "Therefore, my brothers, we need a *new nobility*, which is the adversary of all rabble and all despotic rule and which writes anew the word 'noble' on new tablets" (Nietzsche 2006b, 162).

Nietzsche also attacks those in political power for regurgitating the rabble for conformists to consume. Those coveting power achieve this by appropriating the virtues and moralities of the herd, be it through religion or ideology. These "fire hounds," for Del Caro and Pippin, are exemplified by the "fire-breathing, revolutionary spirit . . . who believes in and foments 'great events' of a political nature" (cited in Nietzsche 2006b, 103). Such people coveting power, who now appear virtuous with carefully catered talking points that pander—a "hellish noise" (that nonetheless impresses followers)—are harshly rebuked by Nietzsche for their disingenuousness. We are warned of their antics and advised to distrust in whom there is an intense need to punish, for from such persons' discontents the need for retribution emerges and "being the judge is bliss to them" (Nietzsche 2006b, 77).

The revanchist attribute of politicians can be understood through Nietzsche's important concept of *ressentiment,* the state of resentment and perpetual victimhood that inspires people to blame others for their own shortcomings, a concept that would later receive greater elaboration in *Genealogy.*[4] In *Zarathustra* the concept is nonetheless still made operative, enough for Nietzsche to warn us about the character disposition of power seekers as they lead their conformists: by employing *ressentiment* to generate one or a myriad of "others." Another theme of those who seek systemic power, these "preachers of equality" are creating rabble with utopianisms such as the notion that full leveling can exist between all peoples in society (2006b, 77). For Tiryakian, one of the earliest proponents of existential sociology, "men are basically unequal, but society cannot stand distinctions, so it debases them into a common mediocrity" (1962, 96). Nietzsche thus condemns power seekers informed by such a view for they cheapen how one should rule: with a noble mindset. Nietzsche rejects the art of statecraft and diplomacy of his day, all of which field political machinations that involve "haggling and bartering for power—with the rabble!" (2006b, 75). For Nietzsche, institutions and their lackeys bent on ensuring full equality should not be trusted due to the problematic inner workings of those who crave power through the herd. Exploiting their vulnerable sentiments, the fire hounds validate the disadvantaged who desire to "exact revenge and heap insult on all whose equals we are not" (Nietzsche 2006b, 77). He urges the overcoming of these rulers, warning how such defeatists "are the overman's greatest danger!" (Nietzsche 2006b, 233).

A wonderful quality in Nietzsche's thinking can be seen explicitly in *Zarathustra*, namely his sloganeering of the merits of solitude for working out problematics of the human condition. Here, one can see not only Nietzsche's view that modernity is toxic, but that the overcomer's formulation of excellence and pathways toward emancipation requires an uncluttered social environment freed from the toxicity of decadence. For example, Nietzsche saw solitude as a place for meditation and reflection, one that invariably compels the overcomer to leave and thus share with society acquired insights and knowledge. Note that the character Zarathustra had descended from the mountains after ten years of contemplation where he did not tire from his isolation. It would be Zarathustra's love for humanity, however, that necessitated him to return to society to spread his wisdom.

Nietzsche embraced another function of solitude, namely its capacity for healing the spirit after it has been exposed to cultural stimuli outputted from a dysfunctional modernity. For Nietzsche through Zarathustra, solitude is therapeutic as can be seen with his proclamation "Flee, my friend, into your solitude! I see you dazed by the noise of the great men and stung by the stings of the little" (2006b, 36). Moreover, Zarathustra encourages those of the herd to experience and embrace solitude as a means to develop one's self-defini-tion. In the work, Zarathustra frequently returns to the mountains for renewal, not unlike Nietzsche's many summer returns to Sils Maria. Nietzsche's desire for solitude can be seen in Zarathustra's proclamation, "Oh solitude! You my home solitude! How blissfully and tenderly your voice speaks to me!" (2006b, 147). Finally, it should be noted that Nietzsche was not setting people up for a sanguine experience with solitude. Through Zarathustra and his forthright view of life, Nietzsche warns about solitude's deleterious effects if harnessed incorrectly, namely that the actor will be trapped in a nihilistic state of loneliness. As a place that can harbor great dangers, Zarathustra warns: "Whatever one brings into solitude grows in it, even the inner beast. On this . . . solitude is ill-advised for many" (Nietzsche 2006b, 237).

Although Nietzsche's favorable and realistic views of solitude can be appreciated for their metaphorical value alone, Nietzsche did ascend some of the peaks of the Swiss Alps, such as Piz Corvatsch at a daunting 11,322 ft.—"Nietzsche's mountain," according to John Kaag (2018, 3)—in hopes of enhancing metaphysical and physical strength, molding his will to power in the process. Even in Nietzsche's later works the themes of mountains and ice are employed to frame his context of solitary profundities. As noted in chapter 2, Nietzsche relies on the symbolism of daunting and inaccessible places, such as high mountains and ice, as solitary contexts to enable sur-render and catches that inform self-authoring. Such symbolisms all serve as anvils for forging a transcending purposing of existence for the overcomer, a process that in *Ecce Homo*, is described as peacefully taking place "in the light" (Nietzsche 2007b, 4). Nietzsche even concedes that from such long and trying exercises of self-making, a process that is a form of "wandering *in the forbidden*," realizations about people and why they moralize surfaced, a frightening prospect that prompted our philosopher to ask, "—How much truth can a spirit *stand*, how much truth does it *dare*?—for me that became more and more the real measure of value" (2007b, 4).

Zarathustra, however, benefitted from such conditions of solitude, but had become bloated with wisdoms from his ten-year hiatus from society. He thus had to return to society to provide insights on how to navigate it as an overcomer, in the process offering a critique on contemporary social life with "unexampled ferocity" (Hollingdale 1999, 154). As a character that predates the tropes one sees today in cultural life about "getting off the grid" or delinking from the rabble of social media, one can appreciate the prescience that Nietzsche exhibited regarding the merits of solitary contemplations as prerequisites for decluttering decadent stimuli accumulated from the lifeworld. Yet the means by which one gets to know the self is a fearsome process, a process that requires the overcomer to exhibit tremendous courage. Expressing this courage, Zarathustra embraces eternal recurrence—a heaviest weight already referenced in *Science*—as a worthy test for determining if the individual can handle the grind of the life experience. The overcomer on the other hand, exposed yet impervious to the weight of the life experience, would simply proclaim after triumphing over the angst of eternal recurrence: "Was that life? Well then! One More Time!" (Nietzsche 2006b, 125).

BEYOND GOOD AND EVIL: PRELUDE TO A PHILOSOPHY OF THE FUTURE (1886/2002)

In *Beyond Good and Evil: Prelude to a Philosophy of the Future*, Nietzsche confronts the dysfunction and decadence of Christianity and religion, along with modernity's *isms*. He begins rudimentary elaboration on the master and slave moralities (to further be developed in his next work, *Genealogy*). Nietzsche also more controversially expresses his concerns about the decadence enabled by democratism. Insofar as the topic of democracy is concerned, Clark notes that although *Beyond* does not offer a sustained critique about the institutions of mainstream society, what it does emphasize about democracy is significant in that Nietzsche viewed such institutions as promoting a "form of the decay of political organization" (2015, 170). Hollingdale observes that *Beyond* is "devoted to an elaboration and explanation of theories put forward in *Zarathustra*" (1999, 180). *Beyond*'s Horstmann forwards an alternative perspective, describing Nietzsche's orientation as still suspicious of knowledge, truth, philosophy, and especially morality and religion since these function in ways that are oppressive when rendered as tradition and custom (cited in Nietzsche 2002, vii). Considered one of Nietzsche's greatest works, Horstmann attributes its popularity to Nietzsche's explication of many themes, including his "prejudices and his preferences, his loathings and his hopes, and above all his deep insights into our situation in the modern world," all of which "are united in an exemplary way . . . and for this reason it is a great book" (cited in Nietzsche 2002, viii). Nietzsche himself reflects in *Ecce Homo* that *Beyond* is essentially a "*critique of modernity*, not excluding the modern sciences, the modern arts, even modern politics"—yet it is also a celebration of an "opposing type, as unmodern as possible, a *noble, yes-saying type* [emphasis added]" (2007b, 77).

I begin our discussion of Nietzsche's views of the internal workings of morality since they will allow us to segue into a discussion of his infamous conceptualization of master and slave moralities. Emphases must be made, however, about why I intend to de-emphasize the term "slave" and replace it with "servant." There are a few important reasons that justify such a decision. The first reason for employing the term "servant" is that in our politically charged era of identity politics, it is important that readers are reminded that Nietzsche was in no way an apologist for any ideas that promoted structural or racial subjugation. The second reason is that Nietzsche *never addressed slavery in a racial or internal colonial sense.* He employed the term figuratively in *Beyond* to refer to those who uncritically and sycophantically follow the moral dicta offered by Christianity and other social institutions of modernity. The third reason is offered by Clark (2015). Her thorough vetting of all of Nietzsche's published works reveals how Nietzsche's accommodation of such servitude is figurative and polemical, and only "in some sense or other" (Clark 2015, 171). Moreover, Nietzsche applied the term only to ancient philosophers, non-philosophers, and "scholars and scientists" as "deserving the status of 'slaves' in relation to philosophers" since these are the ones that lack "true independence and freedom" due to their subservience to demands made by academia (Clark 2015, 171). The term is also used to deride what Nietzsche saw as blind sycophants of the democratic ideal, people who were nothing more than "scribbling slaves" of democratism (II, SEC. 44 / 2002, 40). For Nietzsche, the enslaved are generally seen as dependents of every rank (IX, SEC. 260 / 2002, 154). Conversely, the attributes of a "master morality" mindset should henceforth be conceptualized as attributes of a "noble" mindset as they engage in praxis with just use of their overflowing power. Exhibiting noble power—a type of power that for Nietzsche overflows—and engaging in overcoming action, Nietzsche-style, are thus demanding exercises to refine one's will to power for liberating the self from servitude. And when such noble persons assist the unfortunate, they do so not because of pity, but because they have been optimized by an over-abundance of self-empowerment extracted from and informed by a consciousness that has its origins in the actor's confrontation with all nuances and consequences of life struggle. For Nietzsche, the noble-minded person, by honoring the self in such a process, also honors "those who have power over themselves" (IX, SEC. 260 / 2002, 154).

With this understanding, it is incontrovertible that Nietzsche's praise of aristocratic and noble mindsets in no way advocates for aristocratic political institutions. Philosopher Béla Egyed expresses similar sentiments, noting that a noble mindset's use of the will to power should "not be understood as an endorsement of the *political* domination of the weak by the strong" (2007, 112). In this regard, Nietzsche is for a freedom beyond institutions, conveyed with an enthusiasm that welcomes "anyone who is willing to enter the dangerous world of self-overcoming . . . no one is excluded a priori" (Egyed 2007, 109). This "aristocracy" must be new and comprised by us when we have elevated ourselves to our very best state of being (Egyed 2007). Therefore, Nietzsche never advocated for a resurrection of an aristocratic social class of yesteryear. The significance of this discernment cannot be overemphasized. Understanding this position allows us to not take umbrage with Nietzsche's view that the underlying value orientation of society should consider rank in ways that make finer and finer discernments between the capacities of different people (IX, SEC. 257 / 2002, 151). This is a vital point that will be revisited at the closing sections of our discussion of *Beyond* when the noble mindset is identified as the ethos of the ideal human being. Suffice to say for now, the dichotomy between noble and servant can be seen as a useful figurative lens for vetting modern moralities, a lens that allows us to see how modernity relegates to the periphery of cultural production authentic sovereigns who exist in a state of self-mastery and sovereignty, while promoting scripted values for those who remain deferential to social systems and their manufacturers of consent.

The discussion of the noble and servant moralities offers readers an important and obvious subtext: morality is socially constructed. The dysfunctional moralities of Christianity, religion, and modernity are for Nietzsche indicators of the ever-changing terrain of truth. The essence of Nietzsche's view on this matter echoes Marx since the latter also famously claims that it is those in power that construct the superstructure. Such a process, however, still does not validate claims to truth even though it aims to present information as such, not unlike a father who never questions his right to indoctrinate his child into his value system or a mother who never doubts that in her child she has birthed a sort of property as well. Nietzsche views claims to absolute truth as a sort of quarantining system, a control mechanism, in spite of its relativistic expressions that have, through history, altered the definition of what it means to be good and evil. He laments how "now it is the teacher, the social class, the priest, and the prince who . . . see every new person as an incontrovertible opportunity for a new possession" (Nietzsche V, SEC. 194 / 2002, 84).

Noble morality justifies actions of one's desire for an elevated state of existence. The great human being, the overcomer, needs to establish one's noble mindset even if it means the self must be immoral—a non-pejorative term to Nietzsche—while contesting the servant morality of the status quo.

Noble morality, then, embraces living in a manner that creates new values of excellence and life affirmation. Living an optimized life becomes a means by which a noble mindset will discharge its power and strength, a process that expresses one's will to power according to Nietzsche (I, SEC. 13 / 2002, 15). The noble mindset is therefore seen as functional and instrumental for individuals in society to adopt since modern society is itself constituted by many without the will to power and fortitude to purpose their own existence.

According to Clark, *Beyond* conveys the "doctrine of will to power in Nietzsche's own voice," one that provides a "sustained reflection on the doctrine" but unfortunately "mentioned much less frequently in Nietzsche's later books . . . never again" to receive "sustained discussions or explanations" (1990, 212). By *Zarathustra* and *Beyond*, the notion of the will to power made operative in Nietzsche's thoughts reaches a climax. It is as if Nietzsche expects us henceforth to understand that whatever impediments are put forth by the philosopher, it will be one's will to power that allows the overcoming actor to rise to the occasion of greatness in spite of being emplaced within social systems experiencing impairment. In contrast, servant morality configures righteousness based on whether one's intentions are good or evil, a process that relies on prejudicial pre-judgment and *ressentiment*. Kaufmann explains how those crippled by their servant morality, that is, those "lacking the power for creation . . . and, unable to gain mastery of themselves, seek to conquer others" (1950, 255). A better conceptualization of servant morality in *Beyond* is that it functions as a utility, its instrumentality born from people who have been subjected to repeated violations, oppressions, and exhaustions of all kinds. Those harboring such a morality have a pessimistic—even dystopian or apocalyptic—view of the human condition and are thus full of misgivings and doubts about what society deems as good (Nietzsche IX, SEC. 260 / 2002, 155–156).

Nietzsche's view that those with little fortitude exhibit a servant morality is not surprising to Kaufmann, who argues that "Nietzsche assumed that only the weak need to rely on the rules of others" while those with a will to power "should be able to generate his own standards" (1950, 250). The last human beings, unempowered and unable to overcome, lacking a striving, and lacking the will to power to "transcend and perfect oneself" therefore detest the empowering attributes of the noble-minded (Kaufmann 1950, 248). As such, servant morality exploits *ressentiment* to distort the values of the empowered into something evil. This distorted notion of evil is then perceived as a dangerous existential threat for it has been imbued with, through the reverence of subsequent generations of adherents, a mystical malevolence and power, a profoundly "*awesome quality* [emphasis added]" (Nietzsche IX, SEC. 260 / 2002, 156). In contrast, for those with a noble morality, it is the good that inspires empowerment. Young summarizes Nietzsche's servant morality conveyed in *Beyond* as validating values of failure that degenerate society while dismissing beauty, self-assertion, self-empowerment, that is, "every instinct that belongs to the highest and best-turned-out type of 'human' in favour of an 'unworldly,' 'unsensuous'" conceptualization of the human being (2006, 140).

For Nietzsche, Judeo-Christian morality and religion, in general, are the earliest institutions that advocate and reproduce a servant morality, a disingenuous process that treats its own notion of morality as absolute truth. Such a process functions to stifle overcoming. As will be revisited by Nietzsche in *Genealogy*, the key difference between noble and servant moralities is that "the nobles' morality is essentially affirmative . . . [while] slave morality is fundamentally a denial [of their own empowerment] . . . an expression of all-consuming hatred" (Young 2006, 150). For Nietzsche, the Christian faith has been only about sacrifice of all freedom, pride, and self-confidence of the spirit, and therefore it simultaneously enables the enslavement of its adherents within a life of self-hatred (III, SEC. 46 / 2002, 44). Consistent with my assertion that Nietzsche has lurking in his philosophy profound insights on defective social systems, his discussion that the putrefaction of ancient Greece occurred when great noble-minded people able to effuse gratefulness for life and living were overtaken by religiosity is a case in point. Such a process enabled religion to become fear-ridden, especially with the dawn of Christianity (III, SEC. 49 / 2002, 47).

In such a context, Nietzsche was harshly critical of other faiths, even equating Buddhism—a religion containing many tenets that Nietzsche expresses support for—with Christianity since the former is also seen to be complicit in enabling a servant morality. Conflating a sarcastic critique of Christianity and Buddhism with a dialectic that embraces suffering for one's overcoming, Nietzsche alleges these religions teach the pious to deploy their pieties "to situate themselves in an illusory higher order of things," and in the process ensuring that adherents maintain their acquiescence to convention and the status quo (III, SEC. 61 / 2002, 55).[5] Neither did Nietzsche spare the previous atavism of Christianity, Judaism, from critique, noting how the latter inverted values as well by treating the word for poor "as a synonym for 'holy' and 'friend,'" thus birthing servant morality (V, SEC. 195 / 2002, 84).

Pivotal for this work is how Nietzsche envisioned democratism in *Beyond* to be the successor to Christianity. Like Christianity, democratism enables the oppressed and their servant morality to find historical outlets for redemption, as in, for example, the French Revolution, which Nietzsche felt was but an iteration of a slave revolt to acquire secularized social power. As such, Nietzsche felt democracy promoted a diminished and regressive form of humanity, preventing great and exceptional human beings from emerging.

He did not spare anarchism and socialism either, scathingly noting that the complaints of the herd demanding to be given fish rather than learning how to fish, analogously speaking, can also be heard through these other *isms*, especially in how pity is harnessed by their proponents. Yet in spite of the indignations of anarchists and the "silly philosophasters and brotherhood enthusiasts who call themselves socialists," it was clear for Nietzsche that these groups still did not realize that their attempts to end special claims or rights mean that they are in fact in opposition to any rights, since when all are equal, "no one will need 'rights' anymore" (Nietzsche V, SEC. 202 / 2002, 90). Nietzsche, for lack of a better expression, simply was not buying it: members of such groups are all united in their religions of pity and united in their beliefs in the merits of "*communal* pity" as if it were a bona fide morality (Nietzsche V, SEC. 202 / 2002, 90–91). With nihilism having spread across Western Europe due to the slow decline of religion, alternative self-righteous moralities now exist through their respective *isms* as seen in the above examples, compelling Nietzsche to denounce the European morality of his day as a morality of the herd.

Whether we are here attending to religion or political systems, *Beyond* provides us with the needed narratives about the noble mindset and the aristocratic character that is its embodiment. Sociologically, it is clear such persons are seen as praxian and as having agency, engaged in cultural and moral production on their own terms, while creating a new community informed by noble and aristocratic mindsets. Nietzsche observes how "every enhancement so far . . . of 'man' has been the work of an aristocratic society—and that is how it will be, again and again" (IX, SEC. 257 / 2002, 151). Nietzsche has always remained resolute about this thesis, noting that we must remove our rose-colored spectacles while viewing how society evolves: through the efforts of the few—and that such a truth, he concedes, is brutally harsh. Understandably, Nietzsche beseeches us to "not be deceived" by "how every higher culture on earth has *begun*!" (IX, SEC. 257 / 2002, 151). That said, it is important to heed Clark's (1990) emphasis that Nietzsche's vision of aristocracy is distinct from the view that society *needed* aristocratic political institutions to counter the decadence and putrefaction of Christianity, democracy, and the earlier mentioned *isms*. Clark notes how Nietzsche "in fact says nothing at all in *Beyond* about the kind of political organization or institutions (of the larger society) that are required for the enhancements with which he is concerned" (2015, 170). More importantly, Clark observes that:

> In fact, Nietzsche does not say that the "decay of political organization" is a bad thing. Although he undoubtedly thinks its decay reduces the value of political organization for some purposes, what he actually says is perfectly compatible with believing that this decay makes possible things of even higher value, e.g.,

the development of individuality. I suggest that Nietzsche believes that the enhancement of the human type with which he is concerned depends upon the development of individuality and that he recognizes that such development is made possible by a weakening of political organization. . . . The claim that democracy represents the decay of political organization therefore gives me no reason to concede that Nietzsche is against democratic political institutions or in favor of aristocratic ones. (2015, 170–171)

Clark argues how Nietzsche actually "has no objection to democratic political institutions as long as they are compatible with 'aristocratic values'—as long as they allow the few to posit the goal of human life in something beyond that to which the majority can relate" (2015, 174). Even as far back as in *Human*, Nietzsche cautiously celebrated how European democratization was irresistible because the process provided an "upside for higher culture in which the 'few' see the goal and value of human life" (Clark 2015, 174) in ways that guarded against corporeal and mental servitude (Nietzsche Vol. 2, II, SEC. 275 / 1996, 377). That said, Nietzsche's overall sentiments toward democracy was still critical. Democratism, like socialism, and by implication other *isms* of society, contributed to what Nietzsche saw as a complete degeneration of humanity into what is today considered the perfect, ideal human being: the ignoble conformist, the distinguished member of the herd.

Given the delimitations of Christianity, democracy and the aforementioned *isms*, it is not surprising to see the degree of emphasis Nietzsche places on the will to power in *Beyond*. The will to power, then, is a catalytic and enabling agent that allows the concept of human greatness to have positive implications for contesting the scripts and herd demands of society. The onus is therefore on the aristocratic individual with a noble mindset—made possible by the person's empowerment from purposing existence—to want to be unique by walking one's own path and living "by your own fists" (Nietzsche VI, SEC. 212 / 2002, 107). Nietzsche awaits the arrival of such a new philosopher able to exhibit this will and argues that their epistemology is based on creativity and creation, and that their "will to truth is—*will to power*," yet he also asks whether there are: "philosophers like this today? Have there ever been philosophers like this? Won't there *have to be* philosophers like this?" (VI, SEC. 211 / 2002, 106).

Philosophers aside, other actors with self-defined agency are also ideal types. Such daring adventurers, however, must be the actualization of a will to power that wants to grow and spread, but "not out of any morality or immorality, but because it is *alive*, and because life *is* precisely will to power" (Nietzsche IX, SEC. 259 / 2002, 153). Such a person understands unpretentiously the importance of rank constituted by the overcomer with a will to power and those followers without such a will. In this regard, the overcomer, further enhanced by aristocratic and noble mindsets, is able to rise above conformists that populate the herds of modernity constituted by mediocre last human beings, those followers without such a will. Without such a will to power, herds form around generalized narratives about people, a process which Nietzsche blames for the intensification of anti-Semitism and German nationalism.

The concerns Nietzsche felt for those vulnerable to incipient German nationalism must be elucidated clearly. The vast majority of Nietzsche scholars, especially those in the post–World War II era cited herein, have taken upon themselves to be sufficiently informed about the machinations committed by his sister, Elisabeth Förster-Nietzsche, when she distorted her brother's ideas to support German nationalism. Nietzsche, of course, was well-known for his contempt toward nationalism. Toward the conclusion of *Beyond* one can clearly see Nietzsche's frustrations with and dismissal of the German variant when he observes in the Germany of his day "the anti-French stupidity one moment and the anti-Jewish stupidity the next, now the anti-Polish stupidity . . . these little stupors of the German spirit and conscience" (VIII, SEC. 251 / 2002, 141). Nietzsche's blunt and prescient observation of the Germany of his day arguably illuminates sentiments that enabled the spread of German nationalism:

> Just listen.—I have yet to meet a German who was well disposed towards Jews. And however unconditional the rejection of genuine anti-Semitism might be . . . such prudence and politics are not really aimed at anti-Semitic sentiment in general, but instead at . . . the outrageous and disgraceful expression of this excessive sentiment—this cannot be denied. (VIII, SEC. 251 / 2002, 141)

For Nietzsche, that Germany was only grudgingly accepting their coexistence with its Jewish diaspora evinces a lack of communal and civil society advancement in German culture, one that the Italians, the French, and the British have been able to refine in their respective contexts due to their greater tolerance for coexistence with diverse communities (VIII, SEC. 251 / 2002, 141). We again see in such an observation major discontents Nietzsche had about how the nation of Germany is conceptualized by its nationalists. In Nietzsche's view, such a political infection in the German identity of his day reveals how the German people were still regressive on the many fronts of individual and cultural refinement, and therefore this expressed a disposition of a people that are still seen as weak (VIII, SEC. 251 / 2002, 141–142). Because the Jewish community in Europe has had to endure tremendous oppression, Nietzsche argues they are "without a doubt the strongest, purest, most tenacious race living in Europe today," and "this is why, among the spectators and philosophers, artists like us regard the Jews with—gratitude" (VIII, SEC.

251 / 2002, 141–142). It is appropriate, then, to support the assertion about Nietzsche's view on sectarianism offered by one of his many biographers, Lesley Chamberlain, when she accurately notes that "the only nation against which [Nietzsche] did feel racial prejudice was Germany" (1996, 202). Chamberlain adds that "never had Nietzsche sounded so revolutionary as in those moments when he recollected the harm done to an unfulfilled humanity by priests, by the ideal of chastity, and by racial and class barriers that ignored intrinsic human worth" (1996, 202).

For Clark, Nietzsche's incessant focus on renewal, even if the process is subversive, is meant to set into motion a better society based on "the cultivation of a higher culture . . . a higher type of human being than previous cultures have produced" (2015, 174), but only if free spirits are allowed to become vital members of their new community. Here, Nietzsche considers a pan-ethnic solution that celebrates a larger, more expansive, and ostensibly freer European identity. Nietzsche is fully aware that such an identity exacts a currency, however, in that old and narrow provincial and sectarian identities must be purged in ways that can mitigate, for example, the discontents he sees in German nationalism. Yet Nietzsche was hopeful and enthusiastic about the unbounded possibilities of embracing a greater shared humanity in the guise of a European identity, proclaiming, "We *good Europeans* and free, *very* free spirits—we still have it, the whole need of spirit and the whole tension of its bow!" (Preface / 2002, 4). Shrift thus finds in Nietzsche a prescient disdain of nationalism through the philosopher's pro-European views, noting how Nietzsche's "call for 'good Europeans' is based on ideas that current thinkers, trying to escape the legacy of the European nation-states, would do well to explore" (Bergmann et al. 2007, 37).

ON THE GENEALOGY OF MORALITY (1887/2006A)

Keith Ansell-Pearson describes Nietzsche's *On the Genealogy of Morality* as a "book that retains its capacity to shock and disconcert the modern reader," and that it is "one of the darkest books ever written," a subversive work that must be carefully approached (cited in Nietzsche 2006a, xiii–xiv). Ansell-Pearson also writes that in spite of its disturbing nature and its capacity to shock and disconcert the modern reader, it is also paradoxically "a book full of hope and anticipation" (cited in Nietzsche 2006a, xiii). Clark adds that "from beginning to end, Nietzsche's writings convey his belief that he is saying something about truth that is of the utmost importance for understanding human life and that sets him at odds with the whole philosophical tradition" (1990, 6). Although the profundities and provocations noted by Ansell-Pearson's and Clark's sentiments are accurate, *Genealogy* remains an extension of ideas explicated in *Beyond*, and both highlight how socially constructed ideas about morality have been inverted over time. In spite of its comparatively short length, *Genealogy* is considered one of the most significant works by Nietzsche.

Because the noble and servant moralities, and morality in general, are important themes in Nietzsche thought, they are again visited with much fervor in *Genealogy*. For those with a noble mindset and morality, Nietzsche praises how their empowerment stems from their intelligence, creativity, ambition, and will to power. As such, the nobles have been able to justify their values and place in the social order. This observation is, in itself, not unfamiliar given that *Beyond* already pointed to this orientation. However, in *Genealogy*, Nietzsche makes the historical and important observation that before Christianity, members of society acknowledged the ethos and empowerment of the noble as "good," and conversely, those unable to attain this form of empowerment are thus seen as "bad." Nietzsche argues that those aspiring to become good like a noble-minded person should thus be emulated for they accent the creativity, proactiveness, self-creation of values, and meaning of those with a semblance of a will to power. With the onset of the Judeo-Christian worldview, however, proponents of the faith inverted goodness by relegating the expressions of the empowered toward the periphery, while transforming coping mechanisms of last humans into what is meant to be good: not confronting or overcoming, harboring jealousy and resentfulness, and exhibiting pity and sympathy to the point of creating their own suffering. For Nietzsche, the Jewish nation subjugated by the Romans set into motion this inversion. Consequently, heightened values of power and ambition were discarded so as to promote defeatism with the decadent view that "only the poor, the powerless, the lowly are good; the suffering, the deprived, the sick, the ugly, are the only pious people . . . salvation is for them alone," while to those more noble and powerful, "you are eternally wicked . . . eternally wretched, cursed and damned!" (Nietzsche I, SEC. 7 / 2006a, 17). Because of such defeatist sentiments, Nietzsche concludes that pity or sympathy cannot be the foundation of morality. Yet this apparent deduction betrays a cynicism Nietzsche had long held against notions of pity/sympathy. Even as far back as *Human*, Nietzsche already doubted its efficacy, cynically arguing that had alms been "bestowed only out of pity all the beggars would have starved to death" (Vol. 2, Part 2, Sec. 239 / 1996, 370).

What actors of society are responsible for such a social construction and inversion? For Nietzsche, such a vulgar inversion is unfortunately but an uncritically adopted social construction of decadence indicative of the degeneration of civilization, set into motion by a "priestly aristocracy" that desired to secure and justify power for themselves and religious adherents (I, SEC. 6 /

2006a, 16). To ensure this process proceeds smoothly, they interpret as something good the defeatist sentiments of last human beings under their control. By rendering values of last humans into something good, priests overturned the standards that, until the arrival and embeddedness of Judeo-Christianity, had been accepted as legitimate. For Nietzsche, since those without courage had nothing to offer in terms of an empowering philosophy, religious authorities had to dredge up from the herd reactionary responses toward power based off their fears, bitterness, and *ressentiment*. Because the standard practice of priests is to instill metaphysical fears into their adherents, Nietzsche was highly critical of such a religious stratum, noting that because priests are actually the most powerless in practice, one must be warned about their status as "the greatest haters" in history as well as its most clever operators of *ressentiment* (I, SEC. 7 / 2006a, 17). Nietzsche argues that few people—even the most intelligent—can contest "the intelligence . . . of priestly revenge" (I, SEC. 7 / 2006a, 17).

Religion, if it is not yet already obvious, is viewed as a weakening agent by Nietzsche. As institution, it appropriates the powerlessness of last humans by engaging in cultural production to transform their unempowered human condition into "morality." *Ressentiment* then surfaces from the morality of the unempowered to blame those with power, those who have overcome, as being responsible for the unempowered's precarious existence. Last human beings thus culturally, politically, and spiritually camouflage their intense desires for retribution with the term "justice," which for Nietzsche, was simply a refined justification for retaliation, a justification that is needed to *sanctify* the act of revenge (II, SEC. 11 / 2006a, 48). Thus, the vilest expression of unempowered community, revenge, is reproduced and ensconced as morality, as scripted "tradition." Nietzsche argues that impotence against the powerful becomes warped into goodness by the notion of forgiveness and loving your enemies; similarly, timidity is transformed into humility, submission transformed into servile sycophancy, and passively waiting for outcomes determined by others is celebrated as a virtue we call patience. Such legerdemain perplexes and frustrates Nietzsche, for he feels it is absurd to "ask strength *not* to express itself as strength . . . as it is to ask weakness to express itself as strength" (I, SEC. 13 / 2006a, 26). However, last human beings prefer to wallow in the realm of "subterranean revenge," where they unpack all of life's miseries onto happier and more fulfilled actors, onto their happy conscience, with the outcome being that the latter eventually feel that they are undeserving of life affirmation, and that "It's a disgrace to be happy!" for "There is too much misery!" (Nietzsche III, SEC. 14 / 2006a, 91). *Ressentiment* is thus a defeatist energy driving the moral production of last human beings and their servant moralities. To reinforce this assertion, Nietzsche offers a parable about birds of prey that carry off little lambs as an analogy for the distortions of *ressentiment*: "These birds of prey are evil; and whoever is least like a bird of prey and most like its opposite, a lamb—is good"—a sentiment that is, of course, nonsensical to the bird of prey who harbors no grudges against "these good lambs" (I, SEC. 13 / 2006a, 26). But what of the sentiments of the lambs, the analog of the last human beings? The outcome is rather obvious for Nietzsche: harbor a frail identity for "in this way, they gain the right to make the birds of prey *responsible* for being birds of prey" (I, SEC. 13 / 2006a, 26).

Nietzsche highlights the unfortunate symbiosis between priests and their adherents, noting how the latter are exploited by the former, and thus, how the former's intentions cannot be construed as entirely altruistic as they perform their roles in the community, for "wherever there are herds, it is the instinct of weakness that has willed the herd and the cleverness of the priests that has organized it" (III, SEC. 18 / 2006a, 100–101). Nietzsche reminds us that "the strong are as naturally inclined to strive to be *apart* as the weak are to strive to be together" (III, SEC. 18 / 2006a, 101). The priestly class is thus implicated for warping the ascetic ideals from hitherto sovereign thinkers that wielded them as a means for self-authored liberation. In this regard, Nietzsche appears to sympathize with the Buddha as liberator for sacrificing his family's love and his love for family, all for the purpose of seeking enlightenment, even though this achievement would not have been possible were it not for—and Nietzsche was critical of this—Buddha seeking to live a life of an ascetic ideal based on retreat, a path designed to embrace poverty, humility, and chastity, of life negation, a "nihilistic turning-away from existence" (II, SEC. 21 / 2006a, 63). Holding true to his vision that suffering with purpose promotes an unexamined freedom, Nietzsche still grants the Buddha—perhaps a distant philosophical cousin in the mind of the philosopher—dignified treatment. Buddha thus appears to Nietzsche in *Genealogy* as a sort of ideal type after the ancient Greeks to embrace suffering so explicitly. In beings like Buddha are overcoming tendencies that reveal meaning for life and living. To Nietzsche, individuals like the Buddha remind us that fortitude in the harshness of life and living teaches us all to not deny suffering but to even will it, to seek it out, a process that is not fearsome and nihilistic if the actor is "shown a *meaning* for it, a *purpose* of suffering," for the "meaninglessness of suffering, *not* the suffering, was the curse that has so far blanketed mankind" (III, SEC. 28 / 2006a, 120). For Ansell-Pearson, Nietzsche not surprisingly admired the Buddha "for breaking free from his domestic shackles" to search for distant horizons that could offer him some incontrovertible truth (cited in Nietzsche 2006a, x).

Nietzsche felt that even free-spirited philosophers before the Judeo-Christian era fulfilled their outlook on their own terms: by living their philosophy based on soul-searching within the context of solitude. For Ansell-Pearson, however, when the ascetic ideal becomes a proselytized script that upholds a morality, whether a Buddhist morality or a morality from a well-intentioned conformist philosopher, these still constitute an ideal not authored by the original overcomer. Such an ideal remains but a fraudulent scheme for enhancing life and is offered to last humans so as to shut "the door on a suicidal nihilism by giving humanity a goal: morality" (cited in Nietzsche 2006a, xxvi). Here, Nietzsche's sociological imagination highlights for a Europe curious about Buddhism at the time that the piety, compassion, and pity of Buddhist morality are but a shadowing consciousness of the Judeo-Christian tradition, the latter of which found their iterations and renewed purpose inside modernity's *isms*. Buddhist ideals on communal compassion had gained popularity in cultural circles, and notions of a Euro-Buddhism compassion being employed to herd yet another population into scripted subservience, and to nihilism, had concerned Nietzsche (Preface, SEC. 5 / 2006a, 7).

The ascetic ideal, yet another important concept in Nietzsche's philosophy, refers to a spiritual thinker's path toward liberation and transcendence, believed to be secured through lived experiences of poverty, humility, and chastity, experiences that build morality. However, with the onset of Judeo-Christianity and the institutionalization of religion, the ascetic ideal became seen as disciplined and methodical denial, as self-sacrifice, by last human beings. The ascetic ideal was thus inverted by priests to promote their own sense of righteousness and holiness even though they retreated into the solitude of their quarantining system: faith, custom, tradition, the cave, the monastery, the temple. In the retreat offered by the ascetic ideal, decadence sets in: when threats to the faith of priests are lacking, then the same priests, if there is an "absence of external enemies," will make "necessary the internalization of aggression, hostility, and cruelty in the form of guilt, self-castigation, and various forms of self-punishment," factors that for Nietzsche constitute life negation (Clark 1990, 164). Perhaps an analog to Marx's notion of religion functioning as an opium for the masses, Nietzsche offers a parallel rendering: that priests are engaged in the anaesthetizing of pain through emotions and through *ressentiment*. As such, the priests' proselytizations about humility, chastity, religious doctrine, and whatever religious scripts exist, along with the aesthetics of rituals, are instead meted out to last humans so as to deny them self-authored fulfillment in life itself.[6] Reproduced and reified over time, few human beings have dared challenge let alone abandon the ideals offered by the priestly aristocracy, according to Nietzsche.

Nietzsche emphasizes that the ascetic ideal thus "*springs from the protective and healing instincts of a degenerating life*" (III, SEC. 13 / 2006a, 88). Last human beings and their servant moralities become apologists for these priests and their ascetic ideals, and they reason that one who reflects in a monastery has ostensibly figured out the meaning of life since they dared to live in renunciation and self-denial for their gods, for all else is material and transitory. For Nietzsche, the consummate materialist, such an act is life negating, and arguably even based on the abandonment of the flock that so underpinned the success of the priestly aristocracy. Cast adrift but remaining afloat, last human beings and their servant moralities regurgitate whatever iterations of religious doctrine exist to deaden or justify their collective suffering. For Nietzsche, this is but a reflection of the state of last human beings: to be part of a herd. Not surprisingly, Nietzsche was scathing in his retort, exclaiming: "But enough! enough! I can't bear it any longer. Bad air! Bad air! This workshop where *ideals are fabricated*—it seems to me just to stink of lies" (I, SEC. 14 / 2006a, 28).

For Nietzsche, in the age of philosophers before the rise of the priestly aristocracy the ascetic ideal was healthy when enacted by free-spirited thinkers. They were able to, with such an ideal, make visible "many bridges to *independence* that no philosopher can refrain from inwardly rejoicing . . . on hearing the story of all those who, one fine day, decided to say 'no' to any curtailment of their liberty, and go off into the *desert*" (Nietzsche III, SEC. 7 / 2006a, 77). Nietzsche argues that the lives of self-actualized, optimized, and productive spirits have historically and consistently exhibited such a tendency, a state of being later appropriated by the priests who are hardly the inventive and free spirits that Nietzsche so idealized. The ascetic ideal thus regressed from its capacity to nurture the free-spirited genius, to where in a nihilistic modernity it nurtures, instead, defeatist and life-negating sentiments for its religious adherents. Nietzsche highlights the consequences of such defeatist orientations where adherents are still sick from the "after-effects of these priestly quack-cures" that include rigid scripts moralizing about the merits of chastity, what types of food one should include in their diet, and techniques for fasting—processes that are all "antagonistic" toward our senses (I, SEC. 6 / 2006a, 16). As such, Nietzsche spares not the life negating ascetic from criticism, accusing such a person of reproducing *ressentiment* as a means to compensate for a life with "unfulfilled instinct and power" (III, SEC. 11 / 2006a, 86). As a result, these ascetic individuals "wants to be master, not over something in life, but over life itself" (Nietzsche III, SEC. 11 / 2006a, 86). Ensuring that such an undertaking is not threatened by someone with a potentially more emancipatory narrative, the ascetic individual will attempt to use their power to suffocate new sources of the power, while defeatist sentiments are sought after and found in: "failure, decay, pain, misfortune, ugliness, voluntary deprivation, destruction of selfhood, self-flagellation and self-sacrifice. This is all paradoxical in the extreme," according to Nietzsche (III, SEC. 11 / 2006a, 86).

The frustrations felt by Nietzsche over priestly aristocratic practices that will into existence the fantasy of deity is tempered by his advocacy of how one's will to power is also a deified will to power. Nietzsche may have even become an apologist for our priestly aristocrats, for he proclaims that "a will *to nothingness*, an aversion to life, a rebellion against the most fundamental prerequisites of life" nonetheless "remains a *will*! . . . Man still prefers to *will nothingness*, than *not* will" (III, SEC. 28 / 2006a, 120). But clearly, pride of place is still given to the free-spirited philosopher who serves no faith. Such a status allows the "philosopher smiles because he sees an optimum condition of the highest and boldest intellectuality"; moreover, such an individual "does not deny 'existence' . . . but rather affirms *his* existence and *only* his existence" (Nietzsche III, SEC. 7 / 2006a, 77). Thus, with the quarantining effects of a priestly ascetic ideal, it is no wonder that Nietzsche accorded the free-spirited philosopher's ascetic ideal greater reverence, if only for the fact that it frees the philosopher from torture by religious scripts that enthrall with magic and a pantheon of superheroes in the sky, a torture that is uncritically internalized by last human beings.

It is important to note that for Nietzsche, modern culture and its institutions that rely on political ideologies such as democratism and other ideological *isms* will also generate *ressentiment*. Nietzsche views such cultures with disdain. Nietzsche's notion of *ressentiment* is prescient for framing those today who build their identities around being persecuted while expressing their *ressentiment* through identity politics. In the era under discussion by Nietzsche, the defeatist attributes of last humans, once immoral, have now become moralized as priests and uncritical charismatic leaders find succor through their captive audience, the religious faithful, or political activists. Religious and political moralities for Nietzsche are but a prejudicial yet reified interpretation of life that *dis*empower and enervate their adherents over time. A proponent of tough love, Nietzsche's elegiac observation about how in a more empowered past people "were as ashamed of mildness as people are now ashamed of hardness" deserves serious reflection (III, SEC. 9 / 2006a, 82).

Not explicitly articulated in *Genealogy* but taken for granted beyond the already explicated failures of Christianity and religions as a whole, failure of their priestly aristocracies, and failure of democracy and socialism, Nietzsche's assertions can be seen as highlighting the conditions in modernity for the emergence of nihilism. How the dysfunctions of democracy and the state apparatus enable nihilism at the secular realm, then, will need to be considered in the context of those who desire to prevail by creating new meaning, new values, and new moralities. In *Genealogy*, the life force that is the will to power—conceptualized as that deep and powerful instinct for freedom and sovereignty—is argued to be the mechanism. Most importantly for our work that examines how the self overcomes systemic decadence due to authoritarian and totalitarian tendencies of democracy, and how this robs people of their experience with the meaning of freedom, Hollingdale notes how Nietzsche's ability to link the concept of the will to power with our need to "establish a 'meaning' for life is . . . significant, for just as life is will to power, so the 'meaning' of life is the feeling that the will to power is operative" (1999, 183). And what about the outcome if active nihilists fail in their mission, yielding ground to passive nihilists? Hollingdale provides a penetrating insight that can inform us about, of all things, the notion of failed states since "an individual, a nation, a civilization deprived of positive goals destroys itself by willing the last thing left in its power to will—its own destruction; and it will will this rather than *not* will" (Hollingdale 1999, 184).

> Nietzsche now gained the authority to distinguish between different victorious moralities: that a certain morality had established itself did not imply it was . . . for the enhancement of power—it might be a nihilistic morality, and its triumph the triumph of a will to nothingness. He therefore began to speak of "life-enhancing" or "ascending" and "life-denying" or "declining" morality, and he was able to condemn the latter without self-contradiction. (Hollingdale 1999, 184)

One can only imagine how much more philosophy Nietzsche could have composed had he not suffered his mental collapse in 1889. In the next chapter, we examine his last remaining works exhibiting sociological imaginations, works that constitute the "1888 texts."

NOTES

1. Nietzsche exhibits some ill-humor about the undesirable consequences of accepting eternal recurrence, noting in *Ecce Homo* that his only objection for such a cyclicity is that he would be forced to deal with his mother and sister for perpetuity, a "truly *abysmal* thought" (2005, 78).

2. That said, Nietzsche (I, SEC. 18 / 2001, 42) was realistic about the notion of equality in that although he believes in the "doctrine of human equality," its presence in real lived experiences is simply untenable, a position he would again revisit in *Zarathustra*.

3. A useful way of envisioning this outcome is to realize that many exceptionally brilliant people offer their services to the political machinery and military industrial complex of their day, spheres seeking geopolitical empowerment for their states through the mechanism of conflict.

4. Nietzsche employs the French variant of resentment, or *ressentiment*.

5. By the time the *Anti-Christ* was released two years later, Nietzsche again revisits the merits of Christianity and Buddhism, exhibiting noticeably greater charitability toward the latter.

6. In case it may not have already been obvious, Nietzsche's view of the ascetic ideal is in contrast to Max Weber's view of the Calvinists and their innovativeness as described in *The Protestant Ethic and the Spirit of Capitalism*. That said, Max Weber was an admirer of Nietzsche according to his nephew Eduard Baumgarten, who noted that in February 1920, a few weeks before his death, Max Weber took part in a discussion in which he said to students accompanying him: "The honesty of a present-day scholar, and above all a present-day philosopher, can be measured by his attitude to Nietzsche and Marx. Whoever does not admit that considerable parts of his own work could not have been carried out in the absence of the work of these two, only fools himself and others. The world in which we spiritually and intellectually live today is a world substantially shaped by Marx and Nietzsche" (cited in Solms-Laubach 2007, 79).

Chapter Five

Nietzsche's Sociological Imaginations
The 1888 Texts

The next major works of Nietzsche that exhibit his sociological imaginations were undertaken the year before his January 1889 mental collapse in Turin, Italy. In this period, Nietzsche completed the "1888 texts" that constituted his final set of works. The relatively short texts that are most sociological are *Twilight of the Idols*, *The Anti-Christ*, and *Ecce Homo* (the last of which was completed in 1888 but published posthumously in 1908). Because we have already employed *Ecce Homo* throughout our text as an instrument that makes operative Nietzsche's views in hindsight, it will not be discussed as its own publication in this chapter. Moreover, works such as *The Case of Wagner*, *Nietzsche contra Wagner*, and a collection of poems, *Dionysian Dithyrambs*, along with his frequently overlooked choral and orchestral composition *Hymn to Life* will similarly not be given any sociological treatment.

TWILIGHT OF THE IDOLS, OR,
HOW TO PHILOSOPHIZE WITH
A HAMMER (1888/1997A AND 2005)

Kaufmann argues that Nietzsche readers reflecting on his legacy discern a "tough" Nietzsche who was a prophet of "great wars and power politics" (1950, 412), while the forgiving "tender" Nietzscheans value his penetrating insights into the state, the new totalitarian "idol" in the wake of the death of god. Yet, infrequent mention is made about the significance of the mental collapse in Turin as indicator that Nietzsche's bark is far worse than his bite. Sokol claims that Nietzsche's 1889 mental collapse in Turin, Italy, was Nietzsche's final disenchantment with the world, noting sympathetically that this is evidence not of Nietzsche failing to find truth, "but of his sincerity, and

119

even of his love for humanity" (Bergmann et al. 2007, 41). For a philosopher
who critiques compassion and pity, with the latter attribute again bearing his
scorn in *Twilight of the Idols, or, How to Philosophize with a Hammer,* the
embrace Nietzsche exhibited offers an alternative view of the great philosopher as, in the final instance, a deeply caring yet exhausted human being, one
consumed by the demands and consequences of his epic life project not only
for himself but for a new humanity.

Twilight displays Nietzsche's courage in subverting a variety of idols that
people hold dear. *Ecce Homo* clarifies how the term "idols" refers to hitherto
reified and unquestioned truths, and thus *Twilight* conveys arguments and
themes to usher in the end of the "old truth" (2007b, 80). Nietzsche remarked
that *Twilight* was a declaration of war against all sacralized idols of modernity (2005, 155). The modern human condition, for Nietzsche, is littered with
too many idols, and that these idols are constituted by not only idols of our
age, but eternal idols lurking metaphysically as detritus in a bogus conceptualization of the universe (1997a, 4). Additional denouncements are made
against the idols' proselytization of morality and imaginations of utopia, both
of which emphasize and embody the universality of moral truths, respectively. As idols, democratism, socialism, Christianity, Judaism, Hinduism,
rationalism, and altruism are again chastised by Nietzsche since they promote
but cultures of mediocrity and decadence over the best society can offer
through its overcomers. *Twilight* thus reveals Nietzsche engaged in some of
his most intense critiques. The work is described by the editor of *Twilight*,
Tracy Strong, as one that was written to "make it impossible" for us "to live
with idols" (cited in Nietzsche 1997a, x), while Ridley touts it as an exemplar
of Nietzsche's "mature style at its very best" and therefore "this is hard to
square with the suspicion of mental decline" (cited in Nietzsche 2005, viii).

Twilight, Anti-Christ, and *Ecce Homo,* major works from Nietzsche's later
years prior to his mental collapse, have been seen by some as works that point
to his cognitive decline, with *Ecce Homo* often singled out as the most rec-
ognizable example. Ridley disagrees, and points to Nietzsche's *Anti-Christ*
and even *Ecce Homo* being just as resourceful, as coherent, and rich as his
earlier works. Through the three works Ridley argues that Nietzsche desired
to make readers viscerally feel the intensity of the latter's philosophy (cited
in Nietzsche 2005, ix). In the case of *Twilight,* Nietzsche offered his famous
aphorism "What doesn't kill me makes me stronger" to remind people about
the importance of the will to power (1997a, 6). He also continues his criticism of Christianity and how it disempowers, is life negating, and offers an
illusory morality. As a prelude in *Twilight* of what is forthcoming, Nietzsche
comments how morality, in practice, is simply uncritical condemnation upon
matters and consequences that concern life and living, an egregious situation

against which we must transcend. Moreover, Nietzsche wants us to clearly understand that such an error is committed by adherents who, due to their reification of conventional moralities, have caused much damage toward the development of individual agency and will.

More important for this work is Nietzsche's conceptualization of freedom. As we began our journey by first introducing the overcomer in chapter 1, it behooves us to note that it is arguably in *Twilight* that freedom receives its most creative and intense exposition: Nietzsche argues that freedom can only be experienced and comprehended by how one confronts a variety of struggles. Freedom can be secured in this manner when one confronts a powerful foe or experiences what appears to be an insurmountable life problem, a *worthy* process that will ultimately resolve issues. Our overcomer, the tragic artist, thus wills and purposes their victories in ways that can be glorified, for the heroic individual is always formed on the anvil of tragedy.

For Nietzsche, those who lack freedom are those who lack the mental constitution to confront people, ideas and norms, or institutions that hold power over them. Consequently, institutions that shape public opinion such as academia and the courts are able to reproduce *ressentiment* for such unempowered last human beings. Nietzsche's main concern regarding a lack of freedom is that it allows defeatists and conformists to surface, adding to the ugliness of life, dynamics that point to social decay. For Nietzsche, such characters surface whenever oppression is normalized and reified. Lacking freedom, those who seek it run toward social systems and therefore capitulate to their institutional demands for the sake of receiving guidance. Such a process is for Nietzsche tantamount to the degeneration of life.[1] Nietzsche thus critiques democracy and freedom in *Twilight* for not being able to offer a more authentic emancipation beyond highly rationalized institutions of modernity, blaming it for the state's debilitation and atrophy.

It is not surprising for Nietzsche to segue his focus on personal freedom toward institutions that deny it. In his scathing critique, Nietzsche's sociological imagination reveals again his consistent view that modern institutions and their ideological *isms* are in a degenerative state and are thus stifling the agency of individuals. Nietzsche believed that personal freedoms and democratic institutions are antipodes in a degenerate modernity since the latter require captive audiences that can be made to conform. The prescience of this assertion is rather impressive, and because it displays a rare case where a problem is operationalized and a response is prescribed in short order, it is important to quote the passage in length. In the aphorism titled "My concept of freedom," Nietzsche writes:

Liberal institutions stop being liberal as soon as they have been established: from that point forward, there is nothing that harms freedom more severely and fundamentally than liberal institutions. After all, we know what they bring about: they undermine the will to power, they are the leveling of mountain and valley elevated into a morality, they make people small, cowardly, and pleasure-loving—. . . . Liberalism: in other words, *herd animalization*. . . . For what is freedom? Having the will to responsibility for oneself. . . . Becoming indifferent to trouble, hardships, deprivation, even to life. (1997a, 74)

Because the will to power exemplifies the overcomer who can respond to any life struggle, relying on dysfunctional democratic institutions to define what freedom means is absurd for Nietzsche. All democracy is good for, according to Nietzsche, is its transformation of individuals into a population of conformists indoctrinated to experience freedom in a very scripted and vulgarized sense. The vulgarized personal freedoms under democracy and the free market encourage people to live too quickly and too irresponsibly in only the present for the sake of immediate gratification, and "this is exactly what one calls 'freedom'" (Nietzsche 1997a, 76). Nietzsche's view of socialism as degenerate exhibits parallel sentiments. In a short aphorism in *Twilight* titled "The Labour Question," Nietzsche is frustrated that laborers' instincts to excel are not appreciated, and that their attempts to find their form and purpose, their attempts to still maintain the dignity of being themselves, have been irresponsibly obliterated by operators and proponents, the last humans, of modernity. Although the new workers of the industrialized age are allowed to join the military and given the right to organize and vote, the forces that drive their actions are based on a desperate existence that is expressed morally whenever injustices arise, but not as a desire to overcome. Instead, their formula for liberation through class struggle expresses for Nietzsche a *ressentiment* that Marx frames as righteous and historically imminent. For Nietzsche, workers of capitalist democracies and their Marxist "class consciousness" are exhibiting deference to yet another regulatory script, this time to counter the free market, or, under more desirable conditions, to repress impulses so that they can be "committed to hard work" and remain "disciplined and rationalistic" during employment (Calhoun et al. 2012, 5). Indeed, Frankfurt School theorists such as Erich Fromm and Herbert Marcuse incisively highlight another shift in the twentieth century where capitalist discipline of workers transitioned toward transforming members of the public into incessant consumers. On this matter, Nietzsche appears resigned, noting that "the hope is now completely gone that a modest and self-sufficient sort of human being, a Chinese type, could build itself up into a class here: and this would have been rational, it would virtually have been a necessity" (1997a, 77).

Nietzsche implores us to fight for freedom beyond these decaying political and ideological forms. The will to power needs to be harnessed in this endeavor. Nietzsche emphatically advises us that one must always be empowered to become, and tells us to "understand freedom precisely in the sense in which I understand the word freedom: as something that one has and *does not* have, that one *wills* to have, that one *conquers*" (1997a, 75). The urgency Nietzsche exhibits stems from his concerns about those he deemed as "improvers of humanity" who will employ their institutions to render an audience captive and readied for their transformation into conformists, only to have such conformists do the bidding of the institutions that underscore moralities not authored by them. According to Münz, the authoring of other people's morality sets into motion the deification and reification of the improvers of humanity, even if the processes occur outside of conventionally understood religious environments (Bergmann et al. 2007). Not surprisingly, Nietzsche emphatically proclaims that no moral fact or truth exists and that all moralities from religions have one major recurring commonality: to believe in fantasy. For Nietzsche, morality is nothing more than "sign language, just a symptomatology: you already have to know *what* it's all about in order to get any use out of it" (1997a, 38).[2] Nietzsche thus held that systemically imposed morality, because it is incontrovertibly a social construction, goes against our true nature. In the *Twilight* section titled "Morality as Anti-Nature," Nietzsche condemns the institution of Christianity and the "morality" its adherents are subjected to by its improvers of humanity: "The Church fights passion by cutting it out, in every sense; its practice, its 'therapy' is *castration*. It never asks, 'How does one spiritualize, beautify, deify a desire?' . . .—But ripping out the passions by the root means ripping out life by the root; the practice of the Church is *an enemy to life*" (1997a, 25). Nietzsche's critique continues when he offers another example of the anti-natural component of Christianity by citing Matthew 5:29, where one is instructed that "if your eye offends you, pluck it out" (1997a, 25).[3] He snidely conveys his relief when "fortunately, no Christian acts according to this prescription" and offers a comforting, if not derisive analogy in that "we no longer admire dentists who *pull out* teeth so that they won't hurt anymore" (Nietzsche 1997a, 25).

Nietzsche did not spare Hinduism either, showing much sympathy for the Chandalas, otherwise known as the untouchables, members of the lowest caste in Hindu cosmology. Again, the theme that religion can be a weakening agent through, ironically, its improvers of humanity, can be seen through the life negation and the suppression of instincts experienced by the Chandalas. In this context, Nietzsche highlights the rigid protocol that all Chandalas must follow, such as adhering to a particular diet, where to acquire water, how one attends to laundry, as well as how upper-caste women are not permitted to assist Chandala women during childbirth. Nietzsche condemns such actions and argues that the human condition need not be exposed to such insensibilities and practices, all of which are designed to express socially constructed and elaborate scripts to uphold morality.

Religiously inspired improvers of humanity sloganeer the merits of the "true world" beyond this life to inspire its adherents to focus on the after-life rather than their current, corporeal, materialistic existence as "true." For Nietzsche, this true world vis-à-vis the materialistic corporeal world is just another fabrication—a *"moral-optical* illusion" (1997a, 21) and fan-tasy—dispensed by religion's improvers of humanity. In this regard, Marx's claim of how religion functions as the opium of the masses finds its analog in Nietzsche's condemnation of the true world, one that adds tremendous distortions to understanding life and living since adherents have established a true world that exists in opposition to the actual world. These improvers of humanity, with their good intentions that, in essence, will lead one to ruin, require prejudice and discrimination to make operative their metaphysical views as they set into motion the fabrication of a world beyond the current one, setting into motion *ressentiment* dynamics that include slander, trivial-ization, and overall dismissiveness toward affirming life (Nietzsche 1997a, 21). Such distortions betray how religiosity is in a decadent state, one indica-tive of a symptom of life in the ignoble process of decline.

Nietzsche offers penetrating insights about such improvers of humanity as they engage in the process of domesticating the human being, a process not unlike that of breeding a certain species of animal. Employing the zoo as metaphor for society, Nietzsche argues that were one to examine animals domesticated in zoos one clearly sees that they have been weakened by pain, injury, and hunger, as well as the depressive effect of fear. Nietzsche derives from this analogy the same outcomes that have befallen those noble Teuton knights of the Middle Ages when priests indoctrinated them into morality for the sake of improving the elite martial order. However, Nietzsche scathingly observes that after being subjected to such practices by soul doctors, the once proud Teuton had been reduced into a "caricature of a human being, like an abortion" (1997a, 39). For Nietzsche, the once brave and noble Teuton had turned into a sinner who was then locked in a moral cage and imprisoned with horrific concepts of existence. The Teuton in such a situation became "sick, wretched, with ill will towards himself; full of hate against the impulses to live, full of distrust for everything that was still strong. . . . The Church under-stood that: it *corrupted* human beings, it weakened them—but it claimed to have 'improved' them" (1997a, 39). Not surprisingly, Nietzsche emphatically sums up the entirety of historical efforts by improvers of humanity to save humankind as a thoroughly immoral process.

What can a people do to thwart the improvers of humanity's efforts at inserting dogmatism, absolutism, the desire to control, and the enabling of *ressentiment* upon the people? For Nietzsche, overcomers must engage in a revaluation of all values, defined in *Ecce Homo* as the process of freeing the self from all morality so that we can affirm life by "placing trust in everything that has hitherto been forbidden, despised, condemned" (2007b, 61–62). In *Twilight* Nietzsche begins his employment of the concept and continues to apply it in *Anti-Christ* and *Ecce Homo*. For English novelist Will Self in the BBC documentary on Nietzsche, *Human, All Too Human*, Nietzsche's revaluation of values is essentially a process whereby a "systematized destruction of systems" takes place, one that entails the absolute questioning and disposal of all scripts imposed upon the self by mainstream institutions that cater to the herd (Chu, Morgan, and Wardle 1999). Its significance in *Twilight*, however, lies in how the revaluation process is envisioned: to question and if need be discard all values, demands, and instructions of society, a process that can delink the actor from a past faith and from modernity's idols manifested in the state, its utopianisms, and its politicized improvers of humanity. Nietzsche felt Christianity and later modernity corrupted morality through their own revaluation of values that, unfortunately, birthed a servant morality: for the former, deference was given to a deity, for the latter, the new and false "idols": the new *isms* of modernity. In this regard, Münz celebrates the continued relevance of Nietzsche: "I think that his attacks on monotheistic religion are still topical. Let us mention the difficulties the world is having with Islam today. And, were not Hitler and Stalin worshipped like gods? People's tendency to worship human gods is still very much alive" (Bergmann et al. 2007, 27–29).

In *Twilight*, Nietzsche continues his central argument that Christian, democratic, and socialist practices reproduce collective defeatism even though the doctrines appear to reject one another. Nietzsche figuratively notes how with a hammer, one can hear their hollow yet heavily oppressive nature. In such a context, the overcomer's raison d'etre is to challenge the idols that force the self into lifelong subservience (Nietzsche 2005, 155). The persons who successfully engage with the revaluation of all values thus become a living, physiological embodiment of their own valuation systems when conducting social relations and attending to the vagaries of life and living (Nietzsche 2005, 177). Such persons philosophize with a hammer of authenticity, are the yes-sayers to eternal recurrence, are the free spirits who embrace their suffering through *amor fati* as they self-author and purpose their existence in all its iterations.

That Nietzsche is revolutionary in a manner that does not advocate violence through class, political, and/or sectarian conflict has not tempered critics such as philosophers like Ofelia Schutte who argued that Nietzsche was unable to transcend his own nihilism because of "destructive tendencies in his thought" (cited in Woolfolk 1985, 86). Schutte, however, overlooked Nietzsche's employment of a dialectical view that unites in symbiosis destruction and creation. In fact, Nietzsche felt that Christianity had dialectical value within which the overcomer can excel beyond its precepts. Nietzsche argues that immoralists and anti-Christians can learn from the church's existence because the church is so frightful of its detractors, and that "in every age, the Church wanted its enemies to be destroyed" (1997a, 26). Proud to be an immoralist, Nietzsche argues that such an ideal type is always life-affirming and does not negate easily, since for overcoming immoralists their dignity, integrity, and honor are defined by always being affirmative toward life in all its permutations. He further argues that immoralists have taught humanity how to salvage all that the "holy craziness of the priest, the *sick* reason in the priest, rejects" (Nietzsche 1997a, 29).

THE ANTI-CHRIST:
A CURSE ON CHRISTIANITY (1888/2005)

Nietzsche's *The Anti-Christ: A Curse on Christianity* arguably projects his most intense antagonism toward Christianity, already set into motion in *Beyond* and *Genealogy*. However, were one to dive into work without considering it as an atavism of *Beyond* and *Genealogy* blind spots on comprehending Nietzsche's philosophy would certainly surface. Such a possibility should be seriously considered if one chooses to read *Anti-Christ* exoterically as warns Clark (2012) or, as emphasized in chapter 2, out of chronological order. Nietzsche's mental collapse was not far away, and while his next major work, *Ecce Homo*, was generally autobiographical, *Anti-Christ* revealed his continuing and visceral disdain of Christianity. However, Ridley emphasizes for readers to discern in *Anti-Christ* a work of someone who considers Christianity "genuinely maddening" and not a work of someone "who is already mad" (cited in Nietzsche 2005, ix).

As alluded to elsewhere, in *Anti-Christ* Nietzsche describes Christianity as a religion of pity and faults Christianity for generating nihilism and sycophancy in its adherents. Nietzsche observes how the enslaved Jews under Roman occupation had to reassemble justifications that validated their suffering, and as such, inverted their religious views to allow for a God that accepted their defeatist doctrines born from frailty, subjugation, and poverty, along with the *ressentiment* that accompanies such a human condition. Jesus rebelled against this ethos, according to Nietzsche—and here it bears mention that although our philosopher hurled vitriol against Christianity and its herd adherents, Jesus was praised as one who embodied overcoming attributes of a free spirit (SEC.

32 / 2005, 29). Because Jesus fashioned his own views and launched a rebellion against the religious system of his day, Judaism, Nietzsche celebrated Jesus as a "holy anarchist" who rebelled against manufactured inequalities such as caste and privilege, and "everything priestly or theologian-like" (SEC. 27 / 2005, 25). For Nietzsche, the greatness of Jesus was in how he launched a rebellion against a Jewish morality that assumed to know what was good and just. Jesus, then, was the only "true" Christian for Nietzsche. Christians, on the other hand, were simply conformists and members of the herd.

What must also be appreciated is that Nietzsche elaborates for his readers how modern social institutions and ideologies are also complicit in embedding defeatist analogs of pity into cultural and political systems that regulate society. In a wonderful discussion between historian Bettany Hughes and philosopher Ken Gemes in the BBC documentary *Genius of the Modern World* (2016), Hughes shares how she was troubled by Nietzsche's view of the disempowered, to which Gemes discerns: "It's not that Nietzsche thought we should step on the weak; what he thought was we shouldn't be obsessed with the weak." Nietzsche's view that communism, socialism, democracy, feminism, and the like are but atavisms of the Judeo-Christian worldview is explained by Gemes: "A lot of communists and socialists might no longer believe in God, but they still have this core Christian value of compassion."

Nietzsche's attacks on pity is often taken out of context in ways that ignore the only condition where Nietzsche felt pity should be condemned, already noted in *Dawn*: pity is not useful if it causes the self unnecessary and unresolved suffering, something religion and modern institutions, however, amplify as a value. Nietzsche further reinforces this position in *Anti-Christ*, adding that pity prevents the actor from attaining heightened awareness and feelings of optimization and vitality because it "has a depressive effect" that causes one to become enfeebled (SEC. 7 / 2005, 6). In a variety of statements that again highlights Nietzsche's criticism of pity, he notes how pity is a vice that has been reproduced by Christianity, a process that enables all forms of failures and weaknesses. He thus reminds readers to not be awestruck by the religion's teachings and pageantry, for it has "waged a *war to the death*" against higher and noble human beings, suppressing their instincts and will to power, constructing them as evil and depraved, and as a result, deployed its pieties to glorify enfeeblement as a new "power" meant to counter a sovereign will to live a strong and self-affirming life (2005, 5). In this regard, Nietzsche scathingly argues that the religion of pity that is Christianity—and by extrapolation the plurality of religions and their relationship to pity—employ pity in a manner that regresses human development. For Nietzsche, religion and its deployment of pity actually preserves things that are in the process of decaying "by keeping alive an abundance of failures of every type" (SEC. 7 / 2005, 6).

Pity, upon its transformation into a virtue under Christianity, followed by the ideological *isms* of modernity, "runs counter to the instincts that preserve and enhance the value of life: by *multiplying* misery just as much as by *conserving* everything miserable" (SEC. 7 / 2005, 7). It is one of the main tools used to amplify decadence, writes Nietzsche. More perniciously, pity also became an expression of faith. Not surprisingly, Nietzsche viewed both expressions of pity, that of virtue and faith, as negations of one's own self-authored affirmation for life: the former, where pity is seen as virtue, denies the life affirmation of the self when pitying causes anguish and suffering; where pity is an expression of faith, it denies life affirmation of the self through prayer that exacts deference and capitulation to a supernatural deity. Nietzsche regards pitying neither as virtue nor faith but an expression of pathology, a state where you turn "a blind eye to yourself . . . so you do not have to stomach the sight of incurable mendacity" (SEC. 9 / 2005, 8). Not surprisingly, Nietzsche also argues that one major consequence of Christian moralizing is that it engenders depression (SEC. 20 / 2005, 17).

Through Christian faith and not Jesus per se, explanations and justifications of existence became grossly distorted. For Nietzsche, Christians failed to understand how Jesus was an overcomer that vanquished "every feeling of *ressentiment*" (SEC. 40 / 2005, 37). Nietzsche argues, however, that Christians could not forgive those complicit in Jesus's death and as such revanchist sentiments surfaced in the community whereby retaliation and judgement "(—and really, what could be less evangelical than 'retaliation,' 'punishment,' 'passing judgment'!)" was called for against the Jews and Romans (SEC. 40 / 2005, 37). In this regard, Nietzsche controversially concludes that Jesus and God are both "products of *ressentiment*" (SEC. 40 / 2005, 37). Perhaps Nietzsche's most scathing rejection of Christianity, morality, and religion can be seen in aphorism 15 of *Anti-Christ* where he elaborates on how Christianity and religiosity exhibit a variety of fantasies such as beliefs in imaginary causes, contact between imaginary beings, an imaginary psychology that manifests as an inability to understand oneself, belief in imaginary entities such as God, spirits, and souls, and perhaps most deleteriously, belief in imaginaries teleologies such as the kingdom of God, eternal life, and so forth. Nietzsche demotes Christianity and its mythos into a lesser category than dreams, for dreams are at least about unresolved *realities* that manifest within rather than being about fictitious acts and beliefs that negate reality itself, generating decadence in the human condition *and* experience.

Although Nietzsche considered all religions to be nihilistic, *Anti-Christ* reveals the philosopher's benevolent orientalism[4] toward Buddhism in spite of his view that both Christianity and Buddhism are decadent religions. Buddhism, for Nietzsche, was significantly different than Christianity in that the former did not impose upon adherents a comforting or punitive deity. Instead, it dared to confront the human condition and its climax, mortality. Nurtured over hundreds of years since Buddha offered his teachings, its key tenet that covetous minds generate an illusory reality resulting in self-inflicted suffering, expressed a brutally honest view of life that was beyond good and evil for Nietzsche. Nietzsche praises such an orientation because by not employing some dramatic morality to declare an epic and apocalyptic battle against sin, Buddhism is able to confront reality for what it is, unlike Christianity (SEC. 20 / 2005, 16). It also had the foresight to define into its equation how ignorance of self is a form of *self*-deception, a process unlike Christianity where ignorance of self is repulsed through the embrace in the fantasy that is God.

Nietzsche also credits Buddha for seeing all people as potentially noble and thus sees "goodness and kindness as healthy" (SEC. 20 / 2005, 17). Most importantly for Nietzsche, Buddha's orientation toward the human condition did not harness revanchism. Nietzsche is impressed by how Buddha's teachings rebuke "revenge, aversion, *ressentiment* (—'enmity will not bring an end to enmity': the moving refrain of all Buddhism . . .)" (SEC. 20 / 2005, 17). Nietzsche saw in Buddhism a philosophy for a more "*mature* people, for kindly, gentle races," a philosophy that leads the people back to "peace and cheerfulness, to a spiritual diet, to a certain physical fortification" (SEC. 22 / 2005, 18–19). In this regard, Nietzsche praises Buddhism because it nurtures a mild temperament and engages in a supreme act of life-affirmation by promoting the "complete *absence* of militarism" (SEC. 21 / 2005, 17). Given the attributes of Buddhism and its practices, Nietzsche honors the philosophy as one ideally designed for the "end and exhaustion of civilization" while Christianity "has not even managed to locate civilization yet" (SEC. 22 / 2005, 18–19). In this sense, Nietzsche argues that Buddhism is a far more valid belief system than Christianity because the former accepts the reality of suffering without question, and in this regard it is a "hundred times colder, truer, more objective" (SEC. 23 / 2005, 19).

It would be too simplistic to view *Anti-Christ* as a work that advocates discontents against religion. Nietzsche, instead, was keen on arguing how modern Western civilization is but an atavism of Christianity's life-negating nihilistic system. The *Anti-Christ*'s ultimate purpose is thus "constructive rather than destructive . . . since in . . . *Genealogy* Nietzsche has informed us that the 'Antichrist' is not just the 'conqueror of God' but represents also 'the great health,' that is to say, the 'redemption of . . . reality'" (Young 2006, 177). This is the main reason why Nietzsche advocates in the Preface of *Anti-Christ* a rejection of all systemic imperatives: because they harm people's potential for the will to power. Nietzsche encourages us to "be used to living on mountains—to seeing the miserable, ephemeral little gossip of politics and national self-interest [as] *beneath* you" (Preface / 2005, 3). The overcomer, the free spirit, the elevated and life-affirming being, must "invent his *own* virtues, his *own* categorial imperatives" for a people will be "destroyed when it confuses its *own* duty with the concept of duty in general" (Nietzsche SEC. 11 / 2005, 10). Such sentiments are again emphasized by Nietzsche as he condemned the German nation in his revisit of the revaluation of all values, a concept with which he ends *Anti-Christ.*

Although the conflation that includes a critique against the German nation and its philosophy appears disjuncted given that so much of *Anti-Christ* continues its campaign against Christianity, Nietzsche's justification of such a conflation is insightful, for the German Protestant minister is but the "grandfather of German philosophy" (SEC. 10 / 2005, 9). One senses the link Nietzsche *almost* made in *Anti-Christ*: that the German culture of his day, sacralized through nationalism, revived the nation by enabling *ressentiment* to generate new political enemies through the illusory essentialisms of the "other." Already a nation rendered disingenuous by the cultural philistines singled out in *Meditations*, Nietzsche further laments how German nationalism had appropriated *ressentiment* through their regulation of educational institutions. Headed by German partisans that Nietzsche considers to be deceivers, he calls out their hubris:

> German historical scholarship, for instance, is convinced that Rome was a despotism, that the inhabitants of Germania brought the spirit of freedom into the world. . . . Is it any wonder that all partisans, even German historians, instinctively go around with great moral words in their mouths . . . ? (SEC. 55 / 2005, 55)

From the onset of Christianity to the German culture and nationalism of his day, Nietzsche thus cries for the revaluation of all Christian/German values. He calls for us to use all means possible to promote "*opposite* values" so that "*noble* values" can triumph (SEC. 61 / 2005, 64). Nietzsche thus cheers us onward to become great immoralists as Christianity, culture, ideologies, and the state, and ultimately meaning, continue their inevitable decay in modern society. In the next chapter, we thus focus more exclusively on yet another atavism of systemic decay, democratism, as a false yet reified idol.

On January 3, 1889, Nietzsche experienced a mental collapse in Turin, Italy, upon seeing a horse being whipped by its driver. There are slight variations in the accounts, however, for Nietzsche "may have fallen first or he embraced it [the horse] and then fell himself, briefly losing consciousness" (Chamberlain 1996, 208). Rushing toward the horse in distress, Nietzsche chose in his final moments of sanity, with whatever residual lucidity he had left, to express his compassion and humanitarianism. Hollingdale recounts how "with a cry he flung himself across the square and threw his arms about the animal's neck. Then he lost consciousness and slid to the ground, still clasping the tormented horse" (1999, 237). By now a popular figure in Turin, "A crowd gathered, and his landlord, attracted to the scene, recognized his lodger and had him carried back to his room. For a long time he lay unconscious. When he awoke he was no longer himself: at first he sang and shouted and thumped the piano . . . then he quieted down" (Hollingdale 1999, 237).[5]

NOTES

1. Compare to how Frankfurt School's Erich Fromm (a school from which Jürgen Habermas owes his scholarship) envisions the same topic in his classic *Escape from Freedom* (1969) in which freedom is understood as a context where one freely makes important decisions for living, a *stressor* that forces many to "escape" the demand for a responsible use of freedoms.

2. Solms-Laubach notes the popularity of Nietzsche in postmodern circles because of this view, and how with postmodern sociology, "Nietzsche's reputation is on the rise. Foucault's work, too, and that of deconstructionists like Derrida and de Man have also served to amplify his iconoclastic voice" (2007, 11).

3. Nietzsche was charitable in citing but one phrase in Matthew 5:29. In fact, Matthew 5:29 and 5:30 forwards even more bizarre solutions for the faithful such as "It is better for you to lose one part of your body than for your whole body to be thrown into hell" (Matthew 5:29). In Matthew 5:30, it continues: "And if your right hand causes you to stumble, cut it off and throw it away. It is better for you to lose one part of your body than for your whole body to go into hell" (*Biblegateway.com*).

4. Nietzsche criticizes Christianity as a religion that suppresses human instincts, of which the desire to procreate is part and parcel. Yet Nietzsche exhibited a glaring blind spot in his assessment since the enforcement of chastity upon priests has an explicit parallel in Buddhism. Buddhist monks and nuns in monastic communities, known as the *sangha*, live in chastity. This oversight is excusable, of course, since Nietzsche had never visited Buddhist cultures in Asia and derived his knowledge only from his pedantry.

5. Many casual readers of Nietzsche are unaware of his acumen as a composer. Along with *Hymn to Life*, Nietzsche also composed many piano pieces. These compositions are surprisingly accessible online and are still being performed today by choirs and orchestral musicians. In fact, Nietzsche had begun composing at the age of 14 and later befriended composer Franz Liszt. His celebrated friendship with Richard Wagner would end on a sour note, however, as Nietzsche further developed his line of thinking, one that clashed with the growing anti-Semitism and nationalism of Wagner.

Chapter Six

Nietzsche's Sociological Imagination of Motley Cow

In *Twilight*, Nietzsche offers a critical view of society that informs his assessment of the state in its modern phase. Whereas the first pre-Socratic Greek state ideal praised by Nietzsche ultimately collapsed, only to have new states informed by modernist utopianisms degenerate, one could extrapolate that had Nietzsche remained alive until a much later age he would have witnessed modern dynamics that would have furthered his elaborations on how democratic states decay. Nietzsche almost takes readers to this extrapolation in *Twilight*, although understandably an explicit sociological elaboration about the flaws of democracy is lacking. Nonetheless, the decadence of modernity Nietzsche describes in *Twilight* renders the epoch a mess, a Motley Cow writ large, for our social, cultural, and political institutions have failed society. Yet ever the thinker that emphasizes the merits of being accountable and responsible to the self, Nietzsche argues that societies' institutional failures are of our own making, and after we lose "all the instincts from which institutions grow" we would thus be able to discard them because they no longer enhance our new self-authored and purposed sovereignty (1997a, 75).

Nietzsche saw the coming legitimation crises of modernity and dared to call out dysfunctional institutions that have contributed to them. The main goal of this chapter, then, is to highlight across Nietzsche's published works his critique of the state and democratism, and by implication political articulations emanating from other institutions or social systems of modernity. We will also examine in more detail Nietzsche's views of how mass conformists, or what he pejoratively refers to as the herd, perform their roles for their institutions. Presenting more discussions on such conformists allows us to appreciate the uncanny parallel between Nietzsche's view that people killed god and the view that it is not the fault of institutions for enabling modern decadence but "it's *ours*" (1997a, 75). To fully appreciate the critical sociological imagination exhibited by Nietzsche, I discuss his theoretical cues by assembling concepts from across his works to read democracy's systemic crisis. Such an undertaking requires us in the later parts of this chapter to consider Jürgen Habermas's thesis that the democratic lifeworld is colonized. It is hoped that such an amalgamation will make visible details that are indicative of the decadent modernity Nietzsche saw as leading to societal dysfunctions.

At this stage of our discussion, it is rather clear that Nietzsche views the vast majority of social institutions and systems as weakening agents upon the actor. To ensure these weakening and constraining forces are able to maintain control upon the freedoms available for the self, the notions of custom, tradition, and morality are configured through scripts and repetition—with the blessings of the state—to exact deference and sycophancy. The last human beings, then, are those who uncritically, and with what Nietzsche views as misplaced enthusiasm, concede to these demands. Last human beings are thus the followers, the conformists, the unempowered, the mediocre person who uncritically follows scripts, be they devout Christians with their *ressentiment* or the cultural philistines of modernity, that is, the poseurs who keep up appearances of knowledge and cultured learning. Vulgarizing culture into an aesthetic of words, gestures, decorations, displays, and occasions, Nietzsche observes in *Meditations* how cultural philistines feel the need to adorn themselves with the arts (III, SEC. 6 / 1997b, 166), while sacrificing their freedom for the comfort and safety of cultural validations by other cultural philistines.

With freedom of an empowered spirit serving as one of Nietzsche's most important themes, it is hardly surprising that in *Twilight* he engages in a scathing assessment of institutions since they are seen to undermine our will to power and render us automatons. Whereas the pre-Socratic Greek state was considered ideal by Nietzsche, expressions of community and society have since become decadent. That is, with the decline of Christianity, followed by utopian proclamations of modernist political ideologies that are meant to replace old false idols with new alternatives, a captive audience will still need to be corralled for legitimizing the new utopianisms. Nietzsche argues, however, that were one to observe the history of such utopianisms, brimming with cultural and political scripts meted out by their rational-legal systems, one would see that they act as constraining forces upon social interaction and social life, stifling the emergence within and without the lifeworld of the free-spirited individual with self-mastery, the overcomer. Nietzsche emphasizes in *Meditations* that when powerful societies, governments, and their institutions are tyrannical, the noble power of a free-thinking and free-spirited philosopher will be considered an existential threat to the staying power of social systems. Those among us are rather aware of how this prescient observation frames some of history's more charismatic leaders, leaders that dared to buck the trend. Understandably, such individuals and their philosophy can offer "asylum to a man into which no tyranny can force its way" and this "annoys the tyrants" (Nietzsche III, SEC. 3 / 1997b, 139). Nietzsche, then, was urgently advocating for the emergence of actors with self-authored philosophies and a healthy dose of subversion, one who seeks to discharge the self's power by emerging from a metaphorical cave with profundities that are epiphanic, explosive, and powerful.

Weakened by millennia where Christianity and other religions indoctrinated values and norms that required subservience, Nietzsche sees modernity's manufacture of new institutions exhibiting parallel demands. Therefore, the institutions of modernity are, for Nietzsche, complicit in enabling a human condition that is still defined by its accommodation of collective dependency toward social systems, a process that continues to erode prospects of self-authorship and renewal by the individual. Modernity and its *isms* are thus no better than religious institutions from yesteryear. Notions of progress still demand from their adherents deference to macro-level institutions, not unlike how the Christian era or other religious epochs required deference to its supernatural systems. Young (2006) thus observes how for Nietzsche democratism, socialism, feminism, and anarchism express these destructive values. Yet Nietzsche even observed that one redeeming quality of religiosity is that it can give some people the experiences of an elevated self that expresses a more noble purpose for humanity. Such a noble mindset "is what democratic sensibilities work against, and this opposition is the ground for Nietzsche's criticism of these sensibilities" (Clark 2015, 183). Thus, for Nietzsche, the church and an ostensibly secular modernity are both inferior responses to the human condition, since both indoctrinate people to live through servant moralities, the antipode to actors who are noble, self-affirming, and able to purpose their own existence. Servant moralities, then, create value "only derivatively—by reacting against, negating, the values of the nobles" (Young 2006, 123).

The isomorphic manifestation of decadence in modernity surfaces when citizens fetishize, for example, democracy, capitalism, and socialism, a process that mimics the defeatist orientations of religious adherents. State institutions of modernity, regardless of what *isms* are promoted, thus seek out sycophants and last human beings who will validate the embeddedness of state institutions and how they engage in cultural production. In such a context, the modern state has relegated the worship of god to the periphery yet demands the same types of concessions from citizens within the state: the state must be primordialized, sacralized, and glorified, a process that lays the foundation for an incipient and sacralized nationalism. Nietzsche had issues with capitalism as well, namely its corporatist power over the state. In *Human*, Nietzsche opines how such a relationship, and in a manner that

presciently adheres his themes to Habermas's thesis on lifeworld colonization, enables corporate entities to appropriate the business and economic
dynamics of the state. Whatever residual dynamics in the social contract
between state and self soon transitions toward becoming a contract between
a corporatocracy and self, with the state relegated to being the cheerleader of
the former, enabling its private contractors to launch its benevolent or hostile
takeover of what were once the priorities and raison d'etre of government. In
this context, the disregard for the degeneration of the state and the "liberation of the private person"—not the individual—is therefore the consequence
of democratism practiced by modernist states, as notes Nietzsche in *Human*
(Vol. 1, VIII, SEC. 472 / 1996, 172). Nietzsche was justifiably skeptical of
modern secular culture and its economics when seen in the contexts of such
corporatocracies. Nietzsche argues in *Meditations* that for the above process
to reach fruition, the machinations and avarice of profit-seekers require cultural validation, but on the condition that its improvers of humanity are able
to manufacture consent and values of *gesellschaft* for the general population
(III, SEC. 6 / 1997b, 164). As such, Young (2006) is correct to conclude that
Nietzsche's modernity is defined by an undignified work culture:

> We live harried, harassed, high-speed lives—which means that we view life
> "as from a railway carriage." There is no time for contemplation, a fact which
> breeds conformism since no time is available to contemplate alternatives to the
> status quo. (Well-known trick for manipulating meetings: pack the agenda so
> full that pressure of time kills dissent.) Another reason for the conformist char-
> acter of modernity is that it is a machine culture: alternatively put, a "big city"
> culture. (2006, 61)

Social institutions of modernity, because they echo the regulatory nature of
religious systems, similarly employ their version of the true world, albeit with
secular and/or revolutionary trajectories. Whether we are here speaking of
religious adherents, their soul doctors, or historical materialists like Marxists,
socialists, and capitalists, our improvers of humanity proselytize through their
rabble how increasing prosperity through faith, syndicalism, or the free market reliance on supply and demand, respectively, leads to some sort of utopia.
Whereas in religion the true world is developed over time, a liquefying, high-
speed modernity has enabled its own secular utopias to quickly flow through
the modern state, its institutions, and ideologies. These modern institutions
are seen to offer the self alternative truths, albeit mercurial, for happiness:
wealth and social status. Yet Nietzsche criticizes such outputs of modernity
in *Ecce Homo*, bemoaning how iterations of the hereafter and the true world
are constructions conjured to "devalue the *only* world there is" (2007b, 95).
Nietzsche, then, was not impressed by the legacy of the Enlightenment in

his modernity for the formation of great, noble-minded human beings was already written out of modern culture's raison d'etre, a process that can be seen to accelerate as modernity liquifies.

For citizens to become a captive audience of such a true world, improvers of humanity celebrate the merits of their respective systems to uphold the status quo and to quell resistance and subversion against their tenets. Nietzsche warns in *Human*, however, that if improvers of humanity are not held accountable for their promises of utopia, corruption will arise and flourish "like a fungus" (Vol. 1, VIII, SEC. 468 / 1996, 170). For Nietzsche, last humans in such contexts, the unempowered followers, conformists, and improvers of humanity rendered decadent by secular institutions, forget that those with money and power can and do "transform any opinion into public opinion" (Vol. 1, VIII, SEC. 447 / 1996, 164). Nietzsche also warns of manipulative improvers of humanity who are aware that "most people are weak in small matters," and how leaders from such a group will try to attain goals through them (Vol. 1, VIII, SEC. 447 / 1996, 164). Exacerbating the modern human condition is how in both religious and secular contexts conformity and dependency upon social institutions are aggressively demanded. Over a long chronology, reification toward such institutions occurs and the general population no longer questions the scripts and truths emanating from social institutions approved by the state. In this regard, religious and modern eras offer only life negation in their worldviews, constructed by an inversion of their defeatist attitudes into dignified ideals without eliminating *ressentiment*. For Nietzsche, humanity has not advanced in this regard.

That we can see a continuity in how social institutions or systems in religious and secular contexts operate allows us to appreciate why Nietzsche's concept of the eternal recurrence is so valuable: it reminds overcomers to commit themselves repeatedly to life affirmation and life struggle for perpetuity. The story of struggle exhibits a cyclicity for Nietzsche: the pre-Socratic Greek state met its demise, Christian theocratic cultures met their demise, while modernity and its *isms* are experiencing systemic crises of their own manufacturing. The emergence of a super-human being able to overcome life's rabble and *ressentiment* requires courage, an *amor fati* to love, accept, and continuously overcome such scenarios. This is, in essence, the emancipatory project and obligation of becoming and being an overcomer.

State institutions of modernity are, for Nietzsche, not much more distinct than religious institutions of yesteryear insofar as what the former demands from its adherents. In the *Zarathustra* section titled "On the New Idol," Nietzsche warns that the modern state is a dishonest entity because of its sloganeering of notions such as the state and people are one. Certainly aware of the colonial and imperialist projects of his time, Nietzsche further notes of the state that "whatever it has, it has stolen" (2006b, 34). Nietzsche also criticizes states for being parasitic in more ways than one when they engage in life negation through their modernist projects. He argues that states appropriate the works and ideas of inventors, they spew out spin through journalism in ways that admonish everything within and without society, and they enrich their own coffers at the expense of those they claim to serve. Nietzsche then adds how the adherents of such an idol, or all idols for that matter, need to break out of their constraints, to "leap into the open," so as to distance themselves from the "idol worship of the superfluous!" (2006b, 36). Such sentiments can be seen to stem from the philosopher's early witness of the rise of the German state, one that effectively harnessed nationalism for unification purposes, a foreshadowing of a Germany that would later involve itself in two major world wars.

Nietzsche asserts in *Human* how modern state governments employ two methods for ensuring that the body politic remains a captive audience: the first is the military with its monopoly on violence, the other the educational system that outputs administrators and operators who in turn ensure the continuing reproduction of the state apparatus (Vol. 2, I, SEC. 320 / 1996, 285). To the extent that religious institutions generate a herd mentality, the state is also complicit in an identical process since it is but "*a more complicated version of the herd* [emphasis added]" (Kaufmann 1950, 176). Deference and sycophancy to the state exhibit parallels to those required for legitimating religion. A key outcome of such subservience is that state institutions contribute to the weakening of individuals by "lifting responsibility from their shoulders" (Aspers 2007, 489). Nietzsche proclaims in *Zarathustra* that like religion, the state sees itself as possessing the wherewithal to offer its citizens resources for existing, but only if one worships it as an idol. And like many idols, states repeatedly require their human "sacrifice," however one conceptualizes it—the cost and foregone conclusion when living under state authority (2006b, 35). Nietzsche thus welcomes the end of the modern state if it allows for a regeneration of humanity and community. Through what is arguably an anarchistic pronouncement, Nietzsche proclaims with anticipation: "Where the state ends, only there begins the human being who is not superfluous . . . look there, my brothers! Do you not see it, the rainbow and the bridges of the overman?" (2006b, 36). Where the state degenerates, then, is where Nietzsche's sociological imagination, his existential sociology, has epistemic and ontologic importance for informing how a liminal self prevails.

For Nietzsche, the transplantation of a servant morality from the religious era into modernity was uncritically enabled because religion through history had already predisposed the population toward overarching solutions for the suffering of humankind. In *Science*, Nietzsche bemoans how "humanity has for centuries far too eagerly lent its ear to these doctrines . . . [so] this super-stition of being very badly off has finally stuck, so that they are now only too ready to sigh and find nothing good in life and make sad faces together, as if life were really quite hard to *endure*" (IV, SEC. 326 / 2001, 181–182). Institutions of modernity and their complicity in fostering decadence, then, should be seen as an important theme informing Nietzsche's critique of the state across his works since both Judeo-Christian and modern systems are seen to have failed in their capacities to enhance the actor's will to power. Instead, for Nietzsche they instill *ressentiment* in their respective constituen-cies. Kaufmann's view that Nietzsche detests the state because "it prevents man from realizing himself" as it "intimidates man into conformity" is thus justified (1950, 163–164).

Nietzsche offers readers incisive parallels between the demands of the state and religion: the state is made to be idolized by its decadent, non-noble-minded elites, ensuring that the proto-dynamics of nationalism are established. With their improvers of humanity, the nationalists' love of nation is stoked. Reliant on primordialism and epic victories or defeats as nationalist genres for the invention of tradition, nationalists concerned about the forgetting of their nations' epic histories thus arouse the feelings of the people toward self-sacrifice for the material and symbolic culture of the nation. Elements of cultural diacritica can take the form of a castle, religious ruins, a flag, and/or a territory. However, such a process neglects the need for a balance between the almost exclusive reliance on a monumental approach toward history at the expense of antiquarian and critical views of the state, especially when the state is complicit in a nation-construction that generates discontents or even mass death against the nation's naysayers within and without. The premise for the preservation of the state and church are thus rendered a duty for its citizens and adherents to uncritically uphold. Nietzsche claims in *Meditations* that the individual in modernity has but one purpose: to serve the state and give its ideologies a sacralized mystique, a process that is but a "relapse not into paganism but into stupidity" (III, SEC. 4 / 1997b, 148). The realization of this fact, according to Nietzsche in *Human*, should inspire people toward a non-nationalist identity, one that he saw exemplified in a pan-European identity that would blur, if not erase, boundary markers of ethnicity, race, culture, and religion. Not surprisingly, Nietzsche implores us to consider ourselves as good Europeans who should, instead, actively promote a shared humanity through their respective nations. Writing and warning us about the incipient German nationalism of his day in *Beyond*, Nietzsche maintains his view that one of the first yet explicit signs of political infection in the body politic is nationalism.

To further ensure the embeddedness of nationalism in the population, culture must be universalized for the nation while diversity shunned. The function whereby culture can make or allow for the emergence of great, unique, and elevated human beings is thus lost while a cacophony of institutional demands and scripts acting to sustain convention become embedded. With culture plundered by the state to reproduce the latter's staying power, a rather Marxian perspective, Nietzsche deviates from Marx in highlighting the process as one based not on historical materialism or rational technocratic prerogatives, but on the "embodiment of mediocrity" (Kaufmann 1950, 162). "Greatness" in the population is thus exemplified by those who blindly self-sacrifice for the nation. Their exploits are scripted as heroic by the state's military and cultural apparatuses, further validated by the nationalism expressed by adherents, an ethos that parallels religious notions of self-sacrifice seen through the concept of martyrs. Yet, soldier or crusader, one must still sacrifice one's life for a much higher cause through war, be it holy or for protecting and/or expanding the reach of the state, a process that destroys cultural expression seeking attention for non-nationalistic issues.

Additionally, the state when seen as a protagonist is also criticized for its vanity. With its mechanical and efficient bureaucracies, modernist ideologies, and culture industries, the surplus energies in nation construction are rechanneled for pageantry and conveying different nuances of patriotism for the nation. Nietzsche observes in *Human*:

> When the Romans of the imperial era had grown a little tired of war they tried to gain new energy through . . . gladiatorial combats and the persecution of Christians. Present-day Englishmen . . . seize on a different means of again engendering their fading energies: those perilous journeys of discovery, navigations, mountain-climbings, undertaken for scientific ends as they claim, in truth so as to bring home with them superfluous energy acquired through adventures and perils of all kinds. (Vol. 1, VIII, SEC. 477 / 1996, 176)

Arguably the most prescient observation Nietzsche offers us about the state is how its improvers of humanity require enemies within and without, and that such enemies will be manufactured if unavailable. A discussion of this theme in *Human* reveals an irrefutable anti-war stance in Nietzsche's thinking when he describes how states relate to one another:

> They presuppose an evil disposition in their neighbour and a benevolent disposition in themselves. . . . The doctrine of the army as a means of self-defence must be renounced just as completely as the thirst for conquest. And perhaps there will come a great day on which a nation distinguished for wars and victories . . . will cry of its own free will: "*we shall shatter the sword*"—and demolish its entire military machine down to its last foundations. *To disarm while being the best armed*, out of an *elevation* of sensibility—that is the means to *real* peace. (Vol. 2, II, SEC. 284 / 1996, 380)

Young sympathetically remarks how "in spite of his moustache and the belli-cose language of 'war' and 'will to power,' Nietzsche is deeply anti-militaris-tic. He lost school friends barely out of their teens in the Franco-Prussian War and, as a medical orderly, had regular dealings with men with their brains blown out" (2006, 212). War for Nietzsche was but a panoply of "squabbling dynasties which place the flower of a nation's youth in front of the cannons" (cited in Young 2006, 212), a process where the old send the young to die for old values that sacralize old idols. Karzai's account is memorable:

> While Nietzsche was busy writing against anti-Semitism, national socialism, Bismarckian authoritarian politics, and the Aryan white supremacist ideology of eighteenth- and nineteenth-century Germany and Europe, other European philosophers, historians, anthropologists, colonial travel writers, traders, and missionaries were busy advising their then colonial governments on how to best rule and colonize already colonized people in places like the Americas, Africa, Asia, and in what is known today as the Middle East. (2019, 138)

Highlighting how the social construction of enemies is intimately tied to the political climate of the nation, Nietzsche predates, at least foundationally, observations and assertions put forth by sociologists of knowledge such as Peter L. Berger and Thomas Luckmann in their work *The Social Construc-tion of Reality* (1966), as well as other works such as Benedict Anderson's *Imagined Communities* (1983), Eric Hobsbawm and Terence Ranger's *The Invention of Tradition* (1983), and Michael Omi and Howard Winant's *Ra-cial Formation in the United States* (1986). It is not surprising, then, that Nietzsche's observations in *Meditations* about the decadence of modern cul-ture are sociologically relevant: he implicates the state for having harnessed or exploited culture to further reproduce itself since it is unable to "conceive of a goal higher than its own welfare and continued existence" (III, SEC. 6 / 1997b, 174). In *Human*, Nietzsche argues that if war is engaged to further culture, then the state further exacerbates its own degeneration since war is a concussion against cultural production. War presages culture's winter and hibernation, a scenario in which culture can no longer tame how a hubristic victor generates the national narrative or attend to the inculcation of seeth-ing bitterness in the defeated, with the latter embedding *ressentiment* into its worldviews for posterity (Nietzsche Vol. 1, VIII, SEC. 444 / 1996, 163).[1] Kaufmann highlights Nietzsche's cynicism best, claiming that the state for Nietzsche is "in the hands of the military despots" who "will demand that we should yield to it in idolatry" (1950, 167).

In Nietzsche's view, the need for the state to have enemies for admon-ishment and punishment is a legacy of the Judeo-Christian worldview. Its expression in the population of the modern state is an effective mobilizing force because revanchist calls against a rival within or without the state are enhanced by the *ressentiment* transplanted from the religious era into the modern era. Although the textures of discontent exhibit grossly different assumptions and vernacular, the goal of modernity's *ressentiment* is the same: to elevate mediocrity and the content of the rabble expressed by last humans, at the expense of nourishing excellence in a proactive, benevolent elite aspiring toward greatness with life-affirming and noble-minded values. *Ressentiment* is thus more than a psychic phenomenon. It is shaped greatly by sociological contexts of regulation where unempowered groups can be expected to defer to the state's manufactured discontents by its improvers of humanity, discontents that distract citizens from awareness of their own incapacitation.

That Nietzsche viewed *ressentiment* as institutionally enabled by the modern state is highly prescient, especially when one examines the political terrain in the civil society of the United States. One need not be a social scientist to see that the current American experience is one pockmarked with identity groups that feel historically persecuted in ways that justify their continued indignations against their oppressor. To the degree that *ressentiment* has been translated into violence against the other, within or without the state's boundaries, it needs to be seen as a sign of the degeneration of the modern state, a sign of decadence that adopts the same contours as the decadence offered by religious *ressentiment* regardless of whether the state is democratic or socialistic. Here, we need to heed Bergmann's important observation of Nietzsche's orientation toward egalitarianism, namely that it "identified the danger of a certain type of egalitarianism, namely egalitarianism nourished by resentment [*ressentiment*]" and that this mentality "really exists and in very cultivated forms," a "poison that disintegrates any culture" (Bergmann et al. 2007, 25). Sokol argues that institutionalizing *ressentiment* results in a population unable to "stand on one's own feet and think with one's own head," a sign of "indolent times" among "indifferent people, who have no idea what is happening to them and what is in fact coming to engulf them" (Bergmann et al. 2007, 25). For Schrift, Nietzsche's condemnation of democratic mediocrity echoes concerns of

> Jefferson, Madison, Tocqueville, Emerson, and Mill, all of whom were concerned about a possible "tyranny of the majority." The US Senate and "Electoral College" were both created because the founders of the US Constitution had concerns about giving the "masses" direct political power, and their reasons were quite compatible with Nietzsche's critique of the democratic/socialist/ Christian "herd." (Bergmann et al. 2007, 17)

Additional dysfunctions of the state continue to mimic the decadent system of religion. Nietzsche observes in *Meditations* that like religious institutions, state institutions have no need for truth, relying instead on spin to validate its staying power and supremacy (III, SEC. 8 / 1997b, 190). The neutered population, fielding politicians who validate their servant moralities, thus seeks their revenge against all attributes of the powerful by emphasizing the merits of the desperate, dissolving the prospects for the individual actor to develop their noble orientation and will to power. Like the system of religion, untruths conveyed by the state and errors committed by its institutions are excusable for its proponents since maintaining the staying power of the state and not the individual is an existential priority. And like religions and their holy wars and crusades, the state harnesses its military apparatus and its educational systems to breed sycophants in ways that keep the population subjugated. Spiritual thinker Eckhart Tolle declared in the classic *A New Earth* that in this manner modernity fields intelligent people to serve madness (2005).

Even ostensibly benevolent democratic states did not go unexamined by Nietzsche. That Nietzsche is suspicious of democracy and the other *isms* that claim to benefit humankind in spite of their complicity in promoting decadence and degeneration is well known. To appreciate Nietzsche's specific critique of democracy requires us, however, to recall the central importance Nietzsche placed on the sovereign self's capacity to affirm life through one's will to power, to engage in self-creation of one's own destiny. For Nietzsche, all other social inputs are but scripts meant to confine human beings in the realm of conformity. Yet, how are the prevalence of scripts and socially limiting conditions linked to a system described as a "democracy"? Democracy, if one adopts Robert Dahl's classic conceptualization, is a political system that allows competing constituents to elect leaders (1956, 1961, 1968). Yet for Nietzsche, it is a weakening agent simply because the onus is now on the elected leadership to ensure ideal outcomes for those who demand them, a systemic but not self-authored approach toward emancipation and social change. In *Twilight*, Nietzsche therefore argues that democratism in every age has resulted, in some manner, in social forces that promote social and one's internal decay (2005, 214).

And what about our improvers of humanity in a democratic context? In *Twilight* and *Human*, Nietzsche writes how politicians and political parties are so self-serving that they may not be mindful of their self-destructive inclinations, unwittingly ushering in social forces that accelerate the degeneration of their legitimacy. In *Human*, Nietzsche deduces how such state dynamics seen in modern democracies are but historical indicators of a type of state decay (Vol. I, VIII, SEC. 472 / 1996, 173). Nietzsche claims in *Human* that even an ostensibly perfected state will exact a currency: the mental fortitude of the individual is weakened and the sovereignty of the individual is compromised, with the individual ultimately dissolved in the process of nation-state formation. In this context of *Human*, Nietzsche comments on what he believes are the eventual outcomes of democratist and socialist states: "All political powers nowadays try to exploit the fear of socialism. . . . But in the long run it is democracy alone that derives the advantage: for *all* parties are nowadays obliged to flatter the 'people' and to bestow on it alleviations and liberties of every kind" (Vol. 2, II, SEC. 292 / 1996, 383). Nietzsche suggests that a well-designed socialism is no threat to even a dysfunctional democracy because the former's support for the abolition of property will ultimately alienate the people.

Not surprisingly, Nietzsche views socialism as a highly reactionary ideology derived from its secularizing of *ressentiment*, a process that demands an inordinate amount of state involvement to help—yet unwittingly reproduce—hapless selves. Such a process, however, can transform socialism's sanguine utopianism into extreme despotism. Nietzsche warns that we need to be mindful about how socialism promotes continuing accumulation of state power, a process that ultimately annihilates the individual (Vol. 1, VIII, SEC. 473 / 1996, 173). Nietzsche observes that whereas nationalism can be faulted for reproducing last humans that do not desire to employ or refine their intellect, socialism can be criticized for advocating that last humans engage in as little manual labor as possible (Vol. 1, VIII, SEC. 480 / 1996, 177). Stated tersely, nationalism breeds myopia and socialism, complacency. Socialism thus exists as an antipode to potential overcomers or cultures engaged in the generation of new cultural values that can exist and thrive outside such systemic outcomes. By idolizing a utopia where a comfortable existence can be secured for as many as possible, socialism denies the human condition danger, suffering, and trials and tribulations, crucial life experiences for churning out great individuals, thus destroying the catalytic foundations from which an overcoming individual grows (Nietzsche Vol. 1, V, SEC. 235 / 1996, 112).

Sociologists are familiar with how Western variants of capitalism, socialism, and communism give pride of place to industrial development. Yet the technocratic management involved in fulfilling the emancipatory projects of our aforementioned *isms* require the harnessing of the scientific establishment to serve the state. Nietzsche's criticisms of the scientific establishment in *Human* are noteworthy because science is also seen to contribute to nihilism, especially in how science ultimately adopts a technocratic management of life. The scientific establishment therefore also seeks to ensure that humanity experiences long-term prosperity and access to material resources. This project is achieved through its offering of a scientized utopia with positivist articulations of its own true world (Nietzsche Vol. 1, III, SEC. 128 / 1996, 69). In *Science* Nietzsche notes, however, that the assembly of the overcomer requires pain to test the self's tenacity and fortitude in life. Pain is a catalyst for one's continuing renewal, growth, and self-actualization, processes that set into motion momentous and impactful experiences. In this regard, Nietzsche sees overcomers who prevail over physical, emotional, and life hardships as heroic individuals.

The scientific establishment thus drew the ire of Nietzsche because it dominated life and robbed meaning from actors, a process the philosopher felt was anathema for the development of an elevated, life-affirming self. Having already implicated the sciences as contributing to nihilism, Nietzsche reminds us how its ubiquitous power over individual members of society adds to its problematic presence in social life. Nietzsche laments that a life dominated by the sciences becomes one cheapened insofar as meaning is concerned. In light of these constraints, what then, would the role of the creative individual be? In *Meditations,* Nietzsche is not convinced that emancipation for the free spirit can be secured through the sciences since it is dismissive of the eternalizing and inspirational powers of art (II, SEC. 10 / 1997b, 120). Nietzsche confronts science, asking to what degree a scientized culture should dominate the art and practice of living life, to which he emphatically answers, "Life is the higher, the dominating force, for knowledge which annihilated life would have annihilated itself with it" (II, SEC. 10 / 1997b, 121). Understandably, this explains Nietzsche's welcome for a more life-affirming science, a happier science. Yet to Nietzsche's disappointment, science continues to churn out cold facts through their arithmetic and "laws." In *Human*, an immoral Nietzsche explains how proponents of such laws are simply entranced by nature's "morality" and are secretly enthralled by any iteration of a "creative mechanic who has made the most ingenious clock, with living creatures upon it as decorations" (Vol. 2, I, SEC. 9 / 1996, 216).

The scientific approach is thus implicated for enabling nihilism. Yet Nietzsche forwards a loud proclamation in *Science* that attempts to rectify our nihilistic fate, one that reveals his inspiring embrace of nihilism as an *active*, not passive, nihilist able to overcome his own contexts of hardship. Nietzsche's philosophy thus attempts to declutter a scientized universe to accommodate this new human being and human becoming, to allow for their arrival or emergence. Such a new being should not be daunted by the anthropomorphisms that attribute unnecessary powers to imaginary forces. Neither should such a person subscribe to any mechanical "laws" that describe a mechanical world or universe. For Nietzsche, the world and universe are not machines, nor are they living beings; both are and will be for all eternity exemplified by chaos and disorganization. So how dare we believe, in such contexts, that there are those in society—a social construction—who should objectively command and those who should objectively offer their obeisance. To top off Nietzsche's descent into the abyss of nihilism, one in my view Nietzsche is unafraid to confront, he offers us a final and dire view, noting, "Let us beware of thinking that the world eternally creates new things" (III, SEC. 109/ 2001, 110). We are, in essence, on our own, and Nietzsche is braced to experience whatever consequences may follow. Nietzsche's criticism is thus redirected back to the myopia of the scientific method which he faults for reducing all nuances of the human experience "down to the modesty of a hypothesis, a tentative experimental standpoint, a regulative fiction" (Nietzsche V, SEC. 344 / 2001, 200). For Nietzsche, unless a science emerges to affirm life, to elevate life, to give life immeasurable meaning as idealized in *Science*, the scientific enterprise overall remains decadent, life negating, and nihilistic.

In this context Nietzsche expresses his disdain toward the known sociologists of his time, Auguste Comte and Herbert Spencer, as both promoted a positivism based on enhancing the collective rather than the self and society.[2] Of importance is Nietzsche's attack on the stagist trajectory of Spencer's sociological view of humanity, where a higher human ideal based on a moral man is possible as society inevitably progresses forward. Such an ideal discussed in *Genealogy* requires the self to be consistently efficient in coping with stressors in society, a process that requires deference to manufactured expectations for us to cope and evolve—and at this juncture we are familiar with Nietzsche's views on deference toward life projects not generated on our own accord (II, SEC. 12 / 2006a, 52). The self-proclaimed immoralist, Nietzsche emphatically disagrees with such stagist linearity in *Anti-Christ*, arguing that "progress" is but a false modern idea, and that "today's European is still worth considerably less than the Renaissance European; development is *not* linked to elevation, increase, or strengthening in any necessary way" (SEC. 4 / 2005, 5). With a Nietzsche lens, one can envision that scientists, technocrats, improvers of humanity, soul doctors, and cultural philistines have all squandered their will to power to transcend the socially limiting conditions reinforced by natural "laws" manufactured and embedded by modernity. Seeing Spencer as complicit with such decadence due to his "administrative nihilism," Nietzsche remarks in *Genealogy* how his neglect of the forces of constraint upon the individual overlooks the vital significance "reinterpreting, re-directing and formative forces have" upon those "in whom the life-will is active and manifests itself" (II, SEC. 12 / 2006a, 52).

It should be emphasized that those who exhibit a sense of urgency about responding to Nietzsche's disappointments with sociology can find consolation in that he specifically attacked the discipline only through his criticism of England's Spencer and France's Comte. Our discipline was simply too young at the time to field other thinkers that Nietzsche's radar could target. Nonetheless, the youth of sociology as a discipline is no excuse for Nietzsche. In *Twilight* Nietzsche criticizes the discipline of sociology as rendered by

Comte and Spencer since it has only been able to experience social decay—not social uplift or elevation of its citizens toward a more sovereign existence. As such, the discipline is seen to only employ its own "decaying instincts as the *norm* for sociological value judgments" (Nietzsche 1997a, 74). Exacerbating this observation, however, was Nietzsche's erroneous conflation of the sociology discipline as a discipline for socialism. From this vantage point, Nietzsche accuses socialistic sociologists for being decadent, and that "Spencer is also *décadent*" for "he sees something desirable in the triumph of altruism!" (1997a, 74). Nietzsche's view of Spencer is such that the latter is seen to uphold some iteration of Christian morality *through* a positivistic social science. At a time when religious doctrine and morality are seen to be retreating from the onslaught of industrialized and scientized modernity, the notion of Christian pity, as explains Nietzsche in *Dawn*, is replaced with an atavism by which the notion of "love one's neighbor" becomes a mission for modern improvers of humanity to better society through their promises and utopianisms (II, SEC. 132 / 2007a, 139). For Nietzsche, this is the "secret stimulus" that informs Comte's thinking as he sloganeered the positivistic and mechanistic study of society through sociology (II, SEC. 132 / 2007a, 139). However, Nietzsche condemns such orientations where struggle is assumed to be bad. Struggle is needed for self-perfection, a process that can only be attained through suffering, for the person who has "overcome himself does not exclude suffering" (Kaufmann 1950, 303).

In *Science*, Nietzsche argues that because scientific disciplines are unable to fully inform the human condition of a self and society in crisis, opting for mass outcomes rather than exceptionalism, the conquering of meaninglessness as a form of suffering encounters a roadblock in the scientific discourse, one that promotes a mechanical view of the natural world, a world of dreaded first and final laws. Using music composition as an example, Nietzsche explains how a scientific approach to music—counting and calculating rests, length of notes, tempo, time signatures, etc.—can ruin the undertaking. He remarks "how absurd such a 'scientific' evaluation of music would be" for we would have comprehended and understood nothing about the "'music' in it!" (Nietzsche V, SEC. 373 / 2001, 239). Nietzsche's critique of both sociologists highlights how a more positivistic sociology at the time made few inroads into understanding the human condition of the self and society in crisis, crisis that ultimately robs agency from individuals who are suffering. Such a blind spot means that sociologists, for Nietzsche, "have failed to understand under what conditions the individual grows strong and increases his or her autonomy" in ways that can birth a new human being (Aspers 2007, 478). In Nietzsche's view, like the other sciences that reduce understanding of our universe to its mechanics, sociology thus reproduces decadence through its mechanical reading of social behavior. As seen in chapter 3's discussion of *Human*, Nietzsche later became more hopeful when he considered how the sciences can be made to operate in a fashion that is life-affirming, and in ways that create the conditions for an elevated self and elevated culture, one that frees the repressed from a repressed world. Yet for Clark, Nietzsche ultimately exhibits optimism regarding some aspects of empiricism as discussed in *Science*, *Twilight*, and *Anti-Christ*. In this regard, Nietzsche ultimately "presents science as the great liberator from the falsifications perpetuated by religion and metaphysics" (Clark 1990, 104). Nietzsche's early disdain of the sciences was abandoned when he realized it could be employed to contest religion and the religious establishment. This gradual about-face, then, is no indicator of Nietzsche contradicting himself as much as it is an example of his intensely focused mission to unveil what he perceived to be the charlatanism driving different iterations of religiosity and the worship of modern idols.

The larger context that frames our discussion of the sciences allows us to thus segue toward a critical view of modern education, one which Nietzsche believes, as noted in *Twilight*, is complicit in degenerating the human condition by turning people into machines, into automatons of conformity. In *Human*, Nietzsche explains how the state generates conformity in academia by instilling a culture of academic deference to state imperatives. The rewards for intellectuals who conform include acceptance by society's power brokers dispersed inside various institutions, brokers who in turn bestow back to conforming intellectuals cultural and social capital, reproducing for our adorned conformists value systems that further promote deference and sycophancy to apparatuses of the state (Nietzsche Vol. 2, I, SEC. 320 / 1996, 286).

Nietzsche describes scholars of academia as "anxiously muffled up identical people" in *Meditations* (II, SEC. 5 / 1997b, 83). Ever so covetous for peer recognition, they willingly defer to the scripts and regulations of their institutions in ways that keep them entrapped within their groupthink. Considered conformists and members of the herd, Nietzsche's views of those who populate the educational institutions are hardly charitable. No academic personality is a sovereign personality, according to Nietzsche. Becoming a sycophant to academic demands, their individuality is subsumed inside history so as to ensure that "nothing comes out of it except more history" (Nietzsche II, SEC. 5 / 1997b, 84). He adds in *Meditations* how the scholarly castes, trapped in their academic bubbles and unable to therefore see the bigger picture, therefore exist in their guild by enviously monitoring one another so that their search for truth "shall be baptized with the name of its real discoverer" (Nietzsche III, SEC. 6 / 1997b, 172). Nietzsche criticizes the scientific establishment for not enabling individuals to fully understand the entirety of the human condition, for "only he who has a clear view of the picture of life and existence . . . can employ the individual sciences without harm to himself, for without such a regulatory total picture they are threads that nowhere come to an end and only render our life more confused and labyrinthine" (III, SEC. 3 / 1997b, 141).

Academic improvers of humanity and their conformity to academic culture, celebrated for their good behavior with awards and grants, live a life of groupthink and ideological insularity. Nietzsche warns in *Zarathustra* about such sycophants and improvers of humanity, for although they can claim the moral high-ground because of their configured access to "truth," their "powerlessness to lie is by no means love for truth. Beware!" (2006b, 235). Nietzsche observes in *Meditations* how the glorification of modern education functions as a release valve for venting the angst and desires of a generation in a manner that champions existing social institutions (III, SEC. 6 / 1997b, 165). Not surprisingly, Nietzsche believes that supporters of such a system are oblivious to how they are being exploited to disseminate educational content that is, in the final instance, useful for the state when it competes against other states. Academics are thus seen to reside in gilded yet minimum-security iron cages, readied for action at the behest of the state, according to Nietzsche. In a rather humorous and metaphorically rich retort, Nietzsche in *Zarathustra* thus offers another rendering of such sterile scholars, describing them as having "cold, dried up eyes; before them every bird lies plucked" (2006b, 235).

Nietzsche, ever the proponent of a creative renewal and assembly of a higher self, voices his concern about how universities relegate the arts toward epistemic and ontologic peripheries. In *Birth*, Nietzsche laments how the arts and "so-called education" have been confronting each other with feelings of "estrangement and aversion as the one we now see before our eyes" because education "fears it will be destroyed by it" (SEC. 20 / 1999, 97). That is, what is formulaic is retained while what frees the self for ascendancy is discarded. In *Meditations*, Nietzsche explains that rather than celebrate the creative artist injecting life affirmations through music and philosophy, the educational system instead nourishes the pedantic and traditional intellectual. He argues that such persons only attend to books that reinforce one's prejudices in ways that incite some emotive response, that is, "books in which he himself, or his class . . . are the subject of discussion" (Nietzsche III, SEC. 6 / 1997b, 172). The overcoming free-thinking scholar no longer exists in academia, according Nietzsche. Those who populate academic institutions embrace their own variant of a servant morality, hide in cliques that harbor safe ideas and themes, and from their groupthink and insular spaces of armchair academia ply their "objectivity." In *Ecce Homo*, Nietzsche writes of a typical scholar engorged by this approach to thinking: "If he does not skim, he does not think. He *responds* to a stimulus (—an idea he has read) when he thinks—he ends up just reacting. The scholar expends all his strength in saying 'yes' and 'no,' in critiquing what has already been thought—he himself no longer thinks" (2007b, 31).

Although much has already been illuminated about Nietzsche's view toward religion, I revisit his sentiments to highlight his concerns about those who blindly defer to religious demands that parallel their deference to state demands, in spite of their enabling of institutional decadence and dysfunctions in the process. The impressive consistency of Nietzsche's disdain toward conformists and the regulatory scripts manufactured by social systems can again be seen in *Science* where religious prayer is criticized for being offered to people who cannot think for themselves. And "like the Tibetans," such adherents regurgitate their "'om mane padme hum' countless times" in ways that satisfy the priestly aristocracy's requirement for them to "*keep still* with their eyes, hands, legs and other organs," thus making them a "tolerable sight" (Nietzsche III, SEC. 128 / 2001, 122–123). For Nietzsche, the religious faithful who are unable to truthfully enhance their spirituality compensate by relying on such scripted incantations.

Insofar as how the state and religious institutions exhibit their symbiosis, and to a certain extent exhibit isomorphic similarity in structuring power relations, Nietzsche's insights are remarkably prescient: state and religious institutions need one another for legitimation. Although such an insight is not necessarily original today, its impact upon mainstream thinking in Nietzsche's day was controversial. Religion, then, can be seen to anesthetize the discontents of a population disappointed by the state's incompetence. Whether because of wars, natural disasters, or other forms of systemic crises, religion and its pantheon of spiritual superheroes immediately remove the wounded psychology of adherents and places it in the metaphysical realm for deities to heal. In *Human*, Nietzsche argues that the state's utopianisms, especially when the state fails to honor its social contract, have what can only be conceived of as an insurance policy in the guise of legitimating a religion, a process that reveals how state governments of modernity remain fettered to religious institutions in a politicized and opportunistic manner. Nietzsche thus offers a penetrating, if not somewhat derivative observation, noting that if the state is given a choice to abandon or amalgamate itself with religion in an explicit or implicit manner, the state will select the latter option, for religion "quietens the heart of the individual in times of loss," especially when the government feels unable to offer any respite for conditions of extreme duress (Vol. 1, VIII, SEC. 472 / 1996, 170). In such a context, religion "guarantees a calm, patient, trusting disposition" in the uncritical populace—adherents are made to think God is always at work for them and out of faith will "patiently submit to instructions from *above*," thus ensuring the functioning and stability of communities (Nietzsche Vol. 1, VIII, SEC. 472 / 1996, 170–171).

Nietzsche's allusion about how an ineffectual state utilizes religion to placate the larger population surfaces again in *Beyond*. The state, then, employs religion and religiosity to fulfill roles it is unable to fulfill, namely to attend to problematics that a highly rationalized modernity has omitted from its project of modernization: issues related to meaning, depth, and purpose. In this condition of existential impoverishment, religion makes its grand entrance, offering calm and transcendence as antipodes to government and the "necessary dirt of politics" (Nietzsche III, SEC. 61 / 2002, 54). Religion thus ensures that adherents experience institutionalized contentment with their lot in life by minimizing their anxieties, praising their pieties, embracing their joys and pains, and most importantly, offering a justification "for everything commonplace, for all the lowliness, for the whole half-bestial poverty of their souls" (Nietzsche III, SEC. 61 / 2002, 55). That state leaders allow the priestly aristocracy to employ religious morality to legitimate a ruler is not a new idea even in Nietzsche's day, but his observation of how such a process affects adherents is unique: followers sacrifice their inner selves even though normally one "would very much like to escape obedience" to religion and state (III, SEC. 61 / 2002, 54). Nietzsche thus continues to take no prisoners in his scathing critique of religious systems, arguing that this is how the Brahmins of South Asia harnessed faith as "they assumed the power to appoint kings . . . while they themselves kept and felt removed and outside, a people of higher, over-kingly tasks" (Nietzsche III, SEC. 61 / 2002, 54).

Such a relationship allows the state's purveyor of illusions, the priests, the soul doctors—the "*professional* negater, slanderer, poisoner of life," according to Nietzsche in *Anti-Christ*—to focus their ascetic ideal energies upon metaphysical and not empirical truths (SEC. 8 / 2005, 8). In *Anti-Christ*, Nietzsche writes how truth "has already been turned on its head when someone who consciously champions nothingness and negation passes for the representative of 'truth'" (SEC. 8 / 2005, 8). Christianity is implicated in the process of pushing the truth of *ressentiment* in its faithful, reproducing a powerless servant morality so adherents hand over power and legitimation to their soul doctors and priestly aristocracies. Moreover, Christianity "rewards" last humans by "granting 'immortality' to every Tom, Dick, and Harry," a most "vicious attempt to assassinate *noble* humanity" (Nietzsche SEC. 43 / 2005, 40). In the same work, Nietzsche responds to the metaphysical realm sloganeered by priests—a heaven that is for children (SEC. 32 / 2005, 29)—and further asserts that the notion of a kingdom in heaven is but a state of being within the heart (SEC. 34 / 2005, 32). Moreover, in the *Twilight* section titled "How the 'True World' Finally Became a Fiction" (1997a, 23–24), Nietzsche highlights three more damaging errors committed by the priestly aristocracy and its adherents: the first error was committed by priests as they engaged in the social construction of heaven as the metaphysical destination for the wise, pious, and virtuous. The next error centers on how the priestly aristocracy (a group seen to be amalgamated with the state in *Human*) configured the social order to ensure that culture and supporting institutions are established to repeatedly remind adherents through scripts and rituals that the true world can only accommodate the pious and virtuous, the one who repents—but that everyone can be pious and virtuous, and therefore everyone potentially has a place in the true world.

Although the priests have never proven the existence of the true world and accept it as an overall unknown, the final error now lies in how unempowered adherents dared not hold priests accountable for the latter's punitive, if not obscure, tenets. In *Twilight*, Nietzsche expresses his frustration at the gullibility of such religious adherents for their prostrations to the unknown. To rectify such errors by religion that have shaped humanity for millennia, Nietzsche expects us to consider the notion of the true world as an obsolete, untenable, and in his view, anachronistic idea. Nietzsche enthusiastically assures us that by ridding ourselves of the true world, the religious claim that our real corporeal existence is but an illusion evaporates as well; he thus proclaims how we, "*along with the true world . . . have also done away with the apparent!*" (1997a, 24). The raison d'etre of Nietzsche's philosophy emerges: humanity can now assemble a new path that overcomes the human condition as it lies in the rubble of the supernatural (and later, in the rubble of industrial modernity). For Nietzsche, the time to respond to the defects of modernity is nigh, and soon he hopes, we will be able to reinvigorate humanity so that it reaches a high point in its self-actualization and purposing of existence.

Nietzsche also faults religion for its employment of literal and spiritual violence to validate its raison d'être, arguing that even prior to the onset of Judeo-Christianity, prehistoric religions often sacrificed human beings if not their firstborn. By the time Christianity indoctrinated its morality upon the population, humanity's creative and empowering instincts were sacrificed instead, resulting in an emaciated flock of ascetic priests rendered as community leaders, leaders who, however, no longer knew their own intimate natures, according to Nietzsche. One consequence of such a process is that nihilism is enabled; it becomes the "nothingness," the meaninglessness that last humans and their servant moralities have reproduced through a succession of nihilistic systems that have failed to satiate humanity's understanding of their human condition. In *Beyond*, Nietzsche argues that people ultimately sacrificed "God," and in their betrayal, turned toward religiosity's material culture and other diacritica in hopes that these would now field tangible outcomes that will reward their faith and enhance their existence (III, SEC. 55 / 2002, 50). Such reworkings of faith have nothing to do with the inherent utility of religiosity but reflect last humans' desperate attempts to insert their idealized superhumans into the sky, so to speak, to populate their desperately needed true world of heavenly proportions. Even in modernity's nihilistic state of nothingness, then, conformists continue to engage in self-destruction and the reproduction of meaninglessness by offering up fantastic idols. Nietzsche warns of such a process even before the publication of the *Anti-Christ*. In *Zarathustra* he reminds us about the staying power of such decadents in modernity, the priests and their teachings that have become ensconced within younger generations, teachings that immolate the best of us, for "our flesh is tender, our hide is mere lambskin—how could we not tempt old idol priests!" (2006b, 160).

Due to the disingenuousness and errors of the priests (or politicians for that matter) functioning as improvers of humanity, Nietzsche predicts their demise in *Twilight* and *Human*. Nietzsche argues in *Twilight* that when the population realizes how priests throughout history have devalued the highest types of people if they refuse to be conforming adherents, the time will come, promises the philosopher, when priests are instead considered the "lowest type" and "the most mendacious, most improper sort of human being" (1997a, 81). Moreover, because Christianity through its priestly aristocracies had to first toxify the spirit before claiming the righteous wherewithal to detoxify it, Nietzsche confidently declares in *Human* how the Christian system, because of such disingenuousness, will too perish (Vol. 1, III, SEC. 119 / 1996, 67). Nietzsche's condemnation of religion as a system smoothly segued into his critique of the state, especially the utopianisms and ideological *isms* of secular society that adherents uncritically embrace.

Invariably, when systemic crises and nihilism experienced by their adherents become untenable, the solution is to be seen, ostensibly, within and between states, be they through diplomacy or war, which for Nietzsche is the problem: states are life negaters, destroyers of meaning and purpose, for the state exhibits processes of indoctrination not unlike that of religion. Devotion from state adherents, from civil servants to politicians, must now be directed to idealized but secular analogs: sects have become replaced by political parties, the discourse of the *faithful* becomes political ideology, and both state and religion claim to lead adherents to their variant of a true world (but in fact seduce its actors toward dependency upon systems, exposing them to cultural decadence and, ultimately, nihilism).

In *Human*, Nietzsche observes that as religion's relevance in society became overshadowed by the state, the state's zealots—its nationalists—consequently expressed a fanaticism for the state not unlike that exhibited for deities. The zealotry is compensation for the emergence of nihilism in the wake of the death of god, that is, it is exhibited by those who are drowning in lackluster social outcomes from idealized religiosities that promised to offer greater meaning and purpose for the self. The state in modernity fills in such a void, and thus, devotion to the state is but an isomorphic representation of devotion to a new god (Nietzsche Vol. 1, VIII, SEC. 472 / 1996, 172). In this regard, Nietzsche observes that it is in the interest of a decadent state to, unsurprisingly, exploit religion and its priestly aristocracy for its own end, for the latter is skilled in their "concealed and intimate education of souls" (Vol. 1, VIII, SEC. 472 / 1996, 171). Moreover, Nietzsche offers a penetrating assertion that should the citizenry exhibit too many viewpoints from a faith that could hold the state accountable for its actions, the state will adroitly reconfigure religion into "a private affair" to be handed over to the "conscience and customs of every individual" (Vol. 1, VIII, SEC. 472 / 1996, 171). The outcome of such a maneuver is that sects then reproduce themselves through their private in-group rabble, thus enabling intergenerational sentiments defined by narrow provincialisms and voluntary segregation to flow across time. This is the world of Motley Cow.

The extent to which politicians and their ideologies regarding the state mimic priests and their moralities is uncanny. The isomorphism is not simply an observation by your author, but one that Nietzsche brilliantly, or recklessly, formulated himself. For example, Nietzsche posits in *Human* that people envision some form of divinity in how we practice our politics, a process that ensconces a "sacred mystery in the existence of the state," and that this mystique is incontrovertibly of religious origin (Vol. 1, VIII, SEC. 472 / 1996, 173). One can take a variety of cues from Nietzsche's critique of religion and see their parallels toward his critical views of politics and politicians as early as *Meditations* and continuing into the *Anti-Christ*. In *Meditations*, for example, Nietzsche notes how the egocentrism of profit-seekers, along with executives and operators of military industrial complexes around the world, if one transplants Nietzsche's views toward the twentieth and twenty-first centuries, determine a variety of life dynamics on the planet. This, for Nietzsche, is the power that informs how states relate to one another. Such an epic undertaking by states, their lackeys, and administrators consequently inspires their patriots, their nationalists, to ensure that the populace approach the state with the same reverence they once bestowed upon the church (III, SEC. 4 / 1997b, 150). Nietzsche is similarly scathing in *Anti-Christ* when he describes socialists and their "Chandala-apostles" engaged in acquiring adherents as no better than the anarchists who are argued to have descended from the same lineage as Christianity (SEC. 57 / 2005, 60). As weakening agents, both systems thus employ their respective fantasies to ensure their audience remains captive to faith or ideology. Modern social systems, then, enable *ressentiment* to flourish, enable a life defined by a servant morality, contribute to nihilism, generate unnecessary rabble, and suppress the life-affirming instincts of individuals. In *Human*, Nietzsche thus argues that religious and state institutions are but iterations of each other in terms of how they exert social control. Although he urges us to rid our reliance on improvers of humanity and those who subscribe to the merits of their moralities, Nietzsche offers an uplifting consolation, an opening for the greatness of the self to emerge in light of these systemic flaws: we are now justified in self-authoring our own path, with our own morality, toward excellence, toward overcoming.

Our discussion thus far allows us to draw some important insights about Nietzsche's conceptualization of modernity, the state, and its ideological *isms*. Perhaps most important for the discipline of sociology is how Nietzsche viewed the state as a very mortal and fragile social system. Because of these attributes it needs to, like religious systems, have a true world in the form of *isms* to ensure the project of modernity facilitated through its apparatuses remains legitimate. Unlike Weber's formulation where rational-legal systems are designed to ensure institutional efficiency, survivability, and longevity of state apparatuses in modernity, Nietzsche's formulation saw such a mechanical function of the state as life negation, and therefore unable to provide meaning, purpose, and trajectories for the sovereign and free spirit to emerge. In this regard, the modern secular state and its rational legal institutions are susceptible to rot. The state's putrefaction is evinced by some of the following considerations, considerations that expect citizens to uncritically:

- worship its symbols and material culture, as well as acknowledge its martyrs through some form of nationalism—be they benevolent (for example, Dalai Lama and Tibet) or malicious (for example, Pol Pot and the Khmer Rouge),
- subscribe to their particular *ism*'s utopianism,
- rely on only a monumentalist reading of history (for example, epic victories or defeats that reveal the supposed mettle of the nation's survivors),
- employ the educational institution and its scholars, especially through the sciences, to indoctrinate the individual into its project of nation construction,
- accept the superficial and shallow narratives of the state's cultural philistines,
- accept its cultural production of internal and external enemies,
- accept the state's warmongering in all its iterations (for example, proxy wars, geopolitical wars, colonialism, etc.),
- accept the defeatism established by the democratic state, that is, to turn citizens into utter dependents of state institutions, their values, and their morality,

- accept the complacency established by the socialist state, that is, to turn citizens into utter dependents of state institutions, their values, and their morality,
- accept the economic imperatives of the state,
- repress the overcomer's self-authored morality, freedom, and will to power to purpose their own existence,
- enable *ressentiment* in the cultural discourse,
- accept rabble as a means of political and social discourse for underpinning the imperatives of the state, and
- accept state indoctrination of herds manufactured through its culture industry.

Pertaining to the list, Nietzsche likely agrees that support for such social configurations and conventions would emerge from conformists with a herd mentality. These individuals surrender their will to power to their improvers of humanity, soul doctors, and/or cultural philistines and subscribe to their incessant rabble about imminent utopias. This community of last humans operates in a psychic world of servant morality and *ressentiment*, and offers their subservience and sycophancy to a multitude of socially, politically, and culturally scripted constraints and roles. Only higher humans possessing the creativity to assemble one's own authentic character by critically contesting convention through courage, fortitude, and the harnessing of the will to power can become praxian overcomers. Such overcomers can contest the state and its proponents' toxic injection of perennial enfeeblement into the collective consciousness. The overcomer is thus the actor with the fortitude to prevail, able to author and purpose a life trajectory of one's own composition, unfazed by life's trials and tribulations rendered by flawed social systems of modernity.

For Nietzsche, the consequences of the staying power of such dysfunctional state dynamics are that it will ultimately generate nihilism. Because state systems have compounded the dilemma of living in modern society, citizens will be unable to deploy the state apparatus to provide existential meaning and purpose. In such a situation, Nietzsche's ideal of establishing a benevolent *Volk* community through the reassignment of culture to produce great human beings with an elevated noble mindset will be difficult within our modern globalized systems (Young 2006). Moreover, for overcomers such a scenario renders difficult a self-authoring process that can usher in a paradigm shift in how one reconceptualizes the human condition. According to Nietzsche, the state apparatuses of modernity, and by implication liquid modernity, are thus nihilistic systems. In *Anti-Christ* (SEC. 62 / 2005, 66–67), Nietzsche highlights how the self can respond to such systemic failures, failures that ultimately deprive actors and citizens their sovereignty. To rebel against systemically imposed values with *amor fati* is thus the life project of the overcomer, one who envisions:

- the state's suppression of their nature as a vice,
- the state's suppression of their power as a vice,
- the state's suppression of their nature as an obstacle toward overcoming,
- religious and state leaders as a threat to the individual, the self, *and* society,
- participation in religious or political activities as following a script,
- subscription to religious or political ideologies as following a script,
- religious and political institutions as impediments blocking the self-authoring project of the overcomer,
- any subscription to religious or state ideals/ideologies as self-imposed life negation, requiring us to view
- improvers of humanity—the "savior," the "soul doctor," the "redeemer," or the "saint"—with suspicion if not disdain.

At this juncture, the overcomer should be seen as a type of self-developed actor able to contest decadent forces of democracy that will be elaborated upon in the next chapter, one with agency to respond to the nihilisms of a dying Christianity or a modernity administered by crisis-prone state systems, especially as these continue to seek out captive audiences for control by offering cultural scripts and utopias. A general assertion that can be derived from the aforementioned lists, then, is that Nietzsche envisions the overcomer to engage in a revaluation of all values outputted by decaying religious institutions and decadent state institutions of modernity. In such a capacity, it is obvious that Nietzsche's overcomer is a revolutionary but not of the hammer and sickle variety. Instead, Nietzsche encourages psychical and sociological changes drawn from one's examination of their corporeal place in society, a process that includes setting into motion a paradigm shift to promote a new humanity, a humanity where actors are able to overcome the vagaries of the human condition and nihilism on their own noble terms. He urgently proclaims in *Zarathustra* that such persons must overcome the influences of modernity's dysfunctions *today*. In *Beyond*, Nietzsche opines that modernity's decadent rulers, the dogmatist improvers of humanity, are obstacles to one's capacity for a wholesome and authentic assembly of the self. Nietzsche thus views the human condition as sculpted by the dynamic interplay (or entanglement) of "creature" and "creator," where its flotsam of chaos and abundance of minutiae intertwine with the person's creative energies harnessed for exhibiting one's "hammer-hardness" and "spectator-divinity" (VII, SEC. 225 / 2002, 117). We can thus be saintly in our own intimate acts of self-creation and purposing of existence.

What Nietzsche argues for is a new purview for overcomers of modernity that clearly illuminates how even within democracies, or any state that pitches a bureaucratically enforced understanding of freedom, exists numerous authoritarian spaces and totalitarian practices that do irreparable harm to the sovereignty and freedoms of people in the lifeworld. Modern states and their institutions are thus dysfunctional, placing humanity in a prolonged crisis of nihilism. Jürgen Habermas describes such a modernity as experiencing an "exhaustion of utopian energies" (1986), and thus, modernity remains an "unfinished project" (1987). In such a context, iterations of the modern state, especially the democratic state I hope to examine with a Nietzsche lens next chapter, will be approached as a modern system in crisis, a crisis that is but another atavism following the death of the pre-Socratic Greece and later Christianity.

Nietzsche, through the ideal type of the overcomer, was not thwarted by such social decay, for these are but catalysts able to generate new trajectories for culture to return to its main purpose: to create noble-minded individuals capable of self-mastery in the lifeworld. In *Beyond*, Nietzsche embraces political decay as a prelude to the renewal of the self in society, especially through a reworking of culture. In society's current decadence, nothing would be better than to speed its transformation toward such a new community, a new *Volk*. The issue for Nietzsche is that modernity has not yet configured culture for producing great and elevated human beings; all the *isms* have failed in this regard. Trapped in their scripted lifeworlds of cacophonous rabble, with new idols offered up by the machine that is *gesellschaft* society, the need to maneuver through the herd daily, while exposed to the sales pitches made by its improvers of humanity—the "experts" of Bauman's persuasion—our sovereign being suffocates. And because of the modern condition of complacency and resignation, nihilism becomes embedded in the lifeworld, with state systems their enabler.

The enhancement of Nietzsche's critical views of democracy will invariably compel some to question whether or not his views should be considered conservative, and more importantly, whether my monograph is but an oblique attempt to legitimate conservative views. Such a question is premature, one formed by misinformation and an exoteric oversimplification of Nietzsche's ideas. It should be known that many Nietzsche readers envision him as apolitical—a hyper-individual—even anarchistic. Yet we should heed scholars such as Young who notes that although Nietzsche's view of the state makes him "sound like a classical liberal-conservative (a 'neo-con' in current jargon)," Nietzsche's emphasis on important merits of socialism suggests otherwise (2006, 70). For example, Nietzsche observes that although "communal ownership of wealth will . . . destroy 'initiative' . . . moderate accumulation of wealth through work (though not through inheritance) should be allowed" (2006, 70). Young argues that for Nietzsche, "the accumulation of great wealth is to be forbidden" because it is a breeder of *ressentiment*, "destructive envy, class warfare . . . revolution and collapse" (2006, 70).

Bergmann's (1987) account of Nietzsche's life offers up rich insights into social conditions that allowed our philosopher to exhibit such an incisive sociological imagination, one that does a fine job of situating our philosopher in varying political contexts that shaped his life, contexts that witnessed the transition of states once dependent on traditional authority toward that of rational-legal authority. Examples can be seen in the establishment of the nation state as a variety of principalities in Prussia and other German-speaking kingdoms fused under an authoritarian drive toward nation-construction, a process further amplified by political forces and their modernizing effects upon social development. With Nietzsche situated in the unfolding drama and intrigue of a nascent Bismarckian state that became a unified Germany, his philosophy can be seen as invariably shaped by his responses to the ideologies of the day, all of which Nietzsche resisted as the *isms* tried to appropriate if not condemn him. From being seen as conservative, to being occasionally seen as an apologist to socialism, to being labeled an anti-Semite as well as cosmopolitan, as well as self-labeling himself as "Anti-Strauss, Anti-Darwin, Anti-Wagner, and Antichrist," Nietzsche establishes himself as a thinker with a very expansive politicized purview (Bergmann 1987, 5). Bergmann thus highlights Nietzsche's worldliness and experientials that are often overlooked in our analyses of the philosopher and gives readers social contexts of Nietzsche's maneuverings, contexts where time, place, and dates matter, as are changing political climates.

The social factors that shaped Nietzsche's views on politics and power must thus be considered seriously. Bergmann effectively captures the fluidity of Nietzsche's political orientation in ways that require us to conceptualize the overcomer as an actor with the wherewithal to adapt to and confront any context where dysfunctional power operates:

> While conservatives soon came to see him and his following in the nineties as the principal and most dangerous opponent to their orthodoxy, Nietzsche's effectiveness against them derived from his dispassionate analysis of their decline. Even his atheism was couched in the language of regret: God is dead; we have killed him; nihilism, alas, is our fate; let us be strong and go forward, etc. Nietzsche might be "anti-liberal to the point of malice" but toward conservatives he assumed the pose of the far-sighted decadent who recognized that the game was up, that lapses into resentful demagoguery were dishonorable and ultimately self-defeating. . . . His cult of aristocracy focused on spirit, not genealogy; he justified the coming ruling class in the name of European unity, not

national greatness; he attributed social unrest not to race-mixing, but the mixing of classes. He was anti-democratic, not so much in the sense of wanting to thwart democracy's rise, but rather in assuming the stance of a postdemocratic critic anxious to undermine its hegemony. His anti-feminism similarly assumed the triumph of the new woman. (Bergmann 1987, 161)

That said, Bergmann makes a strong case that Nietzsche's views are radical, noting the philosopher's position "closely resembled that of the anarchists," a position that puts his observations at odds with Young (2006) who saw, instead, Nietzsche emphasize the need for individuals to build new communities of excellence, communities that can monitor and repulse the decadence and nihilism of modernity. Thiele offers a different reading, noting that Nietzsche believed that "to celebrate the best in the human experience is implicitly to redeem the ideal, if not the practice, of democracy"; more significantly, Thiele reminds us—and this position I also share—that "if the practice of liberal democracy and egalitarianism has us assuming the worst rather than the best in human beings, then Nietzsche's critique [of democracy] offers a useful tonic" (Bergmann et al. 2007, 27). Thiele affirms Nietzsche's position, noting that "all too often, we organize ourselves politically in campaigns, parties, policies, and institutions—based on the lowest level to which people in their working-day un-freedom and servitude will stoop. A politics that appeals to the least common denominator is certainly not everything democracy might be" (Bergmann et al. 2007, 27). Regardless of one's position on the matter, Patton is correct in reminding us that Nietzsche's philosophy remains a "significant" yet "underutilised resource" for a "different approach to politics and the political organization of society" (Bergmann et al. 2007, 15).

We thus have offered another reading of Nietzsche not as a conservative, for he had always purported to transcend all systems via the notion of revaluation of all values, but more of a fluid and sovereign philosopher/activist: one who formulates a philosophy of self to withstand, overcome, and discard impaired systems designed by secular modernity as it vacillates between hypocrisies and double standards, at least until overcomers can reestablish a new community that celebrates and makes operative the will to power as a positive force for the lifeworld. Nietzsche, then, is no conservative. This is incontrovertible. He simply wanted actors to reappropriate what it means to be a transcendent overcomer, and thus a victorious and self-actualizing survivor of society's discontents and dysfunctions regardless of political ideology. He cared deeply about *us* needing a higher understanding and appreciation of one's mettle and fortitude. At the risk of oversimplification, Nietzsche simply wanted to see strong, honorable, and dignified people with integrity populate and enhance culture and society again. As it stands, social systems and their numerous scripts, on which society has so long depended for rational-legal and cultural content, are preventing people from being their best, from self-actualizing. Nietzsche almost wanted to celebrate the merits of modernity but felt obliged to proclaim his disappointments and discontents with the modernist project and its dismal failure in nourishing human greatness.

What Nietzsche expects of overcomers of modernity, then, is that they clearly understand how within democracies or any state that pitches an institutionally enforced and regulated understanding of freedom, exists authoritarian and totalitarian dynamics that mutilate the sovereignty of people in the lifeworld. Where freedoms exist, they are segmented and as such democracies remain incomplete, as sociologist Jürgen Habermas famously observes. Such a view applies in a timely manner to the United States at the time of this writing. Due to the country's explicit display of democratic dysfunction, the tragic irony is that forces of totalitarianism: a dictatorial oligarchy, corporatocratic control, political correctness, and voluntarily segregated communities with their petty provincialisms and victim identities, now characterize narratives emblematic of American "democracy." Responding to such an environment, overcoming types will need to construct their own meaning and purpose in a life damaged by modernity's crises and exhausted utopias. In this regard, we will examine more closely the dysfunctions of democracy in the next chapter. By highlighting Nietzsche's concerns on this issue, we can see how Nietzsche is a sociological thinker for a sociology that had yet to take root: one that advocated for the agency of the individual in response to a society experiencing its systemic dysfunctions and crises. Yet I am fully aware that Nietzsche, first and foremost, was not a trained sociologist, and as such, the ideas of Jürgen Habermas and other contemporaries are harnessed to respond to, if not tentatively operationalize, Nietzsche's concerns about a dysfunctional democracy.

NOTES

1. A musical composition born in our modernity, a modernity that so riled Nietzsche, has been able to aptly frame his angst and criticism of political improvers of humanity and their intentions: the lyrics of "Fletcher Memorial Home" by the legendary group Pink Floyd.

2. That Nietzsche never engaged in a sustained confrontation with Karl Marx remains, in my view, one of the most unfortunate missed engagements of late nineteenth-century German philosophy. No records exist of them ever meeting. Although past his prime during Nietzsche's creative years, Nietzsche must have certainly been exposed to Marx's works during the former's life adventures: the early parts of *Zarathustra* were published the year of Marx's death in 1883 (Nietzsche was 39) and *Science* the year previous. When Nietzsche was born, Karl Marx was 26; Nietzsche was 23 and Marx was 49 at the time *Das Kapital* was published in 1867.

Chapter Seven

The Self and
Totalitarian Democracy

Operationalizations for Nietzsche's view of a decadent democracy and its *faux* materialist culture can arguably be extrapolated from the ideas of sociologist and philosopher Jürgen Habermas. The two could not be more different thematically: Nietzsche saw democracy's putrefaction while Habermas was committed to its repair. However, their foundational concerns about human freedom, how it is being suppressed, where to find it, and where it cannot be found, reveals overlapping horizons between the thinkers. Unlike the previous chapter where I examined Nietzsche's discontents with the *isms* of modernity, in this chapter I hope to consider instead Nietzsche's sociological imagination on the self's relationship to the vagaries of primarily the democratic capitalist state so as to read existence within the dysfunctions of democracy and the market, a context where Habermas provides rich insights.

Habermas hails from the Frankfurt School, founded at Goethe University in the period between the world wars. As a scion of an intelligentsia that included legendary thinkers such as Erich Fromm, Herbert Marcuse, Theodore Adorno, and Max Horkheimer, Habermas and his earlier contemporaries engaged in incisive critiques of post–World War II capitalism, Marxism-Leninism, fascism, with important contributions to an existential discourse on freedom and sovereignty. The neo-Marxist community became a dangerous voice from the new left that engaged in a variety of sociological demystifications of modernity. Although an exegesis of Habermas's legacy along with other Frankfurt School members is beyond the scope of this work, I intend to employ Habermas, and in a supporting role Fromm, to synchronize with Nietzsche in ways that reveal how a democratic modernity enables totalitarian and authoritarian tendencies to suppress human freedom, and that there is a bona fide need for thinkers to consider the merits of conceptualizing a totalitarian democracy, not as an oxymoron, but as an incontrovertible social fact. Amalgamating Nietzsche's and Habermas's sociological imaginations about democracy's totalitarian spaces is an important undertaking because the process illuminates the panorama of structural impediments functioning as agents of social decay, exemplars that must be overcome per Nietzsche's persuasion. Nietzsche, however, needs assistance in completing this formulation—he *almost* completed it. It is my view that Habermas, and to a certain extent Fromm, will enable Nietzsche's critique of modernity to reach its fruition. Thus far we can already envision a Nietzsche modernity cluttered with cultural and technical scripts imposed upon society by its improvers of humanity, denying individuals in the population agency, meaning, and purpose. This chapter attempts to elaborate how cluttering the process unfolds.

One of the chief concerns of Habermas in his classic works *The Theory of Communicative Action* (TCA) (Volume 1, 1984; Volume II, 1987) and *The Structural Transformation of the Public Sphere* (1991) is how a low-quality, incomplete democracy can be attended to. For Habermas, the aesthetics, practices, and physicality of democracy manifest only during election cycles. Yet it is the period between election cycles in the lifeworld, however, that is arguably a more valid indicator of democratic and capitalist practices. The lifeworld allows unresolved issues of collective and individual powers to be disentangled therein, a process that, for Habermas, is now stunted by its colonization. Therefore, by disrupting the a priori assumption that democracy equals good governance, both Nietzsche and Habermas are engaged in a much-needed reconceptualizing of democracy and its practices. For example, Habermas reminds us that redeeming democracy may be poorly realized if undertaken through institutional mechanisms from above. The trajectory will need to emanate from actors who grant legitimacy to social systems through "will-formation" from below, from the grass roots, that is, from the lifeworld (Warren 1993: 211). For Habermas there remains untapped potential for democratic articulation in the lifeworld, thus the need to decolonize the lifeworld so that actors can have emancipatory and transformative social experiences (Mezirow 2004). The fight for a more complete democratic capitalism, then, will need to be resurrected and concluded inside the lifeworld and not through the political apparatuses of corporatocracies. This is because the totalitarian spaces of democracy and the market can be seen in the lifeworld's public spheres, sites that have been colonized by macro-bureaucratic forces.

Historically, public spheres of the lifeworld were fettered to monarchical dynamics where king, queen, and aristocrats "largely monopolized public authority" and determined for the court content for public consumption and discourse (Habermas 1991, 68). The country that birthed the Industrial Revolution more so than any other, the United Kingdom, saw its political public spheres emerge at the turn of the eighteenth century. In this context, the propertied and aristocratic classes during the Industrial Revolution remained deferential to royalism and monarchy, employing public spheres as environments to showcase high-value material culture that tied them to different nuances of traditional authority. Consequently, in the case of eighteenth-century Germany, the nobility's cultural capital and sense of self-worth still depended on the validation of the court. Such conventions meant the early bourgeoisie relationship with the aristocrats of their respective societies was ultimately overshadowed by their efforts to ensure economic imperatives favorable to the capitalist class from which the former hails. Exacerbating matters, German aristocrats failed to establish "strong enough lines of communication with bourgeois intellectuals" to create "a strong civil society separate from the state" (Calhoun 1994, 15). Habermas comments: "While the early institutions of the bourgeois public sphere originally were closely bound up with aristocratic society as it became dissociated from the court, the 'great' public that formed in the theaters, museums, and concerts was bourgeois in its social origin. Around 1750 its influence began to predominate" (1991, 43).

For Habermas, the earliest bourgeois publics soon garnered support for their important role in economic production: the secular state had become staffed by members of public spheres hailing from or supportive of bourgeois class interests; that is, they were class allies emanating from a "narrow" segment of Europe's population. Members of this class, "mainly educated, propertied men . . . conducted a discourse not only exclusive of others but prejudicial to the interests of those excluded" (Calhoun 1994, 3). Public spheres, then, have always been exposed to different nuances of lifeworld colonization during their respective time periods. Habermas illuminates how the vulnerability of public spheres to lifeworld colonization has historically been part and parcel to the operating dynamics of democracies.

It should be noted that Habermas's observation of bourgeois dominance as one that still had to defer to the state is distinctly different from Marx, who condemned the intimate links between the state and its capitalist class, one where the former does the bidding of the latter. Habermas saw the public during Western European industrialization as still "state-related" and state-dependent in that the public functioned as an "apparatus with regulated spheres of jurisdiction" (1991, 18). However, percolating in the bourgeois public sphere, journals and literature emerged to address problematics related to the state, and these existed in tension with concerns of intellectuals aligned with merchants, bankers, entrepreneurs, and manufacturers. Yet social changes were underway: the press now had a more significant role as the public sphere transitioned toward being a "reading public," one that brought civil society into existence to further depersonalize state authority. Aided by the press, which Habermas notes had "developed a unique explosive power," the public sphere acquired more sovereignty (1991, 20). However, the state was not yet ready to be relegated to the periphery and opened up its own access to the press, and "very soon the press was systematically made to serve the interests of the state administration" (Habermas 1991, 22). However, with a depersonalizing state that began to concede territory to civil society the bourgeois class then became the "real carrier of the public" (Habermas 1991, 23), one that expressed their iteration of public opinion, consciousness, and conscience (Habermas 1991, 89–90).

> Unlike the great urban merchants and officials who, in former days, could be assimilated by the cultivated nobility of the Italian Renaissance courts, they could no longer be integrated . . . into the noble culture at the close of the Baroque period. Their commanding status in the new sphere of civil society led instead to a tension between "town" and "court." (Habermas 1991, 23)

In spite of its ability to insert itself into society, the bourgeois public sphere declined in influence over time. By the mid-1800s, new social conditions set into motion by the Industrial Revolution and inadequacies of *laissez-faire* capitalism transformed the state into a welfare state, one where provisions were provided for citizens by rational-legal systems, a process that nonetheless did not prevent the private and public from becoming interlocked (Calhoun 1994). This iteration of the public sphere ultimately conveyed concerns of civil society in ways that allowed state authority to "correspond to its needs" (Habermas 1991, 74).

Over time the public sphere was infiltrated by the state and media through juridification, a situation where technical language and laws from social institutions infiltrate the public spheres of the lifeworld with regulatory and, I argue in cultural contexts, politically correct language, rendering it "colonized by abstract principles of formal law" (Frank 2000, 4). Juridification of the lifeworld shares similar horizons with political philosophers Hannah Arendt's (1973) and Sheldon Wolin's (2003, 2008) notions of totalitarianism. Arendt observes how institutions in modern societies are superfluous and adorn the apparatuses of the state, yet offer no means of emancipation from tyranny, a perspective Habermas intimates in his colonization of the lifeworld thesis. Yet in contrast to Wolin, Habermas views an amalgamated state/corporatocratic entity as infiltrators of a lifeworld that can still be redeemed, while for Wolin the state apparatuses instead destroyed those institutions from within, securing their hegemony. Both see the same outcome that Wolin describes as an "inverted totalitarianism," a systemically "managed" democracy where corporatocratic dynamics administer the apparatuses of the state. Wolin's more dramatic assessment, though differing from Habermas and Arendt, can still be appreciated for its shared concerns about the total regulation of the lifeworld, and of existence itself within democracies exhibiting such totalitarian dynamics.

Habermas is concerned by how law develops into "an external force, imposed from without, to such an extent that modern compulsory law, sanctioned by the state, becomes an institution *detached from the ethical motivations* [emphasis added] of the legal person and dependent upon abstract obedience to the law" (1987, 174). A leading pathology of modernity, then, is this gradual infiltration of legal regulations into ever-greater expanses of lifeworld activity. In this regard Habermas is critical of the social-welfare state in its current iteration, an institution that for Chriss (1998) grants so many "rights" on the basis of race, gender, sexual orientation, age, disability, etc., that the actual legal enforcement of such state-sponsored rights enables *more* state encroachment, enforcement, and regulation of the lifeworld. Freedom is deemed good, but only if it is state-defined, state-imposed, and informed by political correctness, constraints of the rabble that troubled Nietzsche greatly. In this regard, Nietzsche's concerns about formal and informal systemic regulation reveals his affinities with Habermas. For Patton, Nietzsche forces us to ask to what extent our political authorities "appeal above all to the fear and impotence of the individuals who make up the political community," forcing us to confront questions about "the nature of political authority and institutions in a community of sovereign individuals" (Bergmann et al. 2007, 23).

A provocative extrapolation can be gleaned from a critique of the social-welfare state and a more decentralized, yet nevertheless faster, moving globalism that is liquid modernity: in its good intentions to be resourceful for every individual citizen, the democratic state—in need of ensuring public policy translates into realizable goals and resources for a variety of dependent and impatient groups—will grow larger, the regulatory apparatuses of the state will grow larger, and the reach of the state into one's sovereignty grows more extensive. What therefore emerges from such an observation are the tragic contradictions of democratism and capitalism: in its attempts to offer freedom to enhance life, the *enforcement* of freedom itself becomes a totalitarian and regulatory process that can incapacitate the self. Patton invokes Nietzsche by noting parallel sentiments from some of his Australian kinfolk, arguing that "Christian charity is one of Nietzsche's favoured examples, but a modern secular equivalent are the varieties of passive welfare payment or what Aboriginal people in Australia call 'sit-down money'" (Bergmann et al. 2007, 23).

Such infiltration into the lifeworld is mimicked by cultural production, as in the "enforcement" of political correctness by the slighted party that first exhibits the standard practice of being offended, followed by the expression of anger through generalized indignations that reinforce their identities.

Invariably, the offenses require a scripted communicative apology by the offending "other," a cultural convention that is now expected by identity groups, particularly in the United States. The crucial material consequences of life and living, its corresponding wisdoms, and potential for the will to power to develop in actors *within* a declining society, evaporate into emotionally politicized semantics further reproduced by political panopticons. Race, ethnicity, religion, and gender have thus become highly politicized victim identities that are used to police citizens of alternative persuasions, since under capitalism such victim identities are highly lucrative and profitable for those who wield them as weapons. Voluntary segregation based on petty provincialisms, nationalisms, and groupthink become the norm, and a new iteration of Motley Cow is established in the ever-cluttered lifeworld as we enter the second decade of the twenty-first century.

Yet another issue of lifeworld colonization requires mention. As juridified infiltration exacerbates the sanctity of the public sphere, cultural philistines and improvers of humanity, along with the market and its rational-legal apparatchiks, enable such social forces because the weakening of the lifeworld grants them access to its control. Fromm argues how such persons sacralize the public as a site of validations, and thus imbue it with a "religious quality for those who do not believe in the traditional hereafter anymore," and that such a public "paves the way to immortality," transforming public relations agents into culture's "new priests" (Fromm 1976, 70). Moreover, such persons offer themselves as a commodity, evinced as yet another manifestation of modernity's decadence. Here, Fromm echoes Nietzsche's concerns about selling out in ways that transform the self from a "use value" into an "exchange value" (1976, 127). Fromm further notes that in such a context, "the living being becomes a commodity on the 'personality market.' The principle of evaluation is the same on both the personality and the commodity markets: on the one, personalities are offered for sale; on the other, commodities" (1976, 127). In the less examined recesses of the *mis*information age signified by, for example, Facebook and social media cultural production, the aforementioned decadent forces synchronize, further crowding out lifeworld sovereignty with outside scripts to lure people toward befouling their consciousness and life narratives through visual excess of the minutiae and mundane.

Habermas laments how such developments enable lifeworld infiltration by a capitalist welfare state intimately tied to market dynamics. For Habermas, the public sphere's ability to repulse such infiltration is contingent upon its contestations of oppressive macro-level institutions. Only in such a manner could democracy complete itself as a project. Garnham argues that Habermas clearly distinguishes the public sphere from that of the state and market and, as a result, advantageously positions the observer to view "threats to democracy and the public discourses upon which it depends" (1994, 361). Public spheres are thus vital for ensuring that conditions for autonomy and sovereignty become salient. However, not all actors are cognizant of this and thus allow large-scale institutions to infiltrate and colonize their communities and freedoms, robbing actors of their autonomy. Such a concern would likely have befallen Nietzsche had he lived long enough to see the discontents of modernity transition toward its liquid state. When such a colonization occurs, regulatory and technical language become emptied of norms, a condition Habermas describes as being norm-free (1987). For Habermas the norm-free colonizing forces of the lifeworld is a deleterious systemic situation, contrasted by a norm-rich condition that is to be found in a decolonized lifeworld. With norm-free and regulatory language flowing down to the populace, into the public spheres of the lifeworld, the colonization of the lifeworld thus leaves but one "freedom" left for members of the community of last humans: the "freedom" to engage in consumption—including the consumption of material culture—with little distinction between healthy and unhealthy consumption. For Fromm, the outcome of this form of lifeworld colonization, one that Nietzsche would certainly validate, is that

> the individual ceases to be himself; he adopts entirely the kind of personality offered to him by cultural patterns. . . . The person who gives up his individual self and becomes an automaton, identical with millions of other automatons around him, need not feel alone and anxious anymore. But the price he pays, however, is high; it is the loss of his self. (Fromm 1969, 184)

Habermas envisions public spheres as contexts of "freedom and permanence" that exhibit emancipation beyond what elections can offer (1991, 4). That public spheres will contain those with personal and collective interests do not disqualify them from being important sites for social discontents to be addressed. It is thus imperative for Habermas that the grass roots reclaim the public sphere if only for the "natural vocation of man to communicate with his fellows, especially in matters affecting mankind as a whole" (1991, 107). Warren's (1993) examination of the utility of Habermas's ideas reveals how autonomous individuals are able to author and be critically decisive of their needs and interests. Because of their sovereignty, autonomous individuals are able to delink the self from systemic demands, one teeming with "traditions, prevailing opinions, and pressures to conform" (Warren 1993, 215), the scripts that so much concerned Nietzsche. Echoing Habermas and Nietzsche, Warren argues that autonomous individuals have agency to "create, to bring new ideas, things, and relations into being," thus enabling for the sovereign actor, the potential overcomer, "some amount of control over one's life history" (Warren 1993, 214–215).

In the current state of modernity, the colonized lifeworld and its public spheres have suppressed key attributes of freedom such as free communication in social life that defines the lifeworld, a process that requires intersubjectivity, a communicative process that can well accommodate overcomers as the educator ideal type envisioned by Solms-Laubach (2007). Yet because democracy remains an unfinished project of modernity, such communicative communities are being severely compromised, ensuring the staying power of nihilism. As such, Habermas was deeply concerned about how the lifeworld, seen as where the self and community deliberate and problem solve, are unable to fully repair the project of democracy. The process of decolonizing the lifeworld is, then, Habermas's sociological thrust into that area of modernity where the energies of communitarian empowerment can again be released. The decolonization process is thus a bottom-to-top trajectory, the trajectory of the overcomer. That said, highlighting major differences between Habermas and Nietzsche (and by implication how the aforementioned share affinities with other Frankfurt School thinkers) is in order before we further make visible their affinities.

The glaring difference between Nietzsche and Habermas, as noted throughout my work, lies in their views of democracy. For Habermas, democracy, in spite of its dysfunctions, remains alive, albeit suppressed, and thus could be made well by decolonizing the lifeworld. Nietzsche, on the other hand, had been penning its obituary and in many explicit instances welcomed its decadence as an epochal opportunity for the overcomer, the new elevated human being, to emerge from its rubble stronger than before and able to overcome all life challenges. Yet even Nietzsche appears sanguine about democracy compared to insights shared by political psychologist Shawn Rosenberg.

A timely warning by Rosenberg was conveyed by Rick Shenkman (2019) for *Politico Magazine* when he attended a 2019 conference in Lisbon, Portugal where the former had given a talk, a talk that echoed Nietzsche's concerns about democracy. Rosenberg provocatively argues that "we the people" are to blame for the decline of democracy. Rosenberg reasons that because democratism requires tremendous intellectual labor as inputs for its operations, the transition from elites who are informed enough to "navigate the heavy responsibilities that come with self-rule," to governance by citizens "ill-equipped cognitively and emotionally to run a well-functioning democracy," has degraded democratism. Power is thus handed over to citizens of a Nietzschean Motley Cow, citizens who exhibit "biases of various kinds" while they seek information to confirm and polarize their biases. Rosenberg laments how such a community of democratists lack the acumen to make operative the best of what democracies can offer, something political elites are better, if not more informed, at ensuring.

The elites, as Rosenberg defines them, are the people holding power at the top of the economic, political and intellectual pyramid who have "the motivation to support democratic culture and institutions and the power to do so effectively." In their roles as senators, journalists, professors, judges and government administrators, to name a few, the elites have traditionally held sway over public discourse and U.S. institutions—and have in that role helped the populace understand the importance of democratic values. (Shenkman 2019)

Shenkman conveys Rosenberg's observations with solemnity as the latter points to the imminent end of democracy, one that that will "continue its inexorable decline and will eventually fail." Citing the oft-quoted Fukuyama thesis about the "end of history," Rosenberg extends from this thesis the likely end of democracy as well. That democracy requires tremendous insight into the logistical and procedural details to prosecute elections, combined with the need to discern "large amounts of information" from *mis*information, the average citizen Rosenberg argues does not exhibit the wherewithal to be so incisive and decisive about such discernments. Rosenberg further adds that "the reason for right-wing populists' recent success is that 'elites' are losing control of the institutions that have traditionally saved people from their most undemocratic impulses. When people are left to make political decisions on their own they drift toward the simple solutions . . . *a deadly mix of xenophobia, racism and authoritarianism* [emphasis added]" (Shenkman 2019). In an observation that has eerie parallels to many of Nietzsche's assertions, Rosenberg continues:

The irony is that more democracy—ushered in by social media and the Internet, where information flows more freely than ever before—is what has unmoored our politics, and is leading us towards authoritarianism. Rosenberg argues that the elites have traditionally prevented society from becoming a totally unfettered democracy; their "oligarchic 'democratic' authority" or "democratic control" has until now kept the authoritarian impulses of the populace in check. (Shenkman 2019)

As noted elsewhere in this work, Habermas did not see the imminent end to democracy but instead saw its incompletion, requiring community empowerment to be secured at the communitarian grass roots, while Nietzsche categorically viewed democracy as a weakening agent, to be abandoned for a paradigm shift toward a new sovereignty that will be ushered in by overcomers. Habermas was not speaking of a romanticized new age through his sociology; Nietzsche, more of a romantic, enthusiastically and urgently called for its arrival. Habermas's sociology did not entirely place the onus of liberation on the individual but on the community to compensate for the democracy-robbing dysfunctions of modernity. Nietzsche, in contrast, believed that the catalysts will need to be the individual and community of noble-minded actors, for depending on modern social institutions alone for emancipation will not yield liberatory outcomes due its systemic demands for deference. The noble-minded overcomers can thus be seen as actors possessing what Egyed describes as an "ontology of agency" (2007, 107), one that can ultimately establish a new community of self-authored peoples who have assembled themselves from the crises of modernity, unfettered from old and contemporary scripts hindering their renewal. Finally, Habermas did not undertake an exegesis of religion and its death as catalysts for enabling nihilism, while for Nietzsche, the death of god and other old idols of religion paved the way for new, yet nonetheless false idols of modern systems to disempower actors, resulting in nihilism. Nietzsche, Habermas, and Rosenberg, however, all saw the putrefaction of democratism as it stands.

Where Habermas shares a similar horizon with Nietzsche is that the former is similarly concerned about systemic dysfunctions of modernity. Habermas is also suspicious of the unleashed forces of the market, its technical and institutional regulations, and how these affect the production of self and culture, parallel concerns for Nietzsche. Habermas also positions the actor to contest systemic incompetence by expressing communitarian tendencies, to which Nietzsche expresses parallel affinities, according to Young (2006), made obvious in Nietzsche's idealization of the pre-Socratic, Dionysian Greek community of *Birth*. Yet because of Habermas's ideological affinities with the Frankfurt School which was also critical of failed projects of modernity—for example, fascism, socialism, and capitalism—Nietzsche's disdain of the same aforementioned *isms* renders the amalgamation of his ideas with Habermas, Fromm, and the Frankfurt School ideal for understanding the impact of false idols upon modernity and liquid modernity.

I am of the view however, that Habermas's best sociology, one that fills in Nietzsche's blind spots, can be seen in his identification and explication of how the lifeworld is colonized by the juridification of macro-level institutions, resulting in a human condition where society's participants are denied the autonomy to deliberate ideas and resolve conflicts. For Habermas, the lifeworld context should ideally allow participants to "express themselves in situations that they have to define in common so far as they are acting with an orientation to mutual understanding" (1987, 121). When subjugated to systemic control, and here we see an identical concern exhibited by Nietzsche, a colonized lifeworld enables organs of the state apparatus to intervene and author the trajectories of its citizens in ways that do not enhance the freedoms needed for overcoming.

Habermas's position harks back to *Legitimation Crisis* (1975), a position that is central to understanding his concerns about the constraints macro-level institutions have upon the dynamics of culture and their communicative dimensions. He demonstrates in *Legitimation* how the state initially encountered resistances as it engaged with the cultural system since the former rendered "problematic matters that were formerly culturally taken for granted" (1975, 73). For Chriss (1998), this top-down dynamic thus constrained knowledge production from below, while Frank (2000) similarly argues that advanced capitalist societies have increasingly disabled communicative action in the lifeworld. In its wake, the marketplace dominates the "academy, basic information . . . news, entertainment, and government," destroying community and individualism in the process (Krey 2002, 5). Such social forces are of great interest to sociologists, according to Calhoun et al., many of whom are concerned with how people realize they were "limited by the social conditions in which they found themselves," and how this "was not just a matter of blockages in their way, of course, but often also of the absence of support systems" (2012, 6).

Habermas thus envisions an ideal society where system and lifeworld synchronize through conditions of empowerment that begin in public spheres. The rupturing of this symbiotic relationship he describes as the uncoupling of the system and lifeworld. In Nietzsche's assertion that morality had become decadent, Habermas thus offers an explanation as to how such a process unfolded: with the uncoupling of system and lifeworld, where the former becomes hegemonic against the latter. Communication and moral attitudes thus lose their purpose and become vulgarized (Jütten 2013). For Krey (2002), the uncoupling of system and lifeworld precedes lifeworld colonization by larger systemic forces. In the chasm between the state and the grass roots, systemic forces jockey for position to indoctrinate their worldviews and utopianisms upon actors' lives. Thus, whereas Nietzsche attributes democratism and capitalism's dysfunctions to their manufacturing of conforming and captive audiences, Habermas similarly saw their dysfunctions in how grass-roots articulations of freedom are stifled by dictates emanating from the bureaucratic echelons of democratic society that have infiltrated the lifeworld. In such contexts, Nietzsche was hoping to see the best overcomers freely reassemble new narratives of emancipation and self-mastery, while Habermas saw in historical and empirical detail what prevented such an emergence.

Habermas asserts that capitalist societies rely on the market as a catalyst for system integration. It performs this function through norm-free regulation of potentially cooperative contexts where the "steering of individual decisions is not subjectively coordinated" (1987, 150). In this regard, citizens living under a colonized lifeworld simply do not know they can still "draw on the 'moral resources' that are available to them in the lifeworld" (Jütten 2013, 594). Habermas warns that such system integration of the lifeworld—or more accurately *system appropriation* of the lifeworld by market forces—can create a variety of social pathologies such as alienation, *anomie*, and loss of individual and collective identities: diacritica of Nietzsche's nihilism. The final step of lifeworld colonization by the state apparatus, then, is to appropriate culture, to "vacuum" from its terrain cues to be refashioned for socio-political interests. In fact, juridification of social life is a form of de jure "rule" inside democratic capitalist states in the period between election cycles. Here Habermas saw the insides of an incomplete and colonized democracy in ways that have overlapping horizons with Nietzsche's assertion that democracy is decadent. Indeed, in between election cycles corporate and cultural entities constrain dialog through juridification and identity politics, respectively, thus entrenching their power through the economy and the culture industry, so effectively noted by key Frankfurt School thinkers such as Max Horkheimer and Theodor Adorno (1972) as well as Herbert Marcuse (1964). For Fromm, juridification trajectories are designed to "befog the issues" as if "problems are too complicated for the average individual to grasp," requiring "specialists" to decipher the cryptic regulatory language that emanates from macro-level institutions (1969, 249). This issue is of great importance to sociologist of postmodernity Zygmunt Bauman. He argues in *Wasted Lives* (2004) that one outcome of a liquid modernity across the planet's various lifeworlds is its enabling of cultural nomadism, a process that has decentered humanity even further from realizable outcomes and accepted truths. One can intimate how such a daunting process exhibits a tragic irony: actors, demoralized, are expected to return to social systems, their juridification, and their different improvers of humanity working out of the state apparatus and panopticized lifeworlds. Bauman explains: "What we all seem to fear . . . is abandonment, exclusion, being rejected, blackballed, disowned, dropped, stripped of what we are. . . . We fear being left alone, helpless and hapless. . . . We fear to be dumped. . . . What we miss most badly is the certainty that all that won't happen—not to us" (2004, 128). For Nietzsche's overcomer, such fears are but attributes of last human beings.

Juridification in democracies is a real mechanism engaged in the systemic colonization of the lifeworld; that is, formal legislation and political correctness that define social regulations are imposed upon the actor to "behave." Arguably employing a Nietzschean lens, we might infer that Bauman's subtext of deferring to juridifying improvers of humanity out of fear evinces an actor's lack of fortitude. Therefore, the contestations of such systems by Habermas, Fromm, and Bauman echo Nietzsche's contestations of the systemic analogs of his day: Christianity, the *isms* of Europe at the turn of the nineteenth century into the twentieth century, and the "heavy" modernity of industrial capitalism. Habermas suggests in *TCA* that if we fail to contest such systems, juridification and its concomitant laws, along with in my view, policing cultural scripts that ostensibly promote identity politics, we will engender a totalitarian democracy. Similarly, Stahl points to the juridification of the family "through the educational bureaucracy and family law, as well as the neutralization of the citizen role by the consumer role" in the private sphere as the human condition of a colonized lifeworld (2013, 539). Juridification can also emerge as a consequence of how modernity and especially a liquid modernity are ever-increasingly reliant on technical and cognitive orientations toward comprehending a reality that relies on legalities which, in turn, propagate more technical control of social life. These social forces can emanate from the higher strata of society's establishments and are meted back to the public as factual information, a top-down process that engenders reification over time. Frank's ability to make operative Habermas's juridification can be seen in his assessment of the medical system:

> In my own study of medicine, the lifeworld relationships of patients and those who care for them—doctors and nurses—are increasingly colonized by the demands of third-party payers, whether these are insurance companies in the U.S. or government in the Commonwealth countries. . . . The legitimacy of medicine is in crisis: the popularity of complementary practitioners is one indication of this, and the prevalence of malpractice suits in the U.S. is another. The discontent I hear constantly in medical groups and illness support groups is loud and clear—and yet medicine becomes more exclusively a "system" that excludes lifeworld communicative action. . . . When such talk is excluded and patients are simply told what medicine will offer, take it or leave it, medicine creates the conditions for its legitimacy crisis to deepen. (Frank 2000, 4)

Habermas notes in *TCA* that lifeworld colonization and its subsequent cultural impoverishment points to how "the imperatives of autonomous subsystems make their way into the lifeworld . . . like colonial masters coming into a tribal society," a situation that forces "a process of assimilation upon it" (1987, 355). For Habermas, actors in lifeworld public spheres are unable to respond to such colonization because large institutions overpower individual agency in ways that subject them to the system, a process that "blocks enlightenment by the mechanism of reification" (1987, 355), a situation that greatly concerned Nietzsche. Habermas is similarly concerned, noting how ideally the "lifeworld is always constituted in the form of global knowledge intersubjectively shared by its members," but that under lifeworld colonization "everyday consciousness is robbed of its power to synthesize" and "becomes fragmented" (1987, 355). However, Habermas's critical views of regulation in no way imply that he sloganeered anarchic revolution. Instead, Habermas's concerns gravitate toward how law micro-manages people's everyday lives in ways that replace the "social solidarity of the lifeworld that formerly was forged tacitly" (Chriss 1998, 3). As informal understanding of life gives way to formal rules codified in law, one's search for meaning and purpose in the lifeworld consequently becomes stifled and impoverished of cues (Chriss 1998). Frank is more forthright, noting how such conditions suggest "there is no possibility of reaching a common understanding" (2000, 3). In an affinity with Habermas, Nietzsche appears to envision an active politics at the micro-level taking place in Volkish social environs not unlike Habermas's lifeworld. It is in this lifeworld, presumably, where Egyed sees Nietzsche's will to power applied:

> It is there that the encounters involve the clash, or convergence, of feeling passions, and where drives are alternatively dominating or dominated. . . . It invites suspicion about totalizing party politics, and it is positively hostile to forms of identity politics that confine persons within narrow limits. A Nietzsche inspired politics would focus on local, punctual, issues. (Egyed 2007, 113)

Egyed, then, localizes Nietzsche's praxis, a fortunate scope condition that inspires empowerment in the immediacies of systemic crisis. In such a lifeworld, understandably, there is no expectation for the community to defer to macro-social institutions. Members of this iteration of society are implicitly aware their interactions with macro-social institutions entail dealing with red tape, cryptic legal language, and regulatory policies. There are also spatial manifestations of juridification that can be experienced tangibly. Architect Victor Gruen offers a biting view of the situation, describing how civic centers are "concentration camps for bureaucrats, who are thus prevented from mingling with common folks" (cited in Oldenburg 1999, 69). Gruen explains this is why institutions "lose their touch with and understanding of the problems of the latter" (cited in Oldenburg 1999, 69).

For Habermas, what should be normatively significant for repairing democratic practices is that new approaches to freedom and sovereignty should be generated from a consensus of deliberative citizens "coming together to decide their fate collectively through representation" (Chriss 1998, 2). However, Habermas observes how thus far the process of colonizing the lifeworld has been successful because money, law, and power underpin all institutions and bureaucracies of the state. They exist in a context where few norms and ethics are allowed to inform their allocation and distribution of social resources. Operators upholding systemic supremacy thus employ an immorality of exploitation, not an emancipatory Nietzschean immorality that is informed by a revaluation of all values. For Frank (2000), quantitative media such as money and power are "non-communicative," but when money as power communicates, they do so by communicating at, not to, the populace through juridification. Habermas thus implicates money for exploiting "a social intercourse that has been largely disconnected from norms and values" (1987, 154). The actor's only purpose in such a system is, for Max Weber in *The Protestant Ethic and the Spirit of Capitalism*, to live the capitalist script of investing and saving for the purpose of consumption. In this regard, the market contains no values comparable to those generated at the grass roots. Moreover, the market's lack of values continues to be regularly reproduced through bureaucratic imperatives from above, not below. Yet, in spite of being norm-free, Habermas argues in *TCA* that the medium of money has structure-forming effects due to its capacity to be an "intersystemic medium of exchange" where "the activities of different organizations for the same function and the activities of the same organization for different functions can be clustered together" (1987, 171–172). Money and power thus play out through juridification by establishing complex communicative interactions and exploitative networks in macro-level institutions for which no one can explicitly be held accountable.

It is the power of money, conveyed through juridification, and emanating from different interconnected institutions that allow for the dynamics of lifeworld colonization to be realized. Habermas contends in *TCA* that this rationalization of the lifeworld "makes possible a heightening of systemic complexity, which becomes so hypertrophied that it unleashes system imperatives that burst the capacity of the lifeworld they instrumentalize" (1987, 155). Frank affirms this condition, noting "as advanced capitalist societies have developed, the core integrative function of communication has been increasingly disabled" (2000, 1). Thus, the colonization of the lifeworld reaches its conclusion when the language of the lifeworld is replaced with norm-free and regulatory language, rewards, and punishments, thus "technicizing" the lifeworld (Habermas 1987, 183) and robbing "actors of the meaning of their own action" (Habermas 1987, 302). A relationship between macro-level institutions and the colonized lifeworld's public spheres driven primarily by the arithmetic of money is thus facilitated through a medium where no common understanding can be reached, only a zero-sum approach where social institutions unfurl agendas upon the populace by imposing their scripts, regulation, and language. Understandably, Frank (2000) notes how money and votes are unable to provide existential understanding or political empowerment since these are primarily quantifiable variables. In such a scenario, the lifeworld is bereft of social actors that can reach a common understanding on social problematics. In its place are Nietzsche's *faux* elites: the cultural philistines, improvers of humanity, the soul doctors, even residual priestly aristocracies of a liquid modernity, all of whom engage in ideological manipulation to "control the substance of public deliberation and . . . legislation . . . that reflect and

defend their own interests at the expense of the relatively powerless masses"
(Chriss 1998, 2). The freedoms of an uncolonized public sphere for the overcomer are thus strangled by the juridification of the lifeworld.

In Erich Fromm's *Escape from Freedom* (1969) the human condition of
freedom is outlined historically, beginning with the medieval period. Fromm
contends that freedom is assembled through the process of individuation
that began during the Reformation and continued onward into the twentieth
century. Fromm provocatively argues that although modernity had inspired
people to celebrate their subsequent freedoms derived from their individua-
tions, it exacted a cost: the ultimate loss of an authentic self able to transcend
systemic control. With such a loss, individuals, although freer than those
from the Medieval period, still had their "safe," and if wearing a Nietzschean
lens defeatist, zones of caste, ethnicity, and religion. These identities of
conformity made unnecessary the need to continue the refinement of their
individualism. As such, the individual of today is trapped in a context of despair, desperation, and isolation. In affirmation of Nietzsche's concern about
modernity's generation of nihilism as well as possibilities for purposing one's
existence, Fromm writes:

> Man was deprived of the security he had enjoyed, of the unquestionable feeling
> of belonging, and he was torn loose from the world which had satisfied his quest
> for security both economically and spiritually. He felt alone and anxious. But he
> was also free to act and to think independently, to become his own master and
> do with his life as he could—not as he was told to do. (1969, 99)

Fromm, however, saw a dangerous facet of freedom: even though Prot-
estantism freed man "spiritually" and capitalism "mentally, socially, and
politically" (1969, 106), the need to repeatedly make important decisions as
a requirement of such freedom, because it exists in great multitude within
our lifeworlds, has turned the responsibilities needed to maintain it into a
severe "burden" (1969, 74). The individual thus tries to escape from freedom,
handing over authority to improvers of humanity nested within macro-level
institutions. Fromm thus illuminates the terrain of Nietzsche's sycophantic
and conforming last humans, along with the political malcontents that fashion
themselves as their improvers of humanity.

Fromm examines Hitler and the Nazi Party's rise to power in post-World
War I Germany to substantiate his assertions, citing how pre–Third Reich
Germans escaped the freedoms offered by the fledgling Weimar Republic, a
representative democracy that existed between 1919 and 1933. The population ceded power to the Nazis so the weight of Germany's cultural, economic,
and political travails could be attended to by the paternal despotism of Hitler
and the Third Reich. The rise of the Third Reich indoctrinated the individual

to be "saved from making decisions, saved from the final responsibility for the fate of his self . . . saved from the doubt of what decisions to make" (Fromm 1969, 155). The entrenchment of the Third Reich thus meant that individual and collective freedoms were articulated not by higher humans or potential overcomers, but by the nationalist state. Fromm's observations thus highlight the plight of the passive nihilist when given a surfeit of freedoms: the non-overcoming individual escapes from them and runs toward profane systems that can make decisions on their behalf, even though such systems direct their constituencies through juridification and social policing by identity groups. In the case of Nazi ideology, this regulatory narrative served the interests of jingoists and military industrialists that supported Hitler's rise to power during the pre–World War II period.

In the context of the free market, Fromm argues that capitalism freed the individual to "stand on his own feet and to try his luck" so as to become the "master of his fate," allowing money to become "the great equalizer of man . . . more powerful than birth and caste," such that it influenced people to employ their freedom to seek out only what is quantifiable in corporeal existence (1969, 61–62). Fromm laments how members of society believe this is a bona fide freedom, unaware that such an orientation is a result of manipulation by what Fromm describes as anonymous authorities, that is, decision-making experts and corporatists plying their trade from within their respective bureaucracies. The power they wield is authoritarian in nature, one that limits interaction between lifeworld and system, and one where juridification constrains the ability of the grassroots to formulate counter-responses against formally sanctioned regulations of social control. Anonymous authority, then, can be seen as an effective means for macro-level institutions of democracies to establish their totalitarian hegemony over last humans. Fromm continues:

It is disguised as common sense, science, psychic health, normality, public opinion. It does not demand anything except the self-evident. It seems to use no pressure but only mild persuasion. . . . Anonymous authority is more effective than overt authority, since one never suspects that there is any order which one is expected to follow. In external authority it is clear that there is an order and who gives it; one can fight against the authority, and in this fight personal independence and moral courage can develop . . . in anonymous authority both command and commander have become invisible. . . . There is nobody and nothing to fight back against. (1969, 166)

Fromm argues, however, that although people surrender their freedom to anonymous authorities and begin to function as cogs, "sometimes small, sometimes larger, of a machinery which forces its tempo upon him, which he cannot control" (1969, 125), they nonetheless believe they are still free to make their own decisions to remove their socially limiting conditions on their own terms. How is this possible? That is, how do people stay deluded when a slow reification of macro-level institutions takes place in ways that, in turn, mete out social control upon the populace? Habermas's response likely suggests these actors' lifeworlds have already been colonized over a long chronology: community has weakened, and members of the community are indoctrinated into and distracted by the need to compete against one another by adorning themselves with material culture secured by being a free consumer, a vulgarized freedom if seen from a Nietzschean perspective. Fromm echoes Tönnies's concerns about *gesellschaft* as well as Habermas's concerns about how a colonized lifeworld generates reification and by extrapolation nihilism, noting how "the concrete relationship of one individual to another has lost its direct and human character and has assumed a spirit of manipulation and instrumentality" (1969, 119). Fromm warns how anonymous authorities are able to make actors believe "we can have thoughts, feelings, wishes, and even sensual sensations which we subjectively feel to be ours, and yet . . . these . . . have been put into us from the outside, are basically alien, and are not what we think, feel and so on" (1969, 187). Fromm emphasizes:

> Most people are convinced that as long as they are not overtly forced to do something by an outside power, their decisions are theirs, and that if they want something, it is they who want it. But this is one of the great illusions we have about ourselves. A great number of our decisions are not really our own but are suggested to us from the outside; we have succeeded in persuading ourselves that it is we who have made the decision, whereas we have actually conformed with expectations of others, driven by the fear of isolation and . . . threats to our life, freedom, and comfort. (1969, 197)

Taking us to the precipice of nihilism, Fromm argues that although the individual is "free from all ties binding him to spiritual authorities . . . this very freedom leaves him alone and anxious" and "overwhelms him with a feeling of his own individual insignificance and powerlessness" (1969, 80). Consequently, the "isolated individual is crushed by the experience" (Fromm 1969, 80). For Fromm, people no longer hail from a world where universal frameworks remain uncontested, frameworks that allowed for teleological certainty about transcendental states or fantastic metaphysical places of meaning, purpose, and immortality. Instead, the modern being in a democratic capitalist system is swimming in a surfeit of scripted and squandered opportunities for assembling new freedoms. Moreover, corporatocratic and state-packaged freedoms overwhelm the person who is already fatigued by their incessant demands for all forms of heavy decision-making. A surfeit of this "new freedom" paradoxically generates a "deep feeling of . . . powerlessness, doubt, aloneness, and anxiety" (Fromm 1969, 63). Lost in the self's own world of relativism, nihilism, and subjective motivations, Fromm contends that people are forced to seek the meaning of life from different sites of society—sites which for Nietzsche are primarily decadent—rendering them vulnerable to control by a variety of institutions and their improvers of humanity.

Fromm thus argues that people who escape their freedoms end up becoming automatons living in a world of negative freedom where they display a "marked dependence on powers outside themselves, on other people, or institutions" (1969, 141). These unempowered, however, have yet to realize that institutions of democratic capitalism do not offer its actors any answers for their epistemic or ontologic dilemmas. Instead, they offer those without courage or fortitude a tawdry pageantry of cultural, political, and consumer scripts to follow and repeat as "tradition." Fromm adds:

> A vast sector of modern advertising . . . does not appeal to reason but to emotion; like any other kind of hypnoid suggestion, it tries to impress its objects emotionally and then make them submit intellectually . . . these methods of dulling the capacity for critical thinking are more dangerous to our democracy than many of the open attacks against it, and more immoral—in terms of human integrity. (1969, 127–128)

For Fromm, such citizens become vulnerable to the "factual or alleged orders of these outside forces" (1969, 141). Alas, the contradiction of the human condition in search of freedom is presented: give the passive nihilist too much freedom (which always is accompanied by requirements for decision-making to sustain systems of the state) and that person will run from it, escape from it, a distinctly different trajectory than that of the overcomer with freedoms who will employ them to bolster the will to power. In this regard, Fromm makes visible an important attribute of democratic capitalism: the escape from freedom is precipitated by those free individuals who no longer wish to, or lack the wherewithal to take on heavy responsibilities needed to assemble their lives in an uncertain, liminal, and liquid world. These are the last humans of Nietzsche thought, flocking toward systems and their improvers of humanity for solutions they have denied themselves from finding. They are, in the final instance, just as complicit in establishing a totalitarian democracy as their improvers of humanity.

EPILOGUE

As this work draws to a close, we need to make visible current social contexts that allow us to envision Nietzsche's overcomer as an actor exhibiting their will to power within such confines, a will to power that can ultimately propel them through their confines. Does a Nietzsche sociology, with the overcomer as a key protagonist in a crisis society, remain relevant if data about the global and local tend toward cautious optimism if not sanguine assessments of social progress? To answer this particular question requires us to consider important arguments that illuminate new and old catalysts that are seen to affect the human condition, especially through the ideas offered by Michele Gelfand (2018), Ronald Inglehart (2018), and Nassim Nicholas Taleb (2012).

Gelfand's thoughtful *Rule Makers, Rule Breakers* makes visible the global and historical tendency for "tighter" cultures to embed greater regulatory norms into their social systems. In contrast, "looser" cultures allow for greater communal permissiveness and multicultural finesse. The tight and loose dichotomy, as analytical device, is transplantable to within states, organizations, and workplace environments. By examining over seven thousand respondents from diverse occupations, genders, ages, religions, and social classes from over thirty countries across five continents, Gelfand found that tighter cultures tend to be centralized in their dynamics. They also offer greater degrees of stability, decisiveness, and synchronization of all layers of society. Looser cultures exhibit greater volatility and instability, yet offer many more expansive horizons for agency and innovation. Moreover, Gelfand's tight-loose continuum accommodates the discontents of culture that transition it between tighter and looser modes, generating liminalities and reassurances that further inform cultural production over time. Comparing world cultures across the present as well as across time, Gelfand's optimism is underscored by the view that the human experience is one that needs to understand and negotiate between these two antipodes of the life experience.

Most relevant for our work, Gelfand convincingly argues that a regional unit's experiences with calamities—be they through warfare, disease, scarcity, or natural disasters, compel the cultural diacritica to exhibit more regulatory social norms. Conversely, a region with fewer threats to human security—that is, fewer existential threats and thus greater existential security, in the eyes of Inglehart (2018)—will over time articulate cultural norms that are more tolerant of diversity (and even its associated dissonance). It is Gelfand's illumination of Nietzsche's time, one proximate to the deadly Franco-Prussian War, as well as Germany as a nation-state experiencing the two world wars, along with the Cold War, that allows her to argue that German culture has historically exhibited a tighter legacy of more rule-based motivations, organizational precision, and bureaucratic hegemony—an issue of great concern in Max Weber's prescient sociology—resulting in a society that emphasizes discipline, precision, and predictability in operations and outcomes. That Nietzsche can emerge within the stifling context of the Germany of his day to not only find his voice, but to create a new philosophy to respond to such existence—one that includes powerful anti-war narrative as seen in *Human*, is commendable. At a time when *faux* norms of civilization reproduced by German cultural philistines had informed an incipient nationalism taking root in Germany, Nietzsche projected such *faux* norms as cultural diacritica that had to be overcome. Nietzsche's incisive and prescient sociological imagination thus illuminates a trajectory for the actor to harness maximum sovereignty and their will to power, even in tight historical and social constraints.

Such maximum agency, for Nietzsche, is also needed in modern life experiences, one impoverished in terms of meaning. It is not enough to simply discern social contexts of tightness and looseness as a means to assess the quality of human existence. Transcendent narratives for meaningful existence based on Nietzschean ideals of emancipation, will to power, and one's ability to purpose their existence as active nihilists working from outside convention and constraints, require life experiences to be as unpredictable for developing the overcomer as Gelfand's rendering of existence is predictable when seen within the antipodes of tight and loose cultures. Moreover, by relying on a tight-loose dichotomy for viewing culture, one overlooks the complex *ressentiment* and revanchisms of informal culture—especially its American "democratic" variant—and how these are still able to, even in the loose cultural channels of civil society, embed panopticons for the sole purpose of tightly policing society. In the final instance, both tighter and looser modes of social systems still engender some form of authority meted out by the state apparatus through its ideological *isms*, juridification, and newer (but still false) idols. Nietzsche's overcomer can still be positioned against such a top-to-bottom flow of culture and power, whether emanating from tighter or looser iterations.

Nietzsche remains a useful contrarian to approaches that see tight and loose social contexts as indicators of lesser or greater maneuverability for the sovereign being, since for our philosopher, freedoms cannot be found in modern systems and their *isms*, all of which institutionally and culturally herd an uncritical populace. Gelfand's binary remains a useful perspective, however, for seeing how social and cultural variations "breathe" across the present as well as across time between its tight-loose modes, often shaped by what Taleb terms "Black Swans," the "large-scale unpredictable and irregular events of massive consequences" that afflict both tight and loose systems (2012, 6; see also Taleb 2010). Such systemic crises for Nietzsche and Taleb are needed as catalysts for the emergence of the actor with agency to prevail, to overcome, and to transcend, to "gain from disorder" as noted in the subtitle of Taleb's work. How overcomers can be seen to respond to liminalities that continue to surface in the dynamics of tight and loose cultures, and within each culture's regulation of tightness and looseness in the lifeworld, can add greatly to contingencies unexplored by Gelfand. Indeed, the introduction of the over-coming actor in this work may serve to nourish the human condition when it experiences Gelfand's concession that "in fact, we're a super-normative spe-cies," one that spends "a huge amount of our lives following social rules and conventions—even if the rules don't make any sense" (2018, 8). With such problematics, the utility of a Nietzsche sociological imagination that empow-ers the praxian agent, the overcomer, is even more timely.

Ronald Inglehart's data-rich *Cultural Evolution* argues that as a human species, we have evolved toward greater self-expression and freedoms given that existential threats to our well-being have decreased overall. By citing data between 1981 and 2014 acquired from over 105 countries with 90% of the world's population, the 358 surveys that resulted in the World Values Survey and the European Values Surveys allowed Inglehart to conclude that as a variety of macro-level threats to our safety have decreased over time (for example, conventional military conflicts), resulting in existential security, the tendency will be for cultures to, in varying degrees, move in the direction of internalizing postmaterialist values such as the embrace of self-expression, as opposed to survival values based on "ethnocentric solidarity against outsid-ers" (2018, 10). Such postmaterialist values are not entirely influenced by the material consequences of life which, argues Inglehart, inform survival values responding to outcomes acutely affected by scarcity and mortality, that is, existential *in*security. A proponent of not modernization theory, but evolutionary modernization theory, Inglehart offers a linear reading of hu-man progress. For example, he notes how in the postwar era of the twentieth toward the twenty-first century, "A central feature of modernization is that it makes life more secure, eliminating starvation and increasing life expectancy . . . this brings pervasive changes in human motivations, enabling people to shift from life strategies based on the perception that survival is insecure, to strategies that take survival for granted" (Inglehart 2018, 10).

Do Inglehart's hopeful findings about how existential security results in greater degrees of self-expression in society exonerate us from the need to make operative Nietzsche's overcoming type? After all, life is improving in a variety of ways, with postmaterial self-expression values leading us toward various iterations of democratism. However, that Nietzsche proclaimed in *Science* the need to live dangerously by building homes on the slopes of Mt. Vesuvius and sailing uncharted oceans if need be, Inglehart's existential security did not offer insights on whether postmaterial cultural content and motivations manufactured by the culture industry and the state's propaganda outlets, even in existentially secure contexts, actually give us a herdish (and thus false) "security" that needs to be overcome, even if dangerous, even if it forces the self upon uncharted oceans. If complacency from such security is manufactured through conformist, herd-like behavior influenced by consumption, materialism, improvers of humanity, and soul doctors, then such existential security is not the equivalent of one having found meaning, purpose, and self-actualization in one's existence. In such a context, Inglehart's assertions about a more civil, communicative, and free-spirited future remains inchoate if made to respond to the shadow of modernity, nihilism.

Lastly, Inglehart celebrates the merits of increasing democratization since it empowers ordinary citizens, a view anathema to Nietzsche's rendering of a democratism that should affirm, instead, the excellence of noble-minded elites with their will to power, not those with debased standards representing last humans operating under their servant moralities and *ressentiment*. To what degree Nietzsche's notion of the noble-minded overcomer possesses the ability to repeatedly find meaning and sovereignty against the backdrop of a conforming general populace, assumed to be able to experience "effective democracy" when there are "high levels of societal development" (Inglehart 2018, 119), constitutes a wonderful problematic that can inform future discourse on a Nietzsche sociology. However, that Inglehart amalgamates social development with effective democracy is a difficult argument to sustain if we examine more incisively the frequency of when democratic practices have not yielded good governance, as can be seen under the current administration in the United States as well as the country's history of internally colonizing its indigenous and minority populations through institutional discriminatory policies and lifeworld hostilities that were based on enslavement, lynchings, genocide, and forced transfers of large and unwilling populations to concentration camps (for example, reservations for the United States' indigenous peoples and World War II's Executive Order 9066).

The liminalities that emerge from such disingenuous "democracies," if one adopts a Habermasian view, reminds us that even in Inglehart's rendering of social progress, Nietzsche's sociological imagination and his overcomer type can still be made operative: for overcoming a life experiencing regression due to manufactured existential securities meted upon the populace in ways that ignore existential *in*securities and nihilism amplified by impaired democratism. Indeed, if we respond to these concerns with discernments from a Nietzsche sociological imagination, then it can be argued that there has been no "evolution" and only intermittent, and likely *faux*, existential security in modernity. Thus, even though modernity is suspect in Nietzsche's sociological imagination, his sociological insights can still be made operative to seek out self-authoring and overcoming agents as a means to confront a conformity-defined safe existence, one that appears increasingly shaped by angst born from meaningless fetishization of commodities and blind spots that overlook how incessant proxy warfare (a type of warfare that actually constituted much of the Cold War and military conflicts of today) and sectarian violence born from failed multiculturalisms (former Yugoslavia and current Myanmar are but two examples) continue to obstruct our evolutionary trajectory toward a sanguine postmaterial existence. An evolutionary modernity that does not explicitly expound in its equation whether there is value beyond our current *isms*, ideologies, and religiosities—even if they are hopeful and are believed to have "evolved"—exhibits a blind spot in reading how self-empowerment can still manifest in contestation against state-generated *in*security and conformity that prevent individuals from affirming an overcoming self.

Such omitted discernments by Inglehart can be attributed, of course, to deliberate research design and its employment of much larger-scope conditions. Thus, my critique should not be seen as a faulting process since Inglehart's excellent study sought a reading of the *planet's* geopolitical conditions and their sociological and development trajectories. Inglehart's scope of examination is thus not the point of contention, but in what context can we accurately frame the overcoming person as a valid actor able to discern disingenuous existential "securities" embedded and entangled in the fog of consumerism, materialism, and political charlatanism offered us by improvers of humanity. The particularities and ubiquity of suffering, the frequent yet random appearances of Black Swans, of systemic crises, or of semantics that potentially circle around definitional properties of "security" that too frequently change with political climate and debased oligarchies, compel me to consider Inglehart's assessment as too optimistic. With a Nietzsche reading of modernity, our failure to sever ties with the states' improvers of humanity—their patriots, their nationalists who have now offered their captive audiences the nation as idol and nationalism as script—has now resulted in a situation where around the globe conditions of a "World" War III are already in place, a life negation of epic and tragic proportions. At the time of this writing, tensions between Pakistan and India continue to deteriorate over Jammu and Kashmir; China and the United States engage in saber-rattling in the Pacific and through the trade war; Iran and Saudi Arabia are on the verge of direct confrontation; Syria, Turkey, and Russia are in a tripartite dance of death—Kurdish deaths; and US tensions with Russia, China, Iran, Venezuela, North Korea, and China's tensions with Japan, Taiwan, Philippines, and Vietnam, to name but a few, suggest instead that existential insecurity can also justifiably be seen to frame our current modernity.

With such aforementioned problematics, a more ideal horizon for making operative overcoming dynamics can be seen in Taleb's innovative work *Antifragile: Things that Gain from Disorder* (2012). Taleb offers a means of assessing systems, institutions, politics, and cultural dynamics on a continuum that ranges from states of fragility, to robustness, and antifragility. He argues, among other things, that systemic design needs to incorporate antifragility, or strength that becomes amplified as decay and disorder increase. Antifragility is defined by Taleb as the "property of all those natural (and complex) systems that have survived" (2012, 5). Taleb's formulation of antifragility is meant to be a multiaxial lens that can view across social and ideational contexts of existence, as well as across the present and across time. Taleb argues immediately in his work's Prologue that with situations like randomness, uncertainty, and chaos, one needs to be able to "use them, not hide from them," and that one needs to be like "fire and wish for the wind" (2012, 3). Our mission as humans, then, is to "domesticate, even dominate, even conquer, the unseen, the opaque, and the inexplicable" (2012, 3). In this continuum, even those who remain but only resilient and robust can muster strength to withstand shocks, while the antifragile succeeds in amplifying their power in contexts of such duress. Taleb, inimitably, forwards the notion of post-traumatic growth as a more effective lens for promoting and understanding human advancement, and in purposing what I consider to be overcoming actors exemplified by "people harmed by past events," yet who are still able to "surpass themselves" regardless of their effects (2012, 41).

Extrapolating from Taleb's arguments, we can see how a scion of Nietzsche existentialism is encouraging us to distance ourselves from social systems that are fragile. Taleb's analog to the improvers of humanity, the *fragilista*, is argued to produce culture and social systems that exhibit "blindness to the mysterious, the impenetrable, what Nietzsche called the Dionysian, in life" (2012, 10). The following palette of Taleb's additional analogs to Nietzsche's last humans reveals the smooth segue that can be had from Nietzsche's ideas operationalized for professional malcontents of Taleb's twenty-first century. For example,

> there is the medical fragilista who overintervenes in denying the body's natural ability to heal and gives you medications with potentially very severe side effects; the policy fragilista . . . who mistakes the economy for a washing machine that continuously needs fixing . . . the psychiatric fragilista who medicates children to "improve" their intellectual and emotional life. (Taleb 2012, 10)

Taleb's view of politicians expresses a similar solidarity with Nietzsche; that is, politicians do not offer empowerment for the self in their role as improvers of humanity. Their "speeches, goals, and promises aim at the timid concepts of 'resilience,' 'solidity,' not antifragility, and in the process are stifling the mechanisms of growth and evolution" (Taleb 2012, 10). Giving credence to active nihilists, Taleb further notes that "we didn't get where we are today thanks to policy makers—but thanks to the appetite for risks and errors of a certain class of people we need to encourage, protect, and respect" (2012, 10).

Taleb's assertions offers potential for antifragile overcoming of a variety of modernity's experientials, be they liquid, tight, loose, or postmaterial. Taleb's antifragile thesis also makes visible, insofar as social and disciplinary systems are concerned, how the overcomer can negotiate with fragile systems: by overcoming social systems that proselytize ideology (fragile) with, perhaps, a Dionysian mythology (antifragile); engage in a paradigm shift in ethics where the antifragile (the strong) are celebrated over the fragile (the weak); participate in a science where theory (fragile) is superseded by phenomenology (robust), and later evidence-based phenomenology (antifragile); and finally, establish a collection of decentralized city-states (antifragile) over the nation state (fragile) insofar as political systems are concerned (Taleb 2012, 23–25). Ensuring that Nietzsche's sociological imagination affirms with Taleb's vision of an antifragile existence amplifies existential sociology at many levels. Most crucially, it gravitates our analysis toward a Nietzschean decadence, or in much more current parlance, the notion of failed states. Like Nietzsche, Taleb sloganeers the need for humanity to seek out stressors, harm, chaos, disorder, and the like as catalysts for post-traumatic growth and self-making, scenarios that are readily accessible in a liquid modernity with no center, exhibiting instead fluid cultural production and unpredictable systemic distortions if not destruction. Like Habermas, Taleb observes through his iteration of juridification how "modernity has replaced ethics with legalese, and the law can be gamed with a good lawyer" (2012, 15). A revaluation of values is thus in order, and we can therefore gift Nietzsche's sociological imagination with a newer horizon: a Taleb-inspired understanding of modernity as replete with fragilities that must be overcome with an antifragile will to power, with antifragile social systems.

Nietzsche's sociological imagination, then, offers the self agency in a society experiencing a multitude of systemic scenarios, sanguine, or crisis-ridden. The utility of Nietzsche's prescience can, it is hoped, be seen in how his ideas are still able to be made operative under the conditions illuminated by Gelfand, Inglehart, and Taleb. For Nietzsche, these conditions can still enable the self's successful quest for sovereignty to purpose one's existence with meaning and power beyond the panopticons of a decaying yet still stubbornly scripted existence. Nietzsche was not a perfect human being, yet he understood acutely that a human being must be a work in progress even if the actor's society is in regress, thus his emphasis for the overcomer as one with ultimate agency to prevail even when social institutions of the state distort, renege, and/or vulgarize their social contracts. Nietzsche took nothing for granted in human existence, especially the idealized utopias and teleological ideologies meted out by society's lifeworld-colonizing institutions. Overcoming their inadequacies without *ressentiment* requires tremendous mental strength and noble integrity. The effort Nietzsche outlined for achieving this makes his philosophy and sociological views ideal for understanding individual agency in contexts of acute social dysfunctions and renewal, contexts that Nietzsche believed can assemble a higher ideal type of the actor in the detritus of modernity and its fast-moving liquid variant.

A superficial reading of Nietzsche risks him being judged a philosopher/ social thinker that fetishizes only deficits in society and in human existence. His unflattering rendering of decadence, last human beings, servant morality, cultural philistines, improvers of humanity, the herd, morality, and soul doctors may inspire us to draw such conclusions. Yet it should be noted that Nietzsche's sociological imaginations and horizons have also consistently illuminated the assets of the modern human condition as well, one that inspires us to still find full optimization in social and historical contexts of deficits, one that harnesses a brilliant dialectic: that suffering is catalytic and necessary for finding one's will to power, purpose, and meaning; that is, Nietzsche's critical observations of modernity constituted by putrefying cultures and systems have been rendered by the philosopher into epic catalysts that can usher in higher humans and overcomers.

Because of their exposure and confrontations with adversity, persecution, and sorrow, Nietzsche argues that our praxian, free-spirited, creative, and noble-minded overcomers can remain optimized to attend to any condition of the life experience. Their *amor fati* and successful pass of the eternal recurrence doctrine propel them beyond the dysfunctions of their social systems and a nihilism that rears its head in their shadows. Nietzsche is thus not positioning the overcomer to be a vanguard in the name of anarchy, for such a loose social environment would be relieved or emptied of any cultural impediments that serve as catalysts for overcoming. Nietzsche was even for democracy, but a democracy that affirmed excellence through noble-minded elites, not a democracy that pandered to those lacking fortitude and mettle to author their own lives in a noble-minded and overcoming fashion. As such, the new false idols of modernities: current democratism and the other *isms* following the death of religion and god, had their reifications destabilized and their utopianisms demystified by Nietzsche. Such a move by Nietzsche has allowed my work to offer new interpretations for comprehending the contradictions inherent in democratism: that it has ample room for authoritarian and totalitarian tendencies in the lifeworld and, in the American iteration of its democratism, capitalism, and globalism, functions as a system of panoptic surveillance and corporatocratic cultural production. Surviving these regressive forces will require the complete expenditure of one's will to power, lest one is absorbed by a variety of conformist-based social systems. And herein lies the worth of Nietzsche's sociological insights: social systems do experience glaring contradictions, dysfunctions, and decay, generating a variety of nihilistic challenges for self and society. Chief among these is how modern culture and social structure output but hollowness and meaninglessness that will need to be overcome on one's own terms. Only in such a manner can we anticipate a paradigm shift toward a culture of nobleness where a new and liberated humanity can surface from the rubble of decay, duress, and strife experienced by people who lead lives as automatons, as last humans desperately dependent on their social systems.

Relying on society's improvers of humanity to convey panaceas and scripts reified by followers has undesirable implications for one's sovereignty in society. For Nietzsche, if one cherishes sovereignty and self-authoring in a social system experiencing a variety of crises and dysfunctions, the improvers of humanity, cultural philistines, and the rest of the poseurs whose sense of self-worth can only be validated by our tawdry consumerist and herd culture, one will need to be relegated from being agents of contemporary cultural production—a *good* scenario for Nietzsche. Nietzsche's notion of an overcoming individual was never meant to embody a neoliberal individual as consumer, producer, and product in the larger economic framework of capitalism. Nietzsche's notion of the individual is envisioned as a person who transcends the self from all types of hypocritical social scripts, especially those that transform a captive audience of conformists into automatons. It is therefore important if a Nietzschean sociology were to offer a discourse for our discipline, that it continues to make room for individual agency in ways that allow the self to withstand the nihilism and contradictions in the *isms* of modernity and liquid modernity.

The question sociology will need to address as a discipline is to what extent society is in a state of dysfunction, in decay, and how to operationalize such dynamics in ways that inform us about their effects upon the self in society. Should we preach revolution, which therefore forces us to defer to ideology and utopia, charismatic leaders that can quickly become routinized, and sometimes professional malcontents, all of whom can only thrive if they have their captive audience? Should actors with agency be so willing to hand over their hopes and dreams, their sovereignty, to improvers of humanity, or to a materialist "culture" where humans are indoctrinated to live as automatons seeking safety in incessant consumption and panopticons that police citizen behavior? Nietzsche forces us to think of agency in such volatile social existences, in societies of double standards and hypocrisies, in societies with contradictions reproduced by social systems, in societies that enable stressors that force people to run to their sects, identity groups, and to their groupthink for safety.

Perhaps we have seen self and society through an uncritical reification of a binary that erroneously assumes stability and continuity in the latter is required for the former to operate. I am of the view that we need Nietzsche's voice in the sociological discipline to disrupt the stability of this binary if only because systemic failure is a bona fide and incontrovertible fact of social existence, especially when they rob actors of purpose, outputting nihilism in the process. Throughout my work, Nietzsche's more socially oriented critiques were harnessed to argue that current modernity and many of its *isms*, including democratism, are impaired, if not failing. I ushered the overcomer into a heavy and liquid modernity, both replete with acute discontents and polarizations, and argued that sociology can well do with theoretical perspectives that return agency to the self, especially if systems have failed the population, especially if systems have violated their social contracts. It is in this context that I discussed how social structures of current modernity are exhibiting their dysfunctions and that systemic crises are with us in more ways than one. Nietzsche's ideas were invoked to read how such acute crises ultimately descend upon the self, and how this can inspire an overcoming self to prevail in yet another iteration of a nihilistic and decaying society.

A Nietzsche social theory on overcoming systemic crises is therefore a social theory on how active nihilists, as actors with agency for social change, are able to re-inject meaning and purpose back into the life experience in ways that contest systemically induced conformities and nihilism. Existential sociology, then, is the sociology for actors who experience the human condition in such liminalities, in such structural instabilities and volatilities that enable contradictions of modernity and liquid modernity to maintain their staying power through institutionally-imposed regulations and scripts. Through a Nietzsche sociology we are exposed to this dreary *and* radiant world, both of which simultaneously serve as contexts for the non-conformist with a keen sense of one's will to power—the overcomer—to emerge and prevail in self-actualization and victory. It is a sociology that dares to consider new ideal types of a praxian actor with agency, one who dares to confront and overcome the dysfunctions and mortality of social structure, one who dares to purpose existence in the self and a new community that can wrestle itself from the forces of systemic decay and nihilism while experiencing post-traumatic growth in the process. Nietzsche, then, reminds us that when society fails to deliver, there remains only the self's will to power to secure continuity, meaning, and purpose, to be achieved by outmaneuvering or completely rejecting society's dysfunctional yet regulatory outputs that suppress one's sovereignty. A sociology that emerges from such a focus is existential sociology, one that cheers a Nietzschean free-spirted self onward with aplomb, through constraining, decaying, and very mortal social systems.

References

Anderson, Benedict. 1983. *Imagined Communities*. London: Verso.

Antonio, Robert J. 1995. "Nietzsche's Antisociology: Subjectified Culture and the End of History." *American Journal of Sociology* 101(1): 1–43.

Arendt, Hannah. 1973. *The Origins of Totalitarianism*. Orlando: A Harvest Book, Harcourt, Inc.

Aspers, Patrik. 2007. "Nietzsche's Sociology." *Sociological Forum* 22(4): 474–499.

Bauman, Zygmunt. 2000. *Liquid Modernity*. Cambridge: Polity.

———. 2004. *Wasted Lives*. Cambridge: Polity.

Bergmann, Peter. 1987. *Nietzsche, "The Last Antipolitical German."* Bloomington: Indiana University Press.

Bergmann, Peter, Teodor Münz, Frantisek Novosád, Paul Patton, Leslie Paul Thiele, Richard Rorty, Alan D. Schrift, and Jan Sokol. 2007. "What Does Nietzsche Mean to Philosophers Today?" *Kritika & Kontext: A Journal of Critical Thinking* No. 35, 8–41.

Berger, Peter L. and Thomas Luckmann. 1966. *The Social Construction of Reality*. New York: Anchor Books.

Calhoun, Craig. 1994. *Habermas and the Public Sphere*. Cambridge: MIT Press.

Calhoun, Craig, Joseph Gerteis, James Moody, Steven Pfaff, and Indermohan Virk. 2012. *Contemporary Sociological Theory, Third Edition*. West Sussex: Wiley-Blackwell.

Chamberlain, Lesley. 1996. *Nietzsche in Turin: An Intimate Biography*. London: Quartet Books.

Chriss, James J. 1998. "Review Essay of Jürgen Habermas's Between Facts and Norms." *Sociology & Criminology Faculty Publications*. Paper 100.

Chu, S., J. Morgan, and L. Wardle (Directors). 1999. *Human, All Too Human: Friedrich Nietzsche* [Documentary]. United States of America, Films for the Humanities & Sciences.

Clark, Maudemarie. 1990. *Nietzsche on Truth and Philosophy*. Cambridge: Cambridge University Press.

———. 2015. *Nietzsche on Ethics and Politics*. Oxford: Oxford University Press.

Clark, Maudemarie and David Dudrick. 2012. *The Soul of Nietzsche's "Beyond Good and Evil."* Cambridge: Cambridge University Press.

Crease, Robert P. 2018. "Unenlightened Thinking." *Physics World*, May 23, 2018. https://physicsworld.com/a/unenlightened-thinking/ (accessed June 2, 2018).

Cox, Anna. (Director). 2016. *BBC Four - Genius of the Modern World: Nietzsche* [Documentary]. United Kingdom: BBC Four.

Crosby, Donald A. 1988. *The Specter of the Absurd: Sources and Criticisms of Modern Nihilism*. Albany: State University of New York Press.

Dahl, Robert. 1956. *A Preface to Democratic Theory*. Chicago: University of Chicago Press.

———. 1961. *Who Governs?: Democracy and Power in an American City*. New Haven: Yale University Press.

———. 1968. *Pluralist Democracy in the United States: Conflict and Consent*. Chicago: Rand McNally & Company.

———. 1989. *Democracy and Its Critics*. New Haven, CT: Yale University Press.

Detwiler, Bruce. 1990. *Nietzsche and the Politics of Aristocratic Radicalism*. Chicago: University of Chicago Press.

Egyed, Béla. 2007. "Nietzsche's Anti-democratic Liberalism." *Kritika & Kontext: A Journal of Critical Thinking* No. 35, 100–113.

Eley, Geoff. 1994. "Nations, Publics, and Political Cultures: Placing Habermas in the Nineteenth Century." In *Habermas and the Public Sphere*, edited by Craig Calhoun, 289–339. Cambridge: MIT Press.

Foreign Policy. 2006. "Failed States Index." *Foreign Policy* May/June.

Frank, Arthur. 2000. "Notes on Habermas: Lifeworld and System." *University of Calgary, Dept. of Sociology*. http://people.ucalgary.ca/~frank/habermas.html (accessed June 11, 2014).

Fromm, Erich. 1969. *Escape from Freedom*. New York: Henry Holt and Company, LLC.

———. 1976. *To Have or To Be?* London: Bloomsbury.

Garnham, Nicolas. 1994. "The Media and the Public Sphere." In *Habermas and the Public Sphere*, edited by Craig Calhoun, 359–376. Cambridge: MIT Press.

Gelfand, Michele. 2018. *Rule Makers, Rule Breakers: How Tight and Loose Cultures Wire Our World*. New York: Scribner.

Giroux, Henry A. 2018a. *American Nightmare: Facing the Challenge of Fascism*. San Francisco: City Lights Books.

———. 2018b. *The Public in Peril: Trump and the Menace of American Authoritarianism*. London: Routledge.

Habermas, Jürgen. 1975. *Legitimation Crisis*. Boston: Beacon Press.

———. 1984. *The Theory of Communicative Action, Volume 1, Reason and the Rationalization of Society*. Boston: Beacon Press.

———. 1986. "The New Obscurity: The Crisis of the Welfare State and the Exhaustion of Utopian Energies." *Philosophy & Social Criticism* 11: 1–18.

———. 1987. *The Theory of Communicative Action, Volume 2, Lifeworld and System: A Critique of Functional Reason*. Boston: Beacon Press.

———. 1991. *The Structural Transformation of the Public Sphere: An Inquiry into a Category of Bourgeois Society*. Cambridge: MIT Press.

Hanshe, Rainer J. 2010. "Invisibly Revolving—Inaudibly Revolving: The Riddle of the Double Gedankenstrich." *The Agonist: A Nietzsche Circle Journal* 3(1): 7–26.

Hemelsoet, D., K. Hemelsoet, and D. Devreese. 2008. "The Neurological Illness of Friedrich Nietzsche." *Acta Neurol Belg* 108(1): 9–16.

Hennis, Wilhelm. 1988. *Max Weber: Essays in Reconstruction*. London: Unwin Hyman Ltd.

Hobsbawm, Eric and Terence O. Ranger. 1983. *The Invention of Tradition*. Cambridge: Cambridge University Press.

Hollingdale, R. J. 1999. *Nietzsche: The Man and His Philosophy*. Cambridge: Cambridge University Press.

Horkheimer, Max and Theodor W. Adorno. 1972. *Dialectic of Enlightenment*. New York: Continuum.

Horowitz, Irving. 1983. *C. Wright Mills: An American Utopian*. New York: Free Press.

Inglehart, Ronald F. 2018. *Cultural Evolution: People's Motivations are Changing, and Reshaping the World*. Cambridge: Cambridge University Press.

Jurist, Elliot L. 2000. *Beyond Hegel and Nietzsche: Philosophy, Culture, and Agency*. Cambridge: The MIT Press.

Jütten, Timo. 2013. "Habermas and Markets." *Constellations* 20(4): 587–603.

Kaag, John. 2018. *Hiking With Nietzsche: On Becoming Who You Are*. New York: Farrar, Straus and Giroux.

Karzai, Anas. 2019. *Nietzsche and Sociology: Prophet of Affirmation*. London: Lexington Books.

Kaufmann, Walter. 1950. *Nietzsche: Philosopher, Psychologist, Antichrist*. New York: Vintage Books.

———. 1974. *The Gay Science: With a Prelude in Rhymes and an Appendix of Songs*. New York. Vintage Books.

Klein, William. 1997. *Nietzsche & the Promise of Philosophy*. New York: State University of New York Press.

Krey, Peter. 2002. "The Life-World and the Two Systems." *Scholardarity*. http://www.scholardarity.com/?s=krey+life-world+two+systems (accessed November 28, 2015).

Kotarba, Joseph and Andrea Fontana. 1984. *The Existential Self in Society*. Chicago: University of Chicago Press.

Kotarba, Joseph and John M. Johnson. 2002. *Postmodern Existential Sociology*. New York: Rowman and Littlefield Publishers, Inc.

Loeb, Paul S. 2006. "Identity and Eternal Recurrence." In *Companion to Nietzsche*, edited by Keith Ansell Pearson, 171–188. Hoboken, NJ: John Wiley and Sons, Ltd.

Lomax, J. Harvey. 2000. "Nietzsche and the Eternal Recurrence." *Philosophy Now: A Magazine of Ideas*. https://philosophynow.org/issues/29/Nietzsche_and_the_Eternal_Recurrence (accessed August 19, 2016).

Löwith, Karl. 1997. *Nietzsche's Philosophy of the Eternal Recurrence of the Same*. Berkeley, CA: University of California Press.

Magee, Bryan. 2001. *The Great Philosophers: An Introduction to Western Philosophy.* Oxford: Oxford University Press.

Marcuse, Herbert. 1964. *One-Dimensional Man.* Boston: Beacon Press.

Mezirow, Jack. 2003. "Transformative Learning as Discourse." *Journal of Transformative Education* 1(1): 58–63.

Middleton, Christopher. 1996. *Selected Letters of Friedrich Nietzsche.* New York: Hackett.

Mills, C. Wright. 1959. *The Sociological Imagination.* Oxford: Oxford University Press.

———. 2000. *Power Elite.* Oxford: Oxford University Press.

Murphy, Timothy F. 1984. *Nietzsche as Educator.* London: University Press of America.

Nehamas, Alexander. 1988. "Who are 'the Philosophers of the Future'?: A Reading of Beyond Good and Evil." In *Reading Nietzsche,* edited by Robert Solomon and Kathleen Higgins, 46–67. Oxford: Oxford University Press.

Nietzsche, Friedrich. 1996. *Human, All Too Human.* Cambridge: Cambridge University Press.

———. 1997a. *Twilight of the Idols.* Indianapolis: Hackett Publishing Company, Inc.

———. 1997b. *Untimely Meditations.* Cambridge: Cambridge University Press.

———. 1999. *The Birth of Tragedy.* Cambridge: Cambridge University Press.

———. 2001. *The Gay Science.* Cambridge: Cambridge University Press.

———. 2002. *Beyond Good and Evil.* Cambridge: Cambridge University Press.

———. 2004. *Dionysian Dithyrambs.* Manchester: Carcanet Press Ltd.

———. 2005. *The Anti-Christ, Ecce Homo, Twilight of the Idols and Other Writings.* Cambridge: Cambridge University Press.

———. 2006a. *On the Genealogy of Morality.* Cambridge: Cambridge University Press.

———. 2006b. *Thus Spoke Zarathustra.* Cambridge: Cambridge University Press.

———. 2007a. *The Dawn of Day.* London: George Allen & Unwin Ltd.

———. 2007b. *Ecce Homo.* Oxford: Oxford University Press.

———. 2010. *The Will to Power (Volumes I and II).* Overland Park, KS: Digireads. com Publishers.

Norman, Judith. 2002. "Nietzsche and Early Romanticism." *Journal of the History of Ideas* 63(2): 501–519.

Oldenburg, Ray. 1999. *The Great Good Place.* New York: Marlowe & Company.

Omi, Michael and Howard Winant. 1986. *Racial Formation in the United States: From the 1960s to the 1990s.* Abingdon, United Kingdom: Routledge.

Partyga, Dominika. 2016. "Simmel's Reading of Nietzsche: The Promise of 'Philosophical Sociology.'" *Journal of Classical Sociology* 16(4): 414–437.

Ritzer, George. 1992. *Sociological Theory.* New York: McGraw-Hill.

Ritzer, George and Jeffrey Stepnisky. 2013. *Contemporary Sociological Theory and Its Classical Roots, Fourth Edition.* New York: McGraw Hill.

Runciman, W. G. 2000. "Can There Be a Nietzschean Sociology?" in *Archives Européennes de Sociologies,* XLI:1. Cambridge: Cambridge University Press.

Shenkman, Rick. 2019. "The Shocking Paper Predicting the End of Democracy." *Politico.com.* https://www.politico.com/magazine/story/2019/09/08/shawn-rosenberg-democracy-228045 (accessed September 10, 2019).

Solms-Laubach, Franz zu. 2007. *Nietzsche and Early German and Austrian Sociology.* Berlin: Walter de Gruyter.

Solomon, Robert C. and Kathleen M. Higgins. 1988. *Reading Nietzsche.* Oxford: Oxford University Press.

Sorgner, Stefan L. 2007. *Metaphysics Without Truth: On the Importance of Consistency Within Nietzsche's Philosophy.* Milwaukee: Marquette University Press.

Stahl, Titus. 2013. "Habermas and the Project of Immanent Critique." *Constellations* 20(4): 533–552.

Taleb, Nassim Nicholas. 2010. *The Black Swan.* New York: Random House.

———. 2012. *Antifragile: Things That Gain From Disorder.* New York: Random House.

Tiryakian, Edward. 1962. *Sociologism and Existentialism: Two Perspectives on the Individual and Society.* Englewood Cliffs, NJ: Prentice-Hall, Inc.

Tolle, Eckhart. 2008. *A New Earth: Awakening to Your Life's Purpose.* New York: Penguin.

Van Tongeren, Paul. 2000. *Reinterpreting Modern Culture.* Bloomington, IN: Indiana University Press.

Warren, Mark E. 1993. "Can Participatory Democracy Produce Better Selves? Psychological Dimensions of Habermas's Discursive Model of Democracy." *Political Sociology* 14(2): 209–234.

Wolin, Sheldon. 2003. "Inverted Totalitarianism: How the Bush Regime Is Effecting the Transformation to a Fascist-Like State." *The Nation.* https://www.thenation.com/article/inverted-totalitarianism/ (accessed July 7, 2015).

———. 2008. *Democracy Incorporated: Managed Democracy and the Specter of Inverted Totalitarianism.* Princeton: Princeton University Press.

Woolfolk, Alan N. 1985. "Unmasking Nihilism." *Human Studies* 8, 85–96.

Williams, Linda. 1996. "Will to Power in Nietzsche's Published Works and the Nachlass." *Journal of the History of Ideas* 57(3): 447–463.

Young, Julian. 2006. *Nietzsche's Philosophy of Religion.* Cambridge: Cambridge University Press.

———. 2010. *Friedrich Nietzsche: A Philosophical Biography.* Cambridge: Cambridge University Press.

Index

About the Author

Jack Fong is a political/urban sociologist who has long appreciated integrating philosophy with the discipline of sociology. With works such as the *Death Café Movement: Exploring the Horizons of Mortality*, as well as *Revolution as Development: The Karen Self-Determination Struggle against Ethnocracy (1949–2004)*, along with other publications related to solitude, nationalism, social movements, and urban problems, Fong's orientation toward living by first confronting all forms of mortality, whether community or state-related, have generated much favorable community response. In his current work harnessing the sociological insights of the great German philosopher Friedrich Nietzsche, Fong offers a unique rereading of Nietzsche in ways that synchronize the ideas of one of philosophy's greats with the complex social dynamics of the human condition in the modernities of the twentieth and twenty-first centuries.

www.ingramcontent.com/pod-product-compliance
Lightning Source LLC
Chambersburg PA
CBHW022312280326
41932CB00010B/1078